otection 1998

al Studies 98/99

CHILD ABUSE

wec   e da

95   9

N THE

CHILD ABUSE

Towards a knowledge base

Brian Corby

Open University Press
Buckingham · Philadelphia

Open University Press
Celtic Court
22 Ballmoor
Buckingham
MK18 1XW

and
1900 Frost Road, Suite 101
Bristol, PA 19007, USA

First Published 1993

A catalogue record of this book is available from the British Library

ISBN 0 335 15746 7 (pb) 0 335 15747 5 (hb)

Library of Congress Cataloging-in-Publication Data

Corby, Brian.
    Child abuse: towards a knowledge base/Brian Corby.
        p.   cm.
    Includes bibliographical references (p.   ) and index.
    ISBN 0–335–15747–5 (hb)   ISBN 0–335–15746–7 (pb)
    1. Child abuse.   I. Title.
HV6626.5.C67   1993
362.7′6 – dc20   92–34683
                                                         CIP

Typeset by Type Study, Scarborough
Printed in Great Britain by
Biddles Ltd, Guildford and King's Lynn

This book is dedicated to the memory of family members and friends who have recently died: William Corby, Carroll Patrick O'Daly and Alban Wiseman.

I would also like to thank my immediate family, Gerry, Matthew, Anna and Joe, for their patience with me while I was preoccupied with writing.

Contents

1

Introduction

The aim of this book is to provide a broad knowledge base for practitioners and students who are working or intending to work in the child protection field. At a time when child protection work is under so much public scrutiny, it is important that practitioners are fully conversant with what is known about child abuse and that they are able to weigh up the strengths and weaknesses of that knowledge.

Practitioners already have easy access to a good deal of practice-focused and practice-derived material. For instance, there are many 'child abuse textbooks' in existence, whose aims are to define and promote good professional practice (see, for example, Moore 1985; Jones *et al*. 1987; Glaser and Frosh 1988). There are also many accounts of practice written by practitioners themselves (see, for example, Lynch and Roberts 1982; Dale *et al*. 1986; Ben-Tovim *et al*. 1988) that are considered to be good models for others to follow.

It is to sources such as these that practitioners and trainers in the child protection field are most likely to turn for information and guidance. However, there are other sources of knowledge about the mistreatment of children to which child protection practitioners have less direct access. This knowledge is not largely drawn from practice experience, but derives more from research and theorizing carried out by 'observers' or 'outsiders' from different academic disciplines, such as history, sociology, philosophy, social policy and psychology. Some of these disciplines have had more impact than others. For instance, certain aspects of psychology have had prominence in this field, because their focus on individuals and their immediate environments makes them more directly translatable to practice. Other disciplines, particularly history and sociology, have been given very little attention at all by practitioners and policy-makers, because their concerns seem far removed from the exigencies of day-to-day child protection problems. It will be argued that these knowledge bases do have more to offer those working in the field of child protection than first meets the eye.

In seeking to give greater prominence to these areas of knowledge, I am not arguing that they are superior to the more practice-based material. Indeed, considerable use will be made of such material throughout this book. The dichotomy between these two types of knowledge is less clear cut than I have stressed in order to illustrate the point. This is as it should be, as it is important that they complement each other. Far from arguing for the purity of research-based knowledge, I will be attempting to emphasize its strengths and weaknesses, and particular attention will be paid to how the values and beliefs of researchers influence their findings. Such knowledge is not better *per se* than other forms of knowledge, but it does exist and is worthy of critical consideration by those seeking to understand what child abuse is, why it happens and what best to do about it.

In writing this book I am affirming my commitment to a model of the social worker (and other child protection professionals) as having particular expertise in working with child abuse and a fair degree of autonomy (and accountability). This expertise must, in my opinion, be based on extensive knowledge of a wide range of research and information on several fronts, and on the ability to evaluate that research and utilize it in practice. Clearly such knowledge is not sufficient by itself to ensure a high level of practice. It must be supplemented by an explicit, agreed-upon set of values and standards of intervention and by competent practice skills. However, I would argue that it is a necessary ingredient. At the present time this model of the child protection practitioner does not prevail for a variety of reasons.

First, the climate of fear that has surrounded child protection work since the death of Maria Colwell in 1973 has led to a form of practice that is increasingly system- and management-led. Front-line social workers have been deprived of much of their discretion by departments responding to the recommendations of public inquiry reports and government guidelines. Second, there is a growing trend for professional education and training to be more practice-led and practice-tested. On the face of it, there is nothing wrong with this, in that everyone agrees with the need for competent practitioners. However, there is a danger that the only type of knowledge thought to be required for doing professional work is that which is above all else practical and job-specific. The need for health and welfare workers to have a broader knowledge base, which will enhance their understanding of the nature of their work and ensure more flexibility and judgement in their day-to-day practice, is not a popular cause at the moment. Both these trends are linked to wider social factors whereby control and discretion are being retained more and more by managers, who see their task as providing a consistent, cost-effective service that cannot be left to the whim of practising professional workers.

There are signs of a change of direction, however, particularly with regard to social work. Two main factors have led to this. First, research into general child care work in the early 1980s (DHSS 1985a) criticized social work practice for being too control-oriented and not flexible enough. Second, there was general condemnation of child protection practice in Cleveland in 1987 and later in Rochdale and the Orkneys. Events such as these had an immediate impact on official thinking and are reflected in the 1989 Children Act, which, with its dual emphasis on partnership with parents and children's rights, provides opportunities for more flexible practice. This act will probably also make intervention more complex than before. In such a climate, the need for practitioners to have a comprehensive knowledge base to aid them in their judgements and decision-making will become even greater.

There is a massive amount of research and writing about child abuse by historians, sociologists, psychologists, medical researchers and social policy academics. Inevitably, therefore, the focus of this book is selective. There is a bias towards British and American research, partly because it is most readily available, but also because of its relevance. Research from other countries is included to a lesser degree.

The most fully researched and written about aspect of child abuse is that relating to physical abuse. Sexual abuse literature and research come second in terms of quantity, followed by physical neglect and emotional abuse. As far as possible, I have tried to do justice to all aspects of abuse. In particular I have tried to give as much focus to sexual abuse as to physical abuse and to compare and contrast material from these two fields. I have made considerable use of public inquiry reports into child deaths, which are a rich source of very relevant material provided they are considered from a critical standpoint. I have used extensive notes both to expand on analysis and to point to additional relevant material. The book's outline is as follows.

In Chapter 2 the focus is on how, throughout history, there have been different constructions and understandings of what constitutes childhood and child abuse. Careful analysis of historical research can help in the understanding of the present.

Chapter 3 concentrates on the recent history of child protection policy and practice. Detailed consideration is given to how social and political forces have shaped the way in which we respond to child abuse allegations today. The aim is to help those currently involved in this field of activity to understand the reasons for the complex and often contradictory nature of that response.

In Chapter 4 consideration is given to the issue of child abuse definition and to research into its incidence and prevalence in Britain and the USA. It is argued that by developing a sense of the whole, practitioners can acquire a more realistic view of their particular roles and functions.

Chapter 5 looks critically at research into the question of who is likely to abuse whom and in what circumstances. Knowledge of this research is seen to be of crucial importance for those trying to assess and make decisions about cases of child abuse.

In Chapter 6 a range of social and psychological theories and ideologies that have been applied to child abuse to explain why it happens is considered. It is argued that understanding why abuse may be happening is an important precursor to planning intervention to prevent its recurrence.

Chapter 7 considers research into the consequences and aftermath of abuse of children. This research has implications for both the practice and the policy of ongoing child protection work, which at present is heavily focused on the detection and investigation stages.

In Chapter 8 empirical research into child protection practice is reviewed. Such research can provide direct lessons for improvements in policy and practice.

Chapter 9 considers some of the major issues that currently beset workers and researchers in the child protection field.

2

Childhood, child abuse and history

Social work is a very present-oriented activity. The social work profession is committed to tackling current social and personal problems and is concerned to find useful and pragmatic tools to help in this endeavour. Indeed, in its determination to discover solutions it has been criticized for being too ready to adopt fashionable new theories and approaches (Howe 1980). This here-and-now emphasis has contributed to a lack of enthusiasm for a historical understanding of social problems and responses to them.[1] This lack of enthusiasm is evidenced by the fact that there are few good historical accounts of the profession itself.[2]

If we consider the specific field of child protection work, this ignorance of the past is all too evident. Until recently, most social work accounts of the background to child protection work began with Henry Kempe and his 'discovery' of the child battering syndrome in 1962, as if the problem either did not exist before this or had somehow lain dormant.[3] Similarly, sexual abuse is often described as having been discovered in Britain at the beginning of the 1980s. However, to take just one example, accounts of the child protection movement in the late nineteenth and early twentieth centuries, such as those by Rose (1986, 1991) Behlmer (1982) and Ferguson (1990), demonstrate that very similar things were happening in this field then as are happening today, albeit in a very different social context and climate. Infant life protection protagonists, NSPCC officials and various other philanthropic agents were then emphasizing the widespread nature of child abuse and seeking to convince the public of the need for a change in attitude. In the same way as social workers today, they were decrying the fact that the law was woefully deficient in dealing with the problem and arguing vehemently that children should be more adequately protected. The experiences of these late Victorians, considered in more detail in Chapter 3, in fact provide us with a rich source of useful material for evaluating contemporary responses to child protection issues. As we shall see, however, in order to benefit from this type of approach we have to interpret the historian's word as critically and as objectively as possible.

Interpreting history

Historians themselves are well aware of the difficulties of learning from the past:

> The study of past attitudes, of modes of thought and feeling is one of the most difficult branches of historiography. Not only is evidence patchy and often indirect, particularly where intimate family matters or the mentality of the inarticulate or the illiterate are concerned, but the interpretation of such evidence requires an empathy, a feeling for nuances, and above all an objectivity, a deliberate attempt to set aside one's own cultural assumptions that is not easy to attain . . . Huge generalisations have been hoisted on the slenderest foundations, evidence that is not congenial has been ignored or brushed aside, while other testimony has been crudely or carelessly misinterpreted. All of which suggests the need for a reminder that bad history can still mislead the 'general public' as well as other scholars and students. (Wilson 1984: 198)

All historical writing is inevitably selective. The range of sources available is often vast. Historians have their own viewpoints and theories, which influence the way in which they interpret data, and this results in emphasis on certain types of evidence and lack of attention to others. For instance, historical writing varies considerably with regard to the attention paid to the different forms of structural oppression, such as race, class, gender and age and their impact on attitudes and behaviours. Currently there is considerable reassessment of the past through these filters, particularly in the case of race and gender.[4]

When history is used as a means of casting light on present issues, there seem to be two mainstream perspectives. The first views the present as an inevitable improvement on the past. Adherents of this viewpoint draw comfort from the ignorance and mistakes (as they see them) of previous generations. The second paints a rosy picture of yesteryear and sees the present not as progress from the past, but as retrogressive. The first perspective views the past as barbaric, the second as a golden age. It is important to be aware of and to understand different viewpoints of this kind in order to maximize the usefulness of historical material.

Childhood and history

The issues of childhood and child abuse are closely linked. Views about the status and rights of children are influential in the way in which they are treated by adults and determine to some extent what is considered to be mistreatment. For the purposes of analysis, however, they will be treated separately. This section will consider what historians tell us about childhood.

Childhood as a social construct

While it may not solve the immediate question of whether a social worker should apply for an emergency protection order in the case of a young child left alone and unprotected, or try to rehabilitate a teenage child who is rejecting his or her parents, awareness of the socially constructed nature of childhood can enable the social worker to reflect more fully on the social and political underpinnings to the situation and may ultimately inform the decisions that are finally reached in these and other cases. A historical perspective that demonstrates the different ways in which childhood has been construed in the past reinforces such thinking.

To the lay person the notion of childhood is self-evident. Everyone knows a child when he or she sees one. Of course it becomes a little more difficult in the case of adolescents. Nevertheless, most people consider childhood to be an age-related phenomenon. This is reflected in British law, which prescribes a series of legal rights and responsibilities that take effect at different ages. These statutes provide protection for children, place duties on their parents, impose prohibitions on certain activities and later lift them. There are all sorts of anomalies. For instance, a 16-year-old is deemed responsible enough to marry (with parental consent) and have children, but not responsible enough to buy an alcoholic drink in a public house or to watch a category 18 film. Heterosexuals can consent to sexual acts at the age of 16, but homosexuals cannot do so until they are 21. A boy can legally consent to sexual intercourse at 14, but girls cannot do so until they are 16. While the age of 18 is generally thought to be the beginning of adulthood, there are still prohibitions which last until the age of 21, in addition to those placed on homosexuals. Only at 21 can a young person stand as a councillor or MP, apply for a licence to sell alcohol, have a heavy goods vehicle licence or apply to adopt a child. Such is the power of chronological age.[5]

Despite these tightly age-related demarcations, we know that children develop and mature, both physically and psychologically, at different rates. We also know that in societies other than our own childhood is construed differently. In so-called developing countries in the southern hemisphere, childhood is mostly shorter, particularly if a child is poor, black and female (see Ennew 1986). Children generally assume what we would term adult responsibilities at an earlier age in these societies than in northern indus- trially developed countries, where childhood has tended to be extended to higher and higher ages. The trend in the latter is to keep young people in education longer, because of the reduced demand for manual labour and the increased demand for a better trained workforce as technology and markets develop and become more complex.

Historians have paid far more attention to children and the concept of childhood in the past 30 years than ever before. Sommerville (1982) attributes this concern to our uncertainties about and ambivalence towards children today. Ironically, he goes on to demonstrate that in Mesopotamia in 1800 BC parents were expressing the same sort of concerns about their children as parents are now, i.e. that they were not obedient and that they were not working hard enough at school. However, whatever the reason, there is no doubt that historians' interest in children and in family life has grown considerably since 1960.

Philippe Aries and childhood

The most influential work on childhood of this period has been that of Aries (1962), a French social historian. He, along with De Mause (1976), an American psychohistorian, whose work is considered below, is probably the most often quoted historian in child care textbooks. The popular view put forward by social work writers of Aries's ideas (with one notable exception)[6] is that the notion of childhood is a relatively recent one (a product of the seventeenth century). This is usually used to show that we have become more sensitive to children and their needs than was true in the past. Strangely this is almost a total misreading of what Aries was arguing. In *Centuries of Childhood*, Aries writes:

> In medieval society the idea of childhood did not exist: this is not to suggest that children were neglected, forsaken or despised. The idea of childhood is not to be confused with affection for children: it corresponds to an awareness of the particular nature of childhood, that particular nature which distinguishes the child from the adult, even the young adult. In medieval society this awareness was lacking. (Aries 1962: 125)

Aries did not see the absence of the concept of childhood as detrimental to children. Indeed he thought the opposite to be true. During the Middle Ages, according to him, children mingled with adults as soon as that was physically possible. They spent much of their time together in both work and play. It was only gradually, and most dramatically in the seventeenth century with the advent of a form of education dominated by religion-based morality, that children became separated from adults in the way that we understand it today. This increasing differentiation of children from adults in the public sphere was seen by Aries as a backward step, i.e. it was used to place greater restrictions on children in their formative years. The concept of childhood is not seen by him as improving children's status, but as a limiting force placing children more at the mercy of adults than had previously been the case. Aries can be seen, therefore, as a child liberationist. He would like to undo the chains imposed by this modern concept of childhood and return to a more varied, open and liberated past.

Many historians, however, do not find Aries's account of the development of childhood to be plausible.[7] Pollock (1983) summarizes the criticisms of his work in her excellent study, *Forgotten Children*. Her main argument is that

Aries's sources of evidence are not sufficient to back his wide-ranging claims. First, he placed heavy reliance on paintings that could have been analysed in a variety of ways, although he interpreted them only in ways that supported his views. His second main source was Heroard's diary of the early years of the future Louis XIII of France. He used this work, which shows Louis to have been regarded and reared as a little man from a very early age, particularly in terms of sexuality, to demonstrate his general thesis of the non-existence of childhood. Pollock's view is that this case is atypical and tells us very little about how children in general were viewed and treated at this time. This seems to be a reasonable criticism – consider to what extent the diary of Prince Charles's nanny (assuming that she wrote one) would give people in the twenty-fourth century a true flavour of European child-rearing practices in the twentieth century.

Pollock is critical of Aries's rosy view of family life in the Middle Ages, which suggests full integration of children and adults into an idealized communal life. She also points out that Aries has nothing to say about the care of children who are still physically dependent on their parents. He gives the impression that until children are aged seven they do not count (it is almost as if they have no existence at all) and that once they reach this age they are fully mature and are assimilated into adult life without any problems.

The disputes over Aries's work highlight the potential benefits and dangers of a historical perspective on children's issues. He clearly sensitizes us to the fact that childhood is a social construction and that the 'problems' of childhood can be socially created. However, he is deficient in terms of explaining why this happens and makes rather sweeping statements on the basis of limited sources. As Wilson (1984: 183) points out: 'Unfortunately, Aries expressed himself more categorically than he might have done, and he attracted followers, rather than critics, initially.'

The barbaric past perspective

Many historians have used Aries's argument that childhood did not exist until the seventeenth century to show that in fact children have been subject to, at the least, detached emotional upbringings and, at the most, severe abuse including infanticide.[8] De Mause in particular makes this claim. His argument is that the more remote the period of history the more cruel the treatment of children becomes.

> The history of childhood is a nightmare from which we have only recently begun to awaken. The further back in history one goes, the lower the level of child care, and the more likely children are to be killed, abandoned, beaten, terrorised and sexually abused. (De Mause 1976: 1)

He therefore shares with Aries the belief that childhood is a product of relatively recent times, but there the similarity of view ends. Whereas Aries sees the development of the concept of childhood as repressive, De Mause sees it as highly progressive. For him childhood has evolved from the dark ages to the golden present. He outlines seven evolutionary stages ranging from what he terms the infanticidal mode, which existed until the fourth century, to the helping mode, which commenced in the middle of this century. Gradually over generations of evolution, we have progressed, according to De Mause, from a state where parents were unable to see their children as separate beings with any particular needs to that where they regard them as distinct, different and deserving of a special set of rights that emphasize respect for them as full human beings.

Stone (1977), focusing on the 1500–1800 period, argues that affection and love between spouses and for their children were impossible before the eighteenth century because of the material conditions of pre-industrial life. Adults did not invest emotionally in children because it was not considered to be worthwhile. Child mortality rates were so high that 'to preserve their mental stability, parents were obliged to limit the degree of their psychological involvement with their infant children' (Stone 1977: 70). It was only in the nineteenth century, in his view, that children were first seen as individuals with special needs because of their vulnerability. This change in perception stemmed initially from the upper and middle classes, who had acquired more leisure time to devote to child care concerns, and was gradually filtered down to the poorer classes.

These and similar views have been heavily criticized by other historians. Demos (1986) is critical of De Mause for the selectivity of his material and the fact that he seems to totally ignore the context and, therefore, the meaning of the behaviours which he is condemning. Macfarlane's (1979) review of Stone's work is particularly telling. He quotes many examples of parents expressing love and affection for their children before the eighteenth century. In particular he refers to the diary of a seventeenth-century puritan vicar, Ralph Josselin, and the grief that he expresses at the death of his eight-year-old daughter, Mary.[9] He argues that Stone ignores evidence from modern societies in the southern hemisphere and from social anthropological studies that demonstrate considerable evidence of close child–adult emotional ties despite gross material poverty and high rates of child mortality. He does not accept Stone's neat evolutionary scheme and is unconvinced by his belief that affective relationships are determined totally by economics.

There is a growing body of evidence to suggest that the concept of childhood has always existed. Boswell (1988: 37) in his study of abandonment of children in antiquity argues: 'It is clear, however, that there was no general absence of tender feeling for children as special beings among any premodern European peoples.' Houlbrooke (1984), writing about families in the fifteenth century, states that: 'Children were seen by many as an important source of help and comfort in old age. To all save those engaged in the most brutal struggle for mere survival, they were probably a source of psychological satisfaction which varied in depth according to the individual character' (p. 127). Somewhat more cynically, he says that 'parents delighted in their children, not primarily because of their good qualities, but because they were theirs' (p. 135).

Pollock (1983), drawing from a study of 496 published diaries and autobiographies written between 1500 and 1900, argues that the concept of childhood changed and developed during this period but certainly existed throughout. The sources she considered all demonstrated a certain amount of ambivalence towards their children. All saw them as a mixture of good and bad or of innocence and depravity. All demonstrated human concern and a sense of responsibility, as well as finding their children wearisome and exasperating. In particular, the diaries she examined showed that the death of a child created the same heartfelt reactions throughout the centuries studied.

It must be concluded, therefore, that although there is no doubt that children in former times were expected to work and become what we today would consider to be adult at an earlier age than our own children, claims regarding the non-existence of the notion of childhood as we perceive it now are grossly exaggerated. It seems likely that children have always had a separate status, particularly early on when they are physically dependent. As societies develop economically there is a tendency for childhood to be extended and to gain more attention as a separate category, a process that is testified to by the growth of child protective legislation. However, the views of historians such as Aries, Stone and De Mause, who see childhood as a modern creation, are as much determined by ideology as by historical accuracy.

A major flaw in many historical analyses of childhood is that they tend to generalize about the way in which children are perceived (and, therefore, behave and are treated) as if all children's experiences are similar at a particular time. It is highly likely that this is far from true. Children of different classes, genders and races are likely to have widely different experiences in every period of history. A good example of this variation in experience is provided by the period of industrialization in Britain in the nineteenth century, during which the development of greater sensitivity and sentiment towards middle-class childhood coincided with appalling working conditions for children of the labouring classes in mills, factories and on the street.[10]

Child abuse and history

What do historians tell us about child abuse? As has already been seen, those historians who view childhood as a relatively modern concept (with the exception of Aries) consider children in the past to have been callously treated because they were not afforded a protected status. Thus virtually all children, according to this view, were abused (certainly by modern standards) and generally such abuse was tolerated by society. Historians who do not hold this view accept that standards of care, particularly for older children, may have been low relative to what we expect today, but not abusive. From this point of view it is argued that within the prevailing standards of each age there have been cruel and loving parents and that children who had cruel parents were likely to be abused, but society did not necessarily condone or accept such abuse.

Child abuse in antiquity

De Mause placed the Roman empire in his infanticide mode. Infanticide was not legally a crime until AD 318 (made punishable by death in AD 374). De Mause concludes from this that it was (a) common practice and (b) evidence of the cruelty of the times. Boswell, whose study *The Kindness of Strangers* (1988) is concerned with abandonment rather than infanticide, a distinction he is keen to maintain, is far less critical of the mores of this period. Whereas De Mause judges the Romans by the standards of today (using psychoanalytic theory as his baseline), Boswell takes into account the meaning of forms of behaviour that on the face of it seem barbaric but are more understandable under closer scrutiny. That the Romans practised infanticide is without doubt. However, seen in the light of the fact that there were no adequate contraceptive techniques and the medical knowledge needed for abortion did not exist, it becomes clear that much (not all) infanticide was a crude, though not altogether callous, means of controlling family size. Another method of achieving this was the abandonment of children. Boswell demonstrates that the latter practice was many times more popular than infanticide for two reasons. First, the average Roman probably took no more pleasure in killing new-born babies than you or I would. Second, abandonment, which was usually carried out in a public place, frequently led to a child being rescued and looked after by someone else. This was in most cases a desired and intended outcome.[11]

Boswell's sympathetic account of the process of abandonment contrasts sharply with the more lurid views of De Mause.

> Parents abandoned their offspring in desperation when they were unable to support them, due to poverty or disaster; in shame when they were unwilling to keep them because of their physical condition or ancestry (e.g. illegitimate or incestuous); in self-interest or the interest of another child, when inheritance or domestic resources would be compromised by another mouth; in hope, when they believed that someone of greater means or higher standing might find them and bring them up in better circumstances; in resignation, when a child was of unwelcome gender or ominous auspices; or in callousness, if they simply could not be bothered with parenthood. (Boswell 1988: 428)

The Middle Ages

Boswell's study goes through to the Renaissance period. He argues that throughout Europe abandonment continued to be a common practice, never openly approved of, but never officially outlawed. Gradually the Church became more involved and began to organize and regulate the activity. Monasteries provided havens for unwanted children through the practice of oblation. In the early thirteenth century, foundling homes were established and the process of abandonment became centralized on these institutions. However, what are seen as progressive developments do not always achieve their intended goals. Boswell argues that the death rate through disease in these places was probably higher than that resulting from the previous practice of abandonment.

How common infanticide was during this period is uncertain. There is evidence that such behaviour was of public concern. Hanawalt (1977) refers to synodal legislation of the thirteenth century that tells parents not to sleep with their children and not leave them alone or unattended near fires. Sharpe (1984) points out that by the sixteenth century infanticide was singled out for severe punishment by most European states and comments that 'The infanticide wave in England at least may have resulted in more executions than the more familiar witch craze' (p. 61).

Sexual abuse

There is little clear evidence about sexual abuse of children in antiquity and medieval times. Again De Mause is unequivocal about the former: 'The child in antiquity lived his earliest years in an atmosphere of sexual abuse. Growing up in Greece or Rome often included being sexually used by older men' (De Mause 1976: 43). Wiedemann (1989: 30) is equally unequivocal:

> Nor for that matter do the occasional references to the sexual exploitation of children by perverts prove that Roman society as a whole was imbued either with a psychotic hatred of childhood, or with a degree of sexual freedom to put modern California to shame.

He points out that pederasty was not acceptable to the Romans and that if it involved a boy of citizen status it was apparently a criminal offence.[12]

There is very little information on this subject during the Middle Ages period, which does not mean that such abuse was not happening then. Incest did not become a legal offence in England until the twentieth century (except for a brief period during the regency of Cromwell). However, it was a crime punishable by death in Scotland from 1757 and it is clear that there were strong social and religious taboos throughout Europe. It should not be assumed that the lack of legislation necessarily means lack of concern about or acceptance of behaviour.

From the Middle Ages to Victorian times

Evidence for this period is as scanty as that for earlier ages. Demos (1986) carried out a study of court records in New England in the seventeenth century and found a conspicuous absence of child abuse cases. Such a finding is usually attributed to the belief that cruelty to children in this period of history was so much the norm that court action was a rarity. Demos argues that this could not have been the case because he also found several instances of master–servant violence, which resulted in action being taken to prevent its continuation. He comes to the conclusion that child abuse was probably less prevalent in New England village communities at this time than it is generally in the USA today. He attributes this to the fact that then there were larger and less introverted and intense families, children's labour value was high, filial duty was greater and there was more communal oversight of families.[13] This study runs counter to the generally held belief, put forward by De Mause and others, that child abuse inevitably declines with social progress.

Pollock (1983) demonstrated that public concern about cruelty to children in Britain existed well before the time it is generally thought to have been discovered, i.e. in the last three decades of the nineteenth century. She carried out a study of child cruelty reports in *The Times* between 1785 and 1860 and found 385 tried cases of child neglect, physical and sexual abuse, of which only 7 per cent were found not guilty. She comments that

> The manner in which the cases were reported by the newspaper provides an indication of the attitudes of the time to cruelty to children. The fact that the majority of the cases were also found guilty meant that law and society condemned child abuse long before the specific Prevention of Cruelty to Children Act in 1889. Parents who abused their offspring were generally considered 'unnatural' and the cruelty as 'horrific' or 'barbaric'.
> (Pollock 1983: 93)

Concluding comments

This brief excursion into the early history of child abuse can of course prove nothing definitely. However, it should dispel at least two commonly held beliefs: first, the notion that the further one goes back in history the worse the treatment of children; second, that it is only in recent times that societies such as ours have taken concerted steps to deal with the problem.

With regard to the first point, there is no doubt that there was much harsh treatment of children in previous eras that would not be tolerated now. Nor is there any doubt that today's children as a whole are more likely to survive infancy and enjoy better health than their predecessors as a result of medical, hygienic and material advances. On the other hand, there is evidence that children in every era have been valued, cared for, nurtured and not ill-treated. There can be no doubt that, as was stressed at the start of this chapter, many historians and social work writers have underestimated the degree of concern that parents of previous generations have shown for their children. More discerning analyses of the treatment of children in the past, such as that of Demos (1986), point to the conclusion that there are no guarantees that the quality of all children's lives will automatically improve with time.

On the second point, there is ample evidence of official concern and state action to protect children from abuse by the parents provided by historians such as Boswell (1988), Hanawalt (1977) and Demos again. However, this evidence seems to go unnoticed. This blindness to the efforts of previous generations to regulate cruelty to children by their parents is perhaps explained by the fact that each new generation needs to think that it is improving on the past.

Careful analysis of the history of child abuse can serve to dispel myths and to put current problems into perspective. What emerges is that every society has to deal with the issue of the care of its young and has devised some means of intervention into family life to ensure this. These efforts have been influenced by the cultures, material circumstances, technologies and politics impinging on those societies. Examining these efforts with due regard to these contextual factors can enhance our understanding of current approaches to the problem.

A recent political history of child abuse and neglect

As Chapter 2 showed, child abuse is not a new phenomenon, nor is public or state concern about it. Nevertheless, fresh attempts to tackle child mistreatment are usually accompanied by the declaration that it is a new and as yet undiscovered problem. This 'newness' is seen as an important part of the process of establishing it as an issue requiring resources to tackle it.[1] Often what is new about the problem is the way in which it is being defined or interpreted. This in turn can be linked to wider issues and concerns in society. In this chapter, the focus will be on responses to child abuse between 1870 and today, with particular attention being paid to the way in which social, economic and political forces have shaped these responses. This starting date is chosen because there is a clear thread of social organization around the problem of child abuse between then and now, and not because there was no problem or societal response to it before that.

Late Victorian and Edwardian responses to child abuse

The late Victorian age saw a flurry of activity around the issue of child protection of a similar degree and nature to that which has taken place in the past two decades.

Socio-economic factors

Throughout the nineteenth century there were dramatic changes in terms of population growth, industrialization and urbanization in Britain. Between 1801 and 1861 the population doubled to a total of 20 million, of whom 7 million were under the age of 15. By 1901 the population was 32.5 million, of whom 10.5 million were under the age of 15. Children formed a third of the population throughout most of this period compared with one-fifth today.

Even so, infant mortality rates were around 15 per cent throughout most of the century. Rose (1991: 2) tells us that, 'Even as late as 1895 half the children up to 5 would die in the worst slums, compared with 19% in a healthy district like Dulwich.'

Until the passing of the 1880 Education Act, when schooling became compulsory for children up to the age of ten, the children of the poor were likely to spend more time labouring than being educated. The 1861 census showed that a third of all children aged five to nine and nearly 50 per cent of ten- to fourteen-year-olds were working. Figures for working-class children alone, had they have been collated, would have been much higher.

By any measure, the nineteenth century was a time of great upheaval and traumatic change for poor families and their children. These demographic changes, created largely by the demands of new technologies, led to new problems and concerns about the upbringing of children and new forms of state intervention into family life.

Child care concerns up to 1870

There had been four categories of children causing concern to the state up to the end of the 1860s: children of the street (vagabonds, beggars, street traders), young offenders, children at work and children looked after by the Poor Law authorities. The main pattern of response had been for issues to be initially taken up by philanthropic societies of different religious persuasions acting as pressure groups, followed by government intervention and state legislation.[2]

None of these child care issues involved direct intervention in the internal workings of the family. Although there was considerable concern to control the unruliness of children on the street (prompted by public order anxieties) and to influence the nature and amount of work children were expected to undertake (prompted by concerns about exposure to immorality as well as by concerns about exploitation), there was little thought given at this time to more direct state intervention into family life to protect children from ill-treatment by their parents, other than the sort of court action described by Pollock (1983), and mentioned in the previous chapter. Behlmer's (1982: 9) analysis of the situation then was that 'To patrol industry on behalf of the young was England's Christian duty. To patrol the home was a sacrilege.' While this analysis is generally correct, it is important to note that the sacrosanctity of domestic privacy to which Behlmer refers had always been more applicable to wealthier families than to those of the poor. In the pre-industrialized period the latter were subject to Church and community controls. The breakdown in these mechanisms that accompanied industrialization created a need for new ways of maintaining moral and social order among poor families, which is where the philanthropists came in. The issue for them and for the state was how best to establish this new form of intervention without undermining parents' responsibility for their children.

Baby farming

In the late 1860s and early 1870s this new form of state intervention into family affairs began tentatively, with its focus on the issue of baby farming. This term was used to describe the then common practice of paying for babies to be nursed and reared by substitute parents – the forerunner of today's private foster parents. The practice was widespread because of the absence of adequate contraceptive devices, the illegality of abortion, the stigma attached to illegitimacy and the need for poorer unmarried women to be free to work. The trade was created by unwanted pregnancies. It was a free-market enterprise uncontrolled by state surveillance. While many of the women who undertook this work may have been honest and trustworthy, there were several infamous cases of babies being murdered by their 'carers', which created widespread public concern.[3]

The medical profession played a leading role in this issue. In 1870 the Infant Life Protection Society (ILPS) was established with a view to controlling the practice of baby farming by means of a system of registration and inspection. By 1872, this pressure group had succeeded in pushing through the Infant Life Protection Act, which required any adult who 'fostered' more than one child under the age of one year to register with the local authority and to meet certain required standards. In practice this act proved ineffective as the resources needed to police it were not made available. London County Council was the only authority to take it at all seriously, and it appointed one inspector in 1878 to cover the whole of the metropolitan area! Further acts dealing with this issue followed: the 1897 Infant Life Protection Act, the 1908 Children Act and the 1933 Children and Young Persons Act. The main developments were that registration was required for the first child placed, the protected age was raised to nine and inspection, largely by health visitors, was made more thorough and comprehensive.

The infant life protection movement's concern with baby farming, though seen by some as unnecessary state interference into domestic arrangements, did not meet massive resistance from the establishment. The reason for this is that it was seen as an issue that was only marginal to family life.

The formation of the NSPCC

It was not to be long before the so-called bastions of the family were to be more directly assaulted. The 1880s saw the emergence of the Liverpool Society for the Prevention of Cruelty to Children (SPCC) and then the London SPCC (later to form the core of the National Society for the Prevention of Cruelty to Children). Most of the larger conurbations in Britain followed suit soon after. While other philanthropic societies, such as Dr Barnardo's, had been 'rescuing' children living outside their families, the NSPCC's concern was to 'rescue' children living in their own homes.

The early SPCC protagonists considered existing arrangements for the reporting of child ill-treatment and neglect and the subsequent impeachment of parents to be something of a lottery. They argued that there were no statutory means of protecting children before cases of parental cruelty were tried and no means of ensuring continued protection once convicted parents had served their sentences.[4]

The following steps were taken to remedy this situation. Inspectors, initially very few in number, were appointed to seek out and report to the police instances of abuse and neglect, even though until the passing of legislation in 1889 they had no legal authority or mandate to carry out this task. Shelters were established to provide places of safety for children pending prosecutions. They too were not backed by the force of law until later. Shocking cases of child mistreatment were publicized in order to influence public opinion and generate resources. Parliamentary lobbying to change the law regarding cruelty to children was relentlessly pursued. The outcome of all this pressure was the 1889 Prevention of Cruelty to Children Act. This act defined specific parental misdemeanours against children and created penalties for wilful ill-treatment or neglect leading to unnecessary suffering or injury to health. It empowered police searches for children thought to be at risk, legalized removals to places of safety and enabled 'fit person' orders (the forerunners of care orders) to be imposed on children whose parents had been convicted of offences against them. Further Acts followed in 1894, 1904 and 1908, the effects of which were to consolidate and extend the original Act.

By this time the main components of child protection law that exist today were in place. As Dingwall *et al.* (1984: 220) put it:

> there have been virtually no fundamental changes in the categories of children covered by the interventionist legislation since 1894. Subsequent legislation has consolidated the Victorian statutes and occasionally modernised their wording. It has introduced a few new types of disposition and redistributed enforcement duties. Nevertheless, the issues of principle were mostly settled in Victorian times.

The foundations were set then even for much of the form and style of current intervention practices in child protection work, according to Ferguson (1990). In his lucid account of an NSPCC case in the North-east in 1898, he depicts an inspector grappling with the same contradictions and complexities as social workers today. Even at this early stage in child protection work, there was much emphasis on providing advice, support and material help. Much was being done to prevent court action as far as possible and to use it as a last resort. This style of intervention, which does not fit with the stereotype of the 'cruelty man', developed as a result of two main factors. First, NSPCC inspectors had to gain acceptance in communities if they were to be effective. Second, their ultimate concern and that of the state was to inculcate a sense of responsibility in parents without totally undermining them. Prison and punishment were not seen as the best means of achieving this. Advice, persuasion and the threat of prosecution were methods that were more in tune with these twin goals.

By 1914 the NSPCC had established itself as a national institution. Its officers, together with its Scottish counterparts, covered the whole of the British Isles. Despite being feared in many communities, the NSPCC was also respected and this was reflected in the high percentage of its referrals that came from neighbours and relatives.[5]

Responding to sexual abuse

During this era, child sexual abuse within the family, previously ignored as an issue, was also being tackled by the NSPCC. Behlmer (1982: 70) notes that the London SPCC in its first year dealt with 95 cases involving 'domestic victims', of which 12 concerned 'an evil which is altogether too unmentionable' (sexual assault or incest). However, despite this awareness and recognition, the NSPCC did not bring the issue of child sexual abuse to public attention in the same way as it had publicized physical abuse and neglect. This response reflected the general attitude to the issue, which was one of not wanting to know, a conspiracy of silence.

The more lurid and salacious side of child sexual abuse, i.e. child prostitution, received far more public attention. In 1885, a journalist on the *Pall Mall Gazette*, William Stead, with the backing of influential social purity and child protection philanthropists, wrote an exposé of a child prostitution ring that lured young English girls to brothels in Belgium. The series of articles he wrote were entitled 'The maiden tribute of modern Babylon' (see Bristow 1977; Gorham 1978). The outcome of these events was legislation to raise the age of lawful consent to intercourse for girls from 13 to 16, a response that Gorham views as inappropriate, but typical of the romanticized view of childhood held by middle-class Victorians, and also of their ignorance of the material conditions and pressures experienced by working-class female children.

The issue of intra-familial abuse or incest meanwhile continued to receive little public attention or recognition. Where it was acknowledged, it was seen as linked to low intelligence and as a product of the overcrowded sleeping conditions of the poorer classes (Wohl 1978). Gordon (1989), drawing on the case records of the Massachusetts Society for the Protection of Cruelty to Children between 1880 and 1910, draws the same conclusion from the American experience:

> The NSPCC's ability to recognize incest, if not discuss it publicly, was in part based on its notion that it was exclusively a vice of the poor. Conservative and progressive reformers spoke of the degradation of poverty, as if its victims were animalistic, lacking in standards of family life. (Gordon 1989: 215)

Another popular explanation of this otherwise inexplicable vice was the demon drink.

There were, however, some public developments. The NSPCC, along with the National Vigilance Association, which had been formed in 1885, pressed for a law to criminalize incest, which was not a specific category of crime at this time. This pressure resulted in the passing of the 1908 Incest Act. Although the impact of this act was very limited, at least incest was officially recognized as a crime and this in turn created the potential for more effective intervention given the will to intercede.[6]

Protecting children within the family

As can be seen, there were considerable shifts in thinking about state intervention into family life between 1870 and 1914. I have focused on the child protection aspects, but one could look at a range of other areas, such as education, working conditions and health, and see similar developments taking place. However, child protection was a particularly problematic enterprise because it was at the most instrusive end of the process, in that it called into question behaviour inside the family home.

The responsibility of carrying out this task was taken up by religiously inspired philanthropic societies, most notably the NSPCC. Their workers faced the dilemma that social agencies today still face: how, following liberal traditions, to influence the family without undermining its independence. That agencies did not wish to undermine families at this period is clear from the accounts of Behlmer and Gordon: 'Under trying and occasionally hazardous conditions, therefore, cruelty men tried to stir a sense of parental duty in the adults they cautioned' (Behlmer 1982: 167). 'The SPCCs aimed as much to reinforce failing parental/paternal authority as to limit it' (Gordon 1989: 56). The aim was to change the internal behaviour of the family in order to ensure child protection, but without disrupting the order of things. Similarities between the late Victorian approach and that of the present response to child abuse abound.

Between the two world wars

A shift in focus

In contrast to the amount of change and degree of concern that characterized child protection work, particularly in the first three decades of the 1870–1914 period, there was a definite shift in focus away from this issue between the two world wars. Early on in this period there was a sense that a corner had been turned. The 1923 Home Office Report on the work of the Children's Branch pointed out that, despite the fact that the 1908 Children Act had broadened the grounds for neglect proceedings, the number of prosecutions of parents had dropped from 4106 in 1900 to 2052 by 1921. The work of the NSPCC reflected these changes. In 1913–14 the NSPCC dealt with 54,772 cases. However, the number of prosecutions resulting from these investigations was only 2349 (approximately 4 per cent compared with a prosecution rate of 10 per cent in 1895–6). Why had this shift in emphasis taken place?

Several reasons have been put forward. The 1923 Home Office report attributed the change to improved standards of parenting:

> The children of the poorer classes are better cared for than they used to be, and it is now unusual to see dirty and ragged children in the streets of our great cities. Cases of extreme brutality which were all too common not so many years ago are now becoming less frequent. (Home Office 1923: 69–70)

These improved parenting standards were seen to be the result of better welfare provision (e.g. school meals, health and child maternity services), changes in working-class habits (e.g. reduced alcohol consumption) and the work of agencies like the NSPCC. Rose (1991) attributes the perceived reduction in child abuse to the decline in the birth rate. He points out that the average number of children born to families in 1915 was 2.5 compared with 6 in the 1860s, and comments that 'One may conclude, therefore, that children being born from the Edwardian period were more "expected" and therefore on the whole more wanted than before' (Rose 1991: 243). Behlmer (1982) considers that two factors were at play. First, the First World War and the depression diverted attention from the issue. Second, complacency had set in as a result of undue faith in the powers of the NSPCC to deal with the problem.

Dingwall *et al.* (1984) argue that child protection in itself had never been a major concern of the state, except in the 1880–1900 period. Its real worry was the threat provided by inadequate moral socialization of children to the social order. They argue that neglect was seen as a cause of delinquency and was, therefore, considered to be an important target of intervention for that reason, not because of concern for the well-being of individual children.[7] Employing the work of Donzelot (1980), they contest that throughout the first half of the twentieth century, the state recoiled from the direct attack on the family (and particularly patriarchal authority) that had taken place in the period immediately before this and redirected its efforts to bringing about change by means of support services focused particularly on mothers.

Gordon (1989), drawing from the American scene, argues that the amount and type of child abuse did not, as far as she could judge, differ significantly during the whole period between 1880 and 1960. All that differed was the response to it. She links societal concerns about child abuse and other forms of family violence to the strength of feminist thinking, arguing that when women have a strong voice, as they had in the late Victorian and early Edwardian eras, the effect of their pressure is to create a tougher response to the issue (though she hastens to add that this does not mean that the agencies established to deal with the problem share a feminist analysis of the problem). Her explanation, therefore, of the lack of overt focus on child abuse in the Depression period in America is as follows:

> One of the major characteristics of depression-era social work was a policy of defending the 'conventional' nuclear family . . . A sympathy arose for the unemployed husband, the stress and role-conflict that

frequently engendered his violence; remarkably less sympathy was mustered for the situation of mothers doing double shifts – at home and at work – in attempts to hold the family together . . . Indeed violence altogether was deemphasised, and the SPCCs devoted themselves almost exclusively to child neglect, now conceived primarily in terms of economic neglect, such as malnutrition or inadequate medical care. (Gordon 1989: 22–3)

Apart from the fact that it is highly unlikely that between the wars British NSPCC inspectors delved into social psychological causes of male violence within families, this argument seems to have as good an explanatory value for the British situation as for that in the USA at this time.

All the foregoing explanations have some validity. There is no way of knowing for certain whether the incidence of child abuse during this era reduced or not. If socio-economic factors are taken into account, then despite the recession of the 1930s living standards were higher than in the late Victorian period and the extent of gross material deprivation was probably much less. These factors point to the likelihood of less abuse taking place, as reflected in official figures. However, it is also clear that there was a much less evangelical approach to the problem than in the previous era and a probability that a good deal of abuse went unnoticed.

Sexual abuse

Gordon (1989) provides one of the few accounts of official responses to child sexual abuse during this period. The case records she studied show that such abuse persisted throughout the whole period of her study (i.e. from 1880 to 1960). The 1880–1910 records show that the SPCC workers of that time more readily accepted allegations of sexual abuse and that they judged child sexual abusers as socially and morally inferior beings. From 1910 onwards there was a much less direct, much more tentative approach to this issue, with far greater emphasis on abuse by strangers and on girls' sexual delinquency. In addition there was a good deal of victim-blaming. The problem of child sexual abuse, as Gordon sees it, though never high on the agenda, went underground for much of this time.

In Britain it is hard to find much reference to the subject. Criminal statistics demonstrate the rarity of prosecution under the Incest Act (see note 6). However, it is clear that cases were pursued, judging from NSPCC accounts such as that by Housden (1955).[8]

1945–1970 and the rise of the children's departments

The Curtis Committee

There was an upsurge of interest in the welfare of deprived children after the Second World War. The report of the Curtis Committee (1946), which was set up to enquire into the conditions of children 'deprived of a normal home life with their own parents and relatives' (p. 5), provides a comprehensive and thoughtful account of the child care concerns of the day. However, it is notable that child neglect is only briefly referred to, and seems to win attention more because of its link with subsequent delinquent behaviour than for any direct concern about harm to the child (see note 7). This is despite the fact that one of the catalysts in highlighting the sorry condition of children cared for by the state at this time was the manslaughter by his foster father of a 12-year-old child in care, Dennis O'Neill, a case that was being separately enquired into at the same time as the Curtis Committee was sitting (O'Neill 1945).

The 1948 Children Act and its implementation

The 1948 Children Act was closely based on the findings of the Curtis Committee and paid little attention specifically to child abuse. In the period following its implementation, however, there were some significant developments on the child abuse front.

In 1950 a joint circular was issued to local authorities, proposing the setting up of coordinating committees for overseeing 'problem family' cases that were being visited by a wide range of departments (Home Office 1950). Children's officers were appointed to act as chairpersons of these committees. Under the 1952 Children and Young Persons (Amendment) Act, children's departments' powers to intervene in cases where children were thought to need care and protection were broadened. This Act also empowered authorities to seek fit person orders on children without the requirement that parents first be prosecuted for cruelty or neglect. This change was seen to be beneficial in two ways. It enabled authorities to protect children more easily and it further reduced the need to prosecute parents, which was in tune with the less punitive approach towards families that characterized this period.

The other major development at this time was the push for a preventive approach to children and family work. This notion was attractive to a wide variety of constituencies. Child care officers, as a result of their direct work with families, saw that admissions to care were preventable given sufficient inputs of counselling and support before a crisis point was reached. Central government departments, concerned by a dramatic rise in the number of children in care immediately following the implementation of the 1948 Act, saw it as a cost-effective option. In addition they were concerned about the link between neglect and delinquency and the need to do something about the latter. There was also research support for a change of emphasis. Bowlby's study of institutional care for children and his resulting theories about the deleterious effects of maternal deprivation were prominent in this respect (Bowlby 1951; Bowlby et al. 1965).

Packman (1975) demonstrates how in practice throughout the 1950s child care officers had spent more and more of their time working with families to prevent receptions into care:

> By the 1960s, children supervised in their own homes far outnumbered those 'in care' and departments were involved, not only with a signifi-cant minority of all families with children (one-third of a million children, referred in one year, represents roughly 3 per cent of the total child popu-lation) but with a whole range of other services on their behalf. (Packman 1975: 72)

Such work received legal backing with the passing of the 1963 Children and Young Persons Act, section 1 of which empowered local authorities to pro-vide material and financial assistance to keep children in their own homes where it was thought to be in their best interests.

Child care concerns in the 1960s

The main concern in the child care field for the remainder of the 1960s con-tinued to be delinquency, the cause of which was seen to be neglect, and the solution increased support for the family. The 1969 Children and Young Per-sons Act reflected this concern and analysis of the situation. Neglected chil-dren were treated by the law in the same way as children beyond control, children in moral danger, children refusing to go to school and children com-mitting offences. As will be seen, when in the mid-1970s attention switched more directly to the ill-treatment of children by their parents, this legislation proved to be inadequate in many respects.

With regard to the professional response, there was a move towards a less specialized approach to child care work and to a broader family problem per-spective (see Donnison 1954). Deprived children were seen to be the products of deprived families and a family-based service was considered to be needed, with a broader remit and more powers than before. Influenced by this type of thinking, the Seebohm report of 1968 recommended the formation of new unified social services departments comprising the former health and welfare and children's departments. Generalist social workers were intended to pro-vide a 'community-based, family-oriented service'. These recommendations were made law and implemented in 1971.

Concluding comments

On the face of it, the period between 1945 and 1970 was one in which family policy in general and the response to neglectful families in particular was rela-tively benign.[9] As an extract from the 1960 Ingleby Report shows, the policy style of the time was unequivocally family-oriented and family-sympathetic:

> In dealing with the prevention of neglect in the home, it is, in our opinion, essential to distinguish the following three stages:
> (a) the detection of the families at risk
> (b) the investigation and diagnosis of the particular problem

(c) treatment: the provision of facilities and services to meet the families'
     needs and to reduce the stresses and dangers that they face. (Ingleby
     Report 1960: sec. 38, 17)

It is notable that it is families that are defined as being at risk and it is families
that are expected to be the recipients of the treatment. Whether such a policy
served the interests of children and women in these families is an open
question.

Once again, Gordon's account of the American situation is instructive,
given the dearth of British studies of child protection during this period. She
characterizes the 1940–60 period as follows:

The defend-the-conventional-family policy in social work continued
through the 1940s and 1950s. These decades represented the low point in
public awareness of family-violence problems and in the status of child-
protection work within the social-work profession. (Gordon 1989: 23)

She describes an increasing psychoanalysation of family violence by social
workers. In Britain, the influence of psychoanalytical theory on social work
practice has always been much less than in the USA (see Yelloly 1980).
Nevertheless, there can be little doubt that the work of Bowlby and the
concerns about delinquency helped to focus attention on the emotional
qualities of mothering and motherhood and emphasized the need to bolster
families with advice, support and casework. Far less direct attention was paid
to violence to children and to women within those families.

Sexual abuse, as we perceive it today, seems to have been even further
from social workers' minds – the main forms of perceived sexual abuse at this
time were either incest, seen as a rare and pathological phenomenon, or girls
in moral danger because of insufficient controls being exerted by their
parents.[10]

Thus from a feminist perspective the policy towards child abuse prevalent
during this period is seen as deficient in terms of protecting women and
children from male violence. On the other hand, this period has been viewed
by other commentators as one of some enlightenment with regard to child
care issues rather than one of lack of vigilance. Parton (1985) and Holman
(1988) both view the child protection practices of the period that will be
considered next as retrogressive and over-intrusive into family life in comparison with this one and are critical of the decline in state support for the
family and the loss of emphasis on preventive work.

The rediscovery of child abuse (1970–1985)

Henry Kempe and baby battering

In the USA child abuse was formally rediscovered in 1962. In that year Henry
Kempe, a paediatrician, and his associates coined the term 'the battered child

syndrome', which described and explained the process that led to parents (but essentially mothers) physically assaulting their babies and young children (Kempe *et al*. 1962). Pfohl (1977) demonstrates that the first medical specialism to rediscover the problem was actually that of paediatric radiology. However, Kempe and his colleagues were the first confidently to attribute injuries seen on children to deliberate mistreatment rather than to the outcome of accident or disease. Kempe argued that abuse of children was far more widespread than anyone had previously considered and that professionals (doctors in particular) had been turning a blind eye to it.

Kempe's original thinking stressed the psychological aspects of child abuse. Essentially his view was that child abuse resulted from emotional or psychological problems within the parents (or parent), which in turn stemmed from their own emotionally depriving experiences in childhood. He argued that parents needed psychological treatment or therapy, that their children needed temporary protection and that in most cases rehabilitation should be the goal. The main exceptions to this rule were parents diagnosed as having psychotic illnesses. (For a fuller account see Chapter 6.)

This model of child abuse was remarkably influential throughout the United States in the 1970s and 1980s. Thanks to the tireless campaigning of Kempe and others in this field, physical abuse of children became a major social issue, attracting national publicity and massive funding. As early as 1967, every state in the USA had mandatory reporting laws and the Children's Bureau was spending considerable amounts of money on research into the problem.[11]

It is hard to pinpoint the reasons for the re-emergence of this age-old problem in this new form at this time. Certainly, technological developments, such as the use of X-rays, played a part. However, Pfohl (1977) attributes much to the professional aspirations of paediatricians, who in an era of better physical health were in search of a new role for themselves. Neither explanation seems sufficient to account for the magnitude or persistence of the response to the issue. Broader social factors need to be taken into account as well. The climate was right for a greater focus on the care and upbringing of children. The relative affluence of the 1960s created the conditions for people to pay greater attention to the psychological needs of children and to the quality of parent–child relationships. Kempe's ideas were in tune with the times in that the notion of parents abusing their children as a result of a psychological syndrome was more acceptable than attributing such cruelty to poverty or ignorance. By giving child abuse a medical label and seeing it as a treatable condition, the new forms of intervention into family life were not seen as a threat to the independence of families in general because they were aimed only at the families that had the illness.

The re-emergence of child abuse as a problem in Britain

Parton (1979, 1981, 1985) provides a detailed account of the development of child abuse as a social problem in Britain in the late 1960s and the 1970s. The pattern of development is similar to (and indeed greatly influenced by) that in the USA. He sees the growth of the problem as very closely linked to professional aspirations and to the politics of the family and the state.

There were two main professional groupings involved in the 1960s: medical doctors (most notably paediatricians) and the NSPCC. In 1963, Griffiths and Moynihan, two orthopaedic surgeons, used the term 'battered baby syndrome' in an influential article in the *British Medical Journal*. The amount of medical literature devoted to this topic developed steadily throughout the 1960s but the problem was not responded to at a wider level at this stage.

The NSPCC was facing an identity crisis at this time. Throughout the 1950s and 1960s, the new children's departments grew in size and stature and there was considerable overlap between their responsibilities and those of the NSPCC. Both were tackling similar problems in similar ways, but the children's departments were better resourced and had a broader statutory mandate. The emergence of a direct focus on physical child mistreatment, well established by the late 1960s in the USA, offered the NSPCC the opportunity of developing a more specialist and separate role. Contact was made with Henry Kempe and his associates, who were refining their ideas and developing new practice initiatives in Denver, Colorado. As a result, a project was established in London to provide specialist casework help for families referred for child abuse at a centre named Denver House. The work of this project is described and analysed by Baher *et al.* (1976). During this period the NSPCC was prolific in its publications on the subject of child abuse and was highly influential in placing it firmly on the social problem agenda.[12]

Maria Colwell

What finally settled matters was the Maria Colwell case (Colwell 1974). Maria, aged seven, was killed by her stepfather in 1973. She had been in care for five years following a period of general neglect and low standards of care, and for nearly all of this time she had been boarded out with her aunt. Her mother had in the meanwhile remarried and had given birth to three children. In 1971, she was determined to have Maria back home. East Sussex County Council, in whose care Maria was, agreed to a plan of rehabilitation, supported Maria's mother's application to discharge the care order and recommended that it be replaced by a supervision order. Maria, who had been very resistant to returning to her mother, died 13 months later, grossly under-nourished and severely beaten by her stepfather. This was despite the fact that throughout this period there had been many health and welfare workers involved in the oversight of her welfare who had failed to 'see' the neglect and ill-treatment that she must have been subjected to over some considerable part of this time.

How the Maria Colwell case came to have such an impact is carefully analysed by Parton (1979). He argues that her death did not immediately cause a great deal of national concern. The key factor was the decision of the then Minister of the Department of Health and Social Security, Sir Keith Joseph, to hold a public inquiry into what happened. Parton pinpoints the influence of a group called the Tunbridge Wells Study Group, consisting of paediatricians, lawyers and social workers, as a key factor acting on Joseph to make his decision. Joseph, himself, was very much in tune with the ideas of this group, as he was promulgating a more general thesis about cycles of deprivation among poor families and the need for such families to be targeted for specialist intervention (Joseph 1972).

The resulting inquiry, aided by media reports, especially in *The Times* and *The Sunday Times*, arrested the attention of the public. Diane Lees, Maria's social worker, was vilified. The social work profession was considered to be too soft and permissive. The more benign family approach to child neglect issues, which, as has been seen, had been prevalent since 1948, was thrown into question.

The establishment of a system for dealing with child abuse

As a consequence of the Maria Colwell report, the DHSS, by means of a series of circulars and letters, established the basis of the system that currently exists for protecting children. The aims of the changes were to raise awareness of child abuse, to ensure that any allegation of abuse was promptly responded to, to improve inter-agency cooperation and to put in place more thorough systems for monitoring children considered to be at risk. The mechanisms for achieving these aims were: (a) Area Review Committees, consisting of higher and middle managers from all agencies with a role to play in the protection of children, whose function was to coordinate and oversee all work in this area; (b) case conferences involving all front-line professionals, whose function was to assess new cases and to review ongoing casework; and (c) registers of all children considered to be abused or at risk of abuse.

Intervention into families with children considered to be at risk thus became, at least in form, more focused and intrusive. The concerns of the previous era, i.e. avoidance of separation of parents and children and support of and influence on the family as a whole, were now being officially called into question. The 1975 Children Act, which was largely concerned with more general child care issues, reflected the mood of the times. In particular, drawing on a study of long-term children in care (Rowe and Lambert 1973), it emphasized the needs of children as distinct from the rights of the parents. On the child protection front this Act made two major changes. First, it incorporated among the grounds for care proceedings the fact that a child was or might be living in the same household as a person who had committed offences under schedule 1 of the 1933 Children and Young Persons Act (i.e. offences of violence and indecency towards children). This was a direct result of the death of a child, Susan Auckland, at the hands of her father, who had previously been convicted for the manslaughter of another of his children (Auckland 1975). Second, it required the appointment of guardians *ad litem* to act exclusively on behalf of the child in cases like Maria Colwell's, when parents were seeking to discharge orders and the local authority was not opposing such courses of action. These changes reflect the fact that the new emphasis on abuse of children was already finding the 1969 Children and Young Persons Act deficient for the purpose of protecting them.

Child abuse work from 1975 to 1985

For the remainder of the 1970s the pressure to create a more effective detection, investigation and monitoring system for child abuse continued unabated. From 1973 to 1981 there were 27 inquiries into the deaths and serious abuse of children in Britain caused by their carers. In almost all these cases, various health and welfare agencies were already involved, often in a statutory capacity (see DHSS 1982). Mainly by means of advice and circulars from the DHSS, considerable effort was made to incorporate lessons from these inquiries into the structure of practice. From relatively small beginnings, child abuse work developed into a major preoccupation of social services departments.

The definition of child abuse broadened over time. This is well demonstrated by the changes in terminology. By 1980, the term 'child abuse' had replaced 'baby battering' and the subsequent term 'non-accidental injury'. The 1980 DHSS circular entitled *Child Abuse: Central Register Systems* outlined four categories of abuse or risk of abuse: physical injury; physical neglect; failure to thrive incorporated with emotional abuse; and living in the same household as someone convicted of offences under schedule 1 of the 1933 Children and Young Persons Act. At this time it is notable that sexual abuse of children was not considered to be a category for registration. This issue, already being addressed on a broad front in the USA, was only beginning to emerge as a social problem in Britain (see below).

In the first half of the 1980s there was some relaxation in the drive to establish better systems for responding to child abuse. There were fewer public inquiries (four in the three years from the beginning of 1982 to the end of 1984) and there was generally a consolidation of the rash of changes that had taken place in the 1970s. By this time, social services departments were firmly in the lead role in this field, despite official concern to emphasize the interprofessional aspects of the work.

Intrusive social work practice?

Between 1970 and 1985 state intervention into families to protect children had certainly become more systematic, in the literal sense of the word. Whether it had become more intrusive into families is open to question. The most comprehensive research into practice during this period was that of Dingwall *et al.* (1983). They argued that the 'new' response to child abuse was tougher in aspect than in practice. They tried to demonstrate that, despite greater concerns for children at risk, social workers, by and large, were still operating in a relatively benign way with families (similar to the pre-Colwell era). They identified what they described as a 'rule of optimism' in action, whereby social workers were expected to make the best interpretation of an allegation of abuse. This 'rule', they argued, was not something of social workers' own making, but reflected prevailing liberal democratic views about the respective roles of the state and the family with regard to the upbringing of children: namely that while the state has a legitimate role to play in intervening into families to ensure the protection of children, this should only be done with due regard to the rights of parents as well as to the assessed needs of children. Thus the liberal approach that they identified being adopted by social workers was in general terms in line with the requirements of the state.

Parton cites the increase in the use of place of safety orders in the 1970s and of the gross numbers of children in care as evidence of a more intrusive approach towards families.[13] His view of the situation is as follows:

> It would thus appear that social work practice with children and families has become far more authoritative and decisive and has increasingly come to intervene in ways which can be experienced by threats or punishments. (Parton 1985: 127)

Corby (1987) found from his study of early intervention into families suspected of abusing their children that the form and style of this intervention was, from the parents' viewpoint, punitive and severe. Parents suspected of abusing their children were at first treated with great suspicion, were poorly informed of what was happening and had no rights of attendance at case conferences. However, after the initial stages of intervention, this more proceduralized and apparently punitive approach gave way to a more sympathetic and helpful response in many cases. Relatively few cases resulted in court action and there was evidence to support Dingwall *et al.*'s (1983) view that, overall, intervention was characterized by a cautious optimism.

Arguably, therefore, it can be concluded that increased state intrusion into family life between 1975 and 1985, while being officially encouraged, was in practice being tentatively implemented. The focus was still on working with families as far as possible.

From 1985 to the present

Developments in the general child care field

At the same time that social workers were being encouraged to take a firmer stance on child abuse, there were counter concerns being put forward about the dangers of over-intrusive, heavy-handed practice in the general child care field. Parton (1991) dates these concerns from 1978.

First, a series of studies was commissioned by the DHSS, resulting in a number of publications summarized in a report entitled *Social Work Decisions in Child Care* (DHSS 1985a). These studies, while not directly focused on child abuse, came to the general conclusion that not enough attention was being paid to the needs of families in child care work. In particular, some were critical of what they saw as the overuse of compulsory powers (Packman 1986).

Second, the House of Commons Social Services Committee chaired by Renee Short undertook an inquiry into children in care and reported in 1984 (House of Commons 1984). Parton (1991: 27–39) gives a good summary and analysis of the working and findings of this committee. It took as its major concern the perennial problem of the relationship between the state, children and the family, namely how the state can best ensure the protection and welfare of children and provide support for the family in achieving this goal without undermining its independence. In particular it was vexed by the relative weight to be given to professional discretionary powers (especially those of social workers) and to a legally enforced rights-based approach, and came to the conclusion that there should be a shift towards the latter. Place of safety orders and parental rights resolutions were particular instances of concern. The report recommended the establishment of a working party on child care law, whose report in 1985 (DHSS 1985b) laid the foundation for the 1989 Children Act.

The Jasmine Beckford Inquiry

On the child protection front there was a major development, though in a totally different direction from that being taken in the broader child care field. The year 1985 saw the publication of the Jasmine Beckford report (Beckford 1985). Jasmine, aged four, died in July 1984, emaciated and horrifically beaten over an extended period of time by her stepfather, Morris Beckford. Jasmine and her younger sister, Louise, had both suffered severe injuries in 1981, for which Morris Beckford was given a suspended sentence. The children were committed to the care of Brent Borough Council and lived with foster parents for six months. They were then returned to their parents, who had been helped with rehousing and had been allocated a family aide, on a home-on-trial basis. The social services department supported the family somewhat spasmodically over the next two years. Jasmine was only seen once by the social worker in her last ten months of life. This social worker, Gunn Wahlstrom, was described by the judge at the trial of Morris Beckford and Jasmine's mother as being 'naive beyond belief' and was subjected to the same sort of negative publicity that Diane Lees had been exposed to eleven years earlier.

The inquiry report made 68 recommendations. Its main concerns were that social workers were too optimistic with regard to the families with which they were working. Dingwall *et al.*'s (1983) 'rule of optimism' was mistakenly interpreted to support this view. The report stressed that too much emphasis was placed on the rehabilitation of Jasmine and her sister to their parents, and that, in the process, evidence to suggest the likelihood of further abuse was ignored.[14] Further, it emphasized that although other agencies were to blame to some extent for what happened, the main fault lay with Brent Social Services Department because it was legally *in loco parentis* with regard to Jasmine by virtue of the care order made in 1981. The report was unequivocal in its view that social work's essential and primary task was to protect children and that where necessary social workers should employ the full force of the law to ensure this.

The findings of the Beckford inquiry had an immediate impact on policy and practice. In 1986, the DHSS published draft guidelines setting out recommendations for improving interprofessional coordination in child abuse work and inviting comments (DHSS 1986). The main proposed changes consisted of reframing child abuse work as child protection work, thus emphasizing the statutory obligation placed on local authorities to act primarily on behalf of children wherever risk was perceived. It was proposed that area review committees be re-termed joint child abuse committees (but in the final guidelines issued in 1988 they were in fact renamed Area Child Protection Committees) and that child abuse registers become child protection registers. The key role of social service department workers was again reaffirmed and strengthened. They were allocated the main responsibility to coordinate work (now called a protection plan) with families whose children's names had been added to the child protection register. Among the other changes, it is notable that with regard to parental participation at case conferences, a topic that had been concerning a wide range of professionals and pressure groups (Brown and Waters 1985), the recommendation was that it was not appropriate for parents to attend formal case conferences, although they could attend informal meetings with key professionals who were involved with them. The tone and message of this document were identical with those of the Beckford Report – the focus of attention was to be shifted to the protection of children first and to consideration of the needs and rights of parents second.

The effects of the Beckford inquiry report seem to have been immediate. Statistics regarding child protection registers (see Chapter 4) show a massive rise in the numbers of children being placed on them after 1985. The number of place of safety orders increased dramatically in 1986 and 1987 after nine years at roughly the same level[15] and there was a significant rise in the number of children coming into care as a result of child abuse and neglect (see also Chapter 4).

The Beckford report was followed by a series of other inquiries. Between 1985 and 1989 there were ten in all, the findings of which are summarized in a study of inquiry reports, 1980–1989 (Department of Health 1991a). What all the physical abuse inquiries of this period were at pains to emphasize was the need for a child-focused approach, with much more emphasis on assessing families for potential risk.

Child sexual abuse

The counter concern for a greater family-focused approach coming from those concerned with the general problems of children in care was augmented from an unlikely source. In the summer of 1987, newspapers reported a child sexual abuse scandal in Cleveland. It emerged that 121 children had, over a period of six months, but mostly in the two months of May and June, been brought into care on place of safety orders on the recommendation of two paediatricians who, using a physical test pioneered in Leeds, had diagnosed the majority of them as having been anally abused. The parents of these children were in uproar and had attracted the attention of the local Labour MP, Stuart Bell, to their cause. He raised the matter in parliament and the outcome was the establishment of another, but this time very different, public inquiry.

Up to this time the issue of child sexual abuse had been a relatively minor concern for child protection agencies in Britain. However, a good deal of pioneering work had already been carried out before events in Cleveland in a quieter and less controversial way. As with physical abuse, concerns about the sexual abuse of children originally stemmed mainly from the American experience. The main protagonists there were survivors of sexual abuse,[16] feminist writers such as Rush (1980) who saw such abuse as symptomatic of gender power inequalities, and the medical profession. Among the latter, Kempe and his associates were again prominent (Kempe and Kempe 1978). Another approach to the problem was developed by Giaretto *et al.* (1978) (see Chapter 8).

Giaretto's work was a strong influence on the British approach to the problem developed by a team of child psychiatrists, psychologists and social workers at the Great Ormond Street Hospital for Children (see Ben-Tovim *et al.* 1988; Furniss 1991). Their approach, which will also be considered in more detail in Chapters 6 and 8, was to develop a method of intervention based on family therapy principles. In addition they developed techniques (again pioneered in the USA) for helping children disclose the fact that they had been sexually abused, using drawings, play, anatomically correct dolls and video-recordings. These techniques were taken on by social workers in several statutory agencies and figured in events at Cleveland.

By 1987 child abuse was beginning to clamber on to the official child protection agenda, though the response to the problem throughout Britain was patchy and variable. A Mori Poll survey commissioned by Channel 4 television had demonstrated that one in ten children had experienced some form of sexual abuse by the age of 15 and in half of these cases the abuse had been committed either by a family member or somebody known and previously trusted by the child (Baker and Duncan 1985). In Leeds a child sexual abuse ring had been discovered in the mid-1980s, involving children of a much younger age than had been previously thought to be associated with such abuse (Wild 1986). Paediatricians there developed the anal reflex dilatation test (Hobbs and Wynne 1986), which was seen as a breakthrough in terms of providing definite physical evidence of sexual abuse, which up to this time had been almost impossible to prove in the courts.

The Cleveland affair

These developments set the scene for what happened in Cleveland. The rash of child sexual abuse diagnoses there and the subsequent removal of children into statutory care can be attributed to a combination of factors. First, there was heightened awareness of the possible extent of sexual abuse of children among key social services personnel and community paediatricians. Second, the paediatricians were aware of the newly developed reflex anal dilalation test, convinced of its validity and determined to use it. Third, other agencies, particularly the police and police surgeons, were more traditional in their approach and did not accept the new thinking, thus creating a major split in the inter-professional approach. Fourth, the social services department had recently reorganized its child protection system in response to the findings of the Beckford inquiry. The result of this cocktail of factors was that the paediatricians diagnosed far more cases of sexual abuse than had previously been the norm, the social services department acted swiftly and authoritatively to secure place of safety orders on all diagnosed cases and the police and police surgeons, who would usually have been closely involved in gathering evidence for possible prosecutions, dissociated themselves completely from what was happening.

As a result, large numbers of children were committed to care, many of whom were inappropriately placed for long periods in hospital wards because there were insufficient social services department facilities to cope with such an influx. Although all the children had been diagnosed as being abused, it was not clear who had abused them. Social workers, using the techniques developed by Ben-Tovim and his colleagues, were holding series of disclosure interviews to try to establish facts, and in the meanwhile those parents who were potential suspects were being denied access to their children in order to ensure that they did not influence their evidence.

The main findings of the inquiry report resulting from these events confirmed that child sexual abuse was a more widespread phenomenon than had previously been thought to be the case. The chair of the inquiry, Lord Justice Butler-Sloss, was at pains to stress that, whatever criticism might be levelled at various practitioners, child sexual abuse must remain on the social policy agenda. The report also criticized individuals from every agency and profession for not working together more cooperatively. In particular, social workers were judged to have rushed in too precipitately to rescue abused children (the opposite of the criticism levelled at them in most of the physical abuse inquiries). The report also recommended that greater consideration be given to the rights of parents (in terms of being fully informed of decisions) and to those of children, particularly with regard to medical examinations (because of the disagreements between professionals at Cleveland some children had been examined on four or more occasions[17]). Finally, it criticized the use of the reflex anal dilatation test without supporting social evidence.

These findings and recommendations had an almost immediate effect. The draft 'working together' guidelines issued in 1986 were hastily amended to incorporate its recommendations. Some of the changes created a complete turn-around in policy, most notably that relating to parental participation at case conferences. Whereas the 1986 draft had stated that it was inappropriate for parents to attend, the 1988 view was that

> They should be invited, where practicable, to attend part, or, if appropriate the whole, of case conferences unless in the view of the Chairman of the case conference their presence will preclude a full and proper consideration of the child's interest. (DHSS 1988: para. 5.45)

These guidelines placed greater emphasis on careful inter-disciplinary consultation before intervention in sexual abuse cases and recommended joint police and social services department investigations to be the norm.

The 1989 Children Act

The Cleveland report also had an impact on the passage of the 1989 Children Act through parliament. There were hasty amendments, such as that empowering children to refuse to undergo medical assessments if they so wished[18] and that enabling local authorities to provide or pay for accommodation for alleged abusers so that children could remain at home during investigations.[19] This Act was already very much a mixed bag. The main thrust for change had come through the general concerns about children in care already documented and the need to improve the use of voluntary care to make it more supportive of families. Another influence had been the need to make the law more specifically responsive to child abuse cases and to avoid the use of wardship that had grown apace throughout the 1980s.[20] Another had been to give greater legal rights to parents and less discretionary power to professionals, for example with regard to access to children in care and the use of emergency measures. Yet another aim had been that of consolidating all child care law, public and private, under one piece of legislation. Meanwhile public inquiries like Beckford, Carlile and now Cleveland continued to raise other issues and controversies. All the changes in the legislation that were emphasizing increased parental participation, more voluntaristic approaches and greater control over professional discretion by the courts were reinforced by events in Cleveland.

Child protection work and the double bind

The net effect of the Cleveland inquiry and the subsequent policy and legal changes was (and still is) to leave social workers in a double-bind situation. With regard to physical abuse, they were being enjoined to take no risks at all and to act immediately there was the slightest suspicion of abuse, whereas in the case of sexual abuse they were being told to intervene with caution largely because of the difficulty of proving that it had taken place and also because of the attendant disruption to families, which was only considered acceptable where there was definite evidence.

Clearly in some places the message of Cleveland was not acted on. In the past three years there have been concerns about the phenomenon of ritual or organized abuse. Most notably there has been much press coverage of investigations into allegations of this type of abuse in Nottingham, Rochdale and the Orkneys.[21] While it is too soon to judge these cases in detail, the general impression seems to be that social workers and other involved professionals have intervened impulsively (without first establishing the facts) and over-intrusively (by adopting so-called dawn raid tactics). The response of the Department of Health (1991b) has been to issue a further set of guidelines, which restate and reinforce the need for a more careful, considered and strategic approach to all child abuse cases.

Concluding comments

There are a variety of reasons for the somewhat bewildering developments of the past six years. They can best be understood by reference to the way in which the issue of child abuse has been responded to in earlier years.

Throughout the whole of this century, there has been ambivalence and uncertainty about the best way for the state to intervene in families to ensure that children are properly socialized and not ill-treated, whatever the view about the motives for this concern. Preserving the independence of the family and the rights of parents has always had to be balanced against the welfare of children and their rights to be protected by those sanctioned by the state to carry out child protection work. For many years this task was left to the judgement of inspectors from the NSPCC and later to that of child care officers in children's departments, with backing from the courts as and when required. This approach was deemed to be working well as long as support for the family remained the major goal. The rediscovery of child abuse challenged this consensus position, just as it did in the late Victorian era. Social workers and other professional workers in this field pressed and were increasingly pressed to intervene more authoritatively into families in the light of the knowledge that abuse of children by their parents was more widespread than had previously been thought to be the case. They did this at first rather uneasily and were pressed further following the Beckford Inquiry. However, those concerned with more general child care matters were of the view that social workers were being inappropriately intrusive into families where such an approach was not required, and lobbied for more legal rights for parents and more legal control over social workers.

A major turning-point came with the increased attention being paid to sexual abuse. The more zealous approach that had been encouraged by the state in the case of physical abuse was seen as inappropriate with regard to sexual abuse. Campbell (1988) has argued that the reason for this apparent about-turn is that the extent of child sexual abuse by males that events at Cleveland pointed to was seen as threatening to men, and the response was, therefore, to defend the family against what were seen as outrageous attacks from outside. While this interpretation may have some validity, it is clear that backing for a more family-supportive approach had already developed considerable momentum by the mid-1980s, as evidenced by the findings of the Short report. Economic and broader social changes, as well as gender factors, have also played a part in these developments in the child protection field. The new softening may well be linked to concerns about the family under threat from recession and unemployment, high divorce rates and the growth of lone-parent families (see Chapter 5).

It appears, therefore, that we are about to enter into a new phase of child protection work. There have been times when specific focus on child protection has been the main concern (the late Victorian era and 1970 to the present) and times when a broader family-supportive approach to child care issues has predominated (from 1914 through to the end of the 1960s). On the face of it, the 1989 Children Act points to greater emphasis being placed on family support again. However, the past 20 years have created an awareness of the fact that families can be dangerous and distressing places for many children. It is hard to envisage this message being completely lost. At this point in time, before the Act has been fully tested, it is far too soon to predict how child protection work will proceed. Awareness of how we arrived at today's position will, it is hoped, inform whatever future action is taken.

4

Defining and measuring the extent of child abuse

Clearly any logical approach to a problem entails describing its nature and size, so that the response to it can be appropriate and sufficiently well resourced to ensure an effective solution. However, as was seen in Chapter 3, child abuse is not a phenomenon that lends itself to logical solutions because of its political, cultural and historical underpinnings. Child abuse is a highly complex issue and, as will be seen, is not easily defined or measured. This chapter will consider critically attempts to achieve these difficult tasks of definition and measurement. Although the two topics are closely interrelated, since the way in which abuse is defined influences its extent, for the purposes of analysis they will be considered separately.

Defining child abuse

Before we look at different categories of child abuse, some general considerations should be taken into account.

The cultural context of child abuse definition

First, child abuse is a socially defined construct. It is a product of a particular culture and context and not an absolute unchanging phenomenon. As has already been seen from the historical survey, what is considered to be abusive in a particular society alters over time. Place is another factor. Anthropological studies show clearly that what is viewed as abusive in one society today is not necessarily seen as such in another, Korbin (1981: 4) cites examples of culturally approved of practices in societies in the southern hemisphere that we would almost certainly define as abusive:

> These include extremely hot baths, designed to inculcate culturally valued traits; punishments, such as severe beatings, to impress the child

with the necessity of adherence to cultural rules; and harsh initiation rites that include genital operations, deprivation of food and sleep, and induced bleeding and vomiting.

She points out that the reverse is also true:

Practices such as isolating infants and small children in rooms or beds of their own at night, making them wait for readily available food until a schedule dictates that they can satisfy their hunger, or allowing them to cry without immediately attending to their needs or desires would be at odds with the child-rearing philosophies of most of the cultures discussed.

The lesson to be learned from anthropological studies is that the cultural context within which behaviour takes place and the meaning attributed to it by those sharing that culture are important factors to be taken into account when labelling certain acts as abusive.

Although such comparisons rightly sensitize us to the culturally relative nature of child abuse, this does not mean that there can be no common standards at all. Korbin stresses that the sort of abuse described by Kempe and his colleagues (1962) as the 'battered child syndrome' would not be sanctioned by any society. Finkelhor and Korbin (1988) argue that there are some culturally approved of practices, such as ritual circumcision and clitoridectomy, that should be universally seen as abusive and addressed as such.

The issue of sensitivity to culture applies within societies as well as between them. However, just the same sort of care needs to be taken with a culturally relativist approach in these circumstances. Dingwall *et al.* (1983) were of the opinion that the standards applied by social workers observed in their study ran the risk of being too low. They were so used to dealing with poor families and poor parenting skills that they accepted them as the norm for that culture. Stubbs (1989) shows how misguided assumptions about cultural differences between white social workers and Asian families can lead to a failure to protect children in these families from abuse. Such views are borne out by some of the public inquiry cases and go some way to explaining the extraordinary degree of tolerance shown by social workers in cases like that of Stephanie Fox (Fox 1990), Lester Chapman (Chapman 1979) and Tyra Henry (Henry 1987).[1] Differentiating between culturally normative and abusive or neglectful parenting is a critically difficult but essential task for child protection social workers.

The concerns of the definers

A second general issue relates to the formal definitions of different types of child abuse. There are a bewildering number of such definitions emanating from a wide range of sources. It is important to know who the definers are, what are their aims, goals and interests. For instance, Henry Kempe and his colleagues, in their original definition, deliberately used the emotive term 'battered child' because they wished to draw public attention to the issue. In other aspects, their definition of the phenomenon and account of its causation reflect a clinician's concern with the individual: 'a battered child is any child who receives non-accidental physical injury or injuries as a result of acts (or omissions) on the part of his parents or guardians' (Kempe and Helfer 1980). Contrast this definition with that of Gil, a sociologist, with clear views about the broader political aspects of the treatment of children. He defines child abuse as 'inflicted gaps or deficits between circumstances of living which would facilitate the optimal development of children to which they should be entitled and their actual circumstances, irrespective of the sources or agents of the deficit' (Gil 1975).

These two definitions are poles apart. Were one to take action according to the latter, all the 3.5 million children living in or 'on the margins' of poverty in Britain in 1985 (Bradshaw 1990) would probably be on child protection registers. Kempe's definition would limit the numbers to those identified by health and welfare agencies as being physically abused or exposed to physical abuse by their parents.

Legislators, by and large, favour non-specific definitions of abuse because they allow flexibility and room for manoeuvre. Therefore, most legal definitions of child abuse are phrased in very general terms, such as 'improper treatment' or 'significant harm'.[2] In the USA in the early 1980s there was a reaction against such general definitions on the grounds that they encouraged unwarranted and harmful interventions. Wald (1982) proposed that the legal definition of physical abuse be limited to 'injuries inflicted on a child which cause or create a substantial risk of death, disfigurement or impairment of bodily functioning'. While such a definition achieves the goal of specificity, many might find it unacceptably narrow as a basis for deciding upon intervention.

Researchers into child abuse are very much concerned with achieving precision and consistency. Clear identification of the object of research and common standards of measurement are important ingredients of such work. As will be seen in the section on prevalence, inconsistencies of definition between studies may well account for major differences in findings (Finkelhor et al. 1986). Besharov (1981: 384) considers that definitional inadequacy has had harmful effects on research:

> There are thousands of different and conflicting definitions of 'child abuse' and 'child neglect' in use today. Some describe child maltreatment in terms of proscribed parental conduct; some focus on the harm to the child; and many are couched in both. While many definitions share common approaches, elements, and even phraseology, the different combinations and permutations seem endless.

Defining child abuse in practice

A third general issue relates to the process by which child abuse is actually defined in practice. Here we are considering what Gelles (1982) terms operational as opposed to nominal definitions (i.e. those used in law and research). How do social workers and other professional groups in fact decide what does and does not constitute abuse from the large number of referrals they receive?

Giovannoni and Becerra (1979: 5) were of the opinion that there were no adequate definitions of abuse that could be operationalized by professionals: 'a major thesis of this book is that child abuse and neglect are matters of social definition and that the problems that inhere in the establishment of those definitions ultimately rest on value decisions.' To test this hypothesis, they devised 78 pairs of vignettes briefly describing potentially abusive situations.[3] Half the vignettes outlined the consequence of the potential abuse; half did not. Sixty of these vignettes were assigned at random to four groups of professionals (police, social workers, paediatricians and lawyers) and to non-professional inhabitants of Los Angeles, and they were asked to rate them on a 1 to 9 scale of seriousness.

The main finding was that there was little agreement between the professional groupings about the seriousness of the various types of abuse. Overall, there was most agreement between the police and social workers, who together took a more serious view of nearly all incidents than did the paediatricians and lawyers (in that order). This lack of agreement was attributed to the requirements of occupational roles. Thus the reason for higher ratings on the part of police and social workers was seen to be their greater involvement in the early investigative stages of abuse. The police rated vignettes where a crime had been alleged as more serious than the other professionals. Social workers were ahead of the others with regard to emotional abuse and lawyers tended to rate everything lower than the rest because their concern was whether there was enough evidence to prove a case in a court of law.

With regard to non-professional people, Giovannoni and Becerra found that as a whole they were more likely to judge the scenarios as more serious than all the professionals and that those from the lower social classes 'generally saw mistreatment as more serious than did those of higher socio-economic status' (Giovannoni and Beccera 1979: 189). This is in contrast to the widely held perception that professionals have higher standards in this respect than the general public (see Christopherson 1983).

The conclusion drawn from the study was that there was much confusion among professionals over deciding whether cases were sufficiently abusive to justify intervention. Examination of cases dealt with in the same area showed that this confusion carried over into practice and that there was a good deal of inconsistency with regard to decisions. Smaller-scale studies in Britain have come to similar conclusions (Corby 1987; Higginson 1992). Giovannoni and Becerra advocated the abandonment of the general terms 'child abuse' and 'neglect' and recommended replacing them with more precise legal definitions of the various categories.

On the basis of these studies, the only safe definition of child abuse is that it is a conclusion reached by a group of professionals on the examination of the circumstances of a child, normally (in Britain) at a case conference. Such a definition is usually symbolized by placing the child's name on a child protection register.

Formal definitions of child abuse

In Britain, formal definitions of child abuse derive from Department of Health guidelines and these will be used as a framework for the rest of this section. There are also legal definitions to be found in section 31 of the Children Act.[4] In addition, new types of abuse and concerns not covered by these definitions are emerging and these too will be considered.

The term 'child abuse' was first officially used in Britain in a 1980 government circular (DHSS 1980). As was seen in Chapter 3, four categories of abuse were specified: physical abuse; physical neglect; failure to thrive and emotional abuse (a combined category); and 'children living in a household with, or which is regularly visited by, a parent or another person who has abused a child and are considered at risk'. Where identified, such children's names were to be placed on a register. Prior to this, there had been no clear guidelines or definitions. By 1988, there were five categories of child abuse: physical abuse; neglect; emotional abuse; sexual abuse; and grave concern (DHSS 1988). By 1991, the categories had been reduced to four again, grave concern having been eliminated without any explanation.[5]

Physical abuse

Physical abuse was the original concern of the child protection lobby and in the public mind was synonymous with child abuse until the publicity surrounding intervention into child sexual abuse cases in Cleveland in 1987. In the 1991 guidelines, physical abuse is defined as 'Actual or likely physical injury to a child, or failure to prevent physical injury (or suffering) to a child including deliberate poisoning, suffocation and Munchausen's syndrome by proxy.' This definition differs from the 1988 version in that it includes a future element which is in line with the Children Act definition (see note 4) and presumably explains the reason for there being no grave concern category. It also differs because it specifically refers to suffocation and the Munchausen syndrome by proxy.

As a nominal definition, this category is very broad. As an operational definition it is so general as to be useless. Wald's definition, quoted above, is much more focused and prescriptive but, as stressed before, probably too restricted in scope. Where the Department of Health definition is specific, it refers to categories that are likely to be very small in terms of numbers of cases. In practice, there are many factors taken into account in deciding whether officially to define a situation as abusive (i.e. by registration).

First, the seriousness of the injury plays a part. Minor bruising, for instance, though frequently cited as a precursor to more serious abuse,[6] is generally not seen as sufficiently serious to require registration, even where there is suspicion that it has been non-accidentally inflicted. A series of unexplained bruises, on the other hand, is more likely, under the same circumstances, to be considered sufficient cause for such action. Serious physical abuse in suspicious circumstances is normally defined as abusive with little delay.

As the term non-accidental shows, intention is a key variable in deciding whether an action is abusive or not. Again there is variation with regard to this. Dingwall and his colleagues, in their study of child protection systems (1983: 36), identified among some hospital doctors what they termed a strict liability approach. From this point of view, if a child suffers a serious injury even accidentally, its carer at the time should accept responsibility for the outcome and can be judged to be abusive. Such a view receives some backing from the official definition when it refers to 'failure to prevent injury'. For the majority of child protection workers, however, intentionality is seen as an influential factor. If, for example, a child is accidentally injured during a fight between its parents, the violence in the household would be considered cause for concern, but registration for physical injury would, in my opinion, be unlikely, unless it was a serious injury. I stress that this is my opinion, because there are no guidelines for disentangling this type of scenario and different groups of professionals might come to different conclusions.

Often other factors will be taken into account in the defining process, such as parental character, criminal offences etc. (see Dingwall *et al.* 1983: 152–66; Higginson 1992). In a case such as the one just referred to, the focus would probably soon shift from the actual incident and injury to consideration of the risk to the child in future. Such prediction is another aspect of the operational definition of both physical and all other types of abuse. Greenland (1987) has devised a checklist to this end (see Appendix). Based on his analysis of child death-by-abuse cases in Canada, he has formulated a series of factors relating to children and parents for use in the assessment of a child's future safety. This type of approach, which received much publicity in the Beckford inquiry report, has been heavily criticized by some (Parton and Parton 1989), but given a cautious reception by others (Clark *et al.* 1990). It has been officially endorsed in the Department of Health (1988) guide to the assessment of families in child protection cases.[7]

A further factor often taken into consideration in defining physical abuse is the age of the child. Generally, the younger the child suspected of being physically abused, the greater the likelihood of official registration. This response is frequently justified by the fact that young children (particularly those under school age) are physically more vulnerable and less open to being monitored by health and welfare professionals. Physical abuse of older children can also sometimes be seen to be an over-zealous use of physical punishment that, while disapproved of, is considered understandable within a culture that supports some forms of physical correction (see Freeman 1988). Such an explanation is not acceptable in the case of very young children.

Last, but not least, is the issue of proving physical abuse in court. The standard of proof obviously has to be higher for care proceedings than for deciding whether or not to place a child's name on the child protection register. Medical evidence is the key factor. X-ray material, blood-clotting tests and expert opinion are the main sources of evidence. Paediatricians have largely been cautious in their assessment of cases and have thereby gained credibility in courts. There are still controversial issues, the most notable of which is whether brittle bone disease might be the cause of some symptoms diagnosed as being the outcome of abuse (see Carty 1988; Paterson and McAllion 1989).

As has been seen, the official definition of physical abuse includes deliberate poisoning, suffocation and Munchausen's syndrome by proxy. It is not clear why these particular forms of abuse are specified, other than to alert professionals to their possibility. The deliberate administration of harmful substances was included in Kempe's early descriptions of child abuse. The issue of suffocation has received a good deal of publicity because some doctors (Meadow 1989; Newlands and Emery 1991) believe that up to 10 per cent of cot deaths may be the result of this form of abuse.[8] Such a viewpoint has been condemned by others because there is no clear-cut evidence for such a belief and the suggestion is thought to be highly insensitive to relatives of cot death children (see letters in the *British Medical Journal* (1989) vol. 299, pp. 178–9 and 455–6).

There is a growing body of medical literature about Munchausen's syndrome by proxy (see Meadow 1977, 1985; Mehl *et al*. 1990). First diagnosed in 1977, the syndrome is characterized by a child presenting with an illness that has been fictitiously produced by a parent, typically the mother. The child is subjected to abuse by exposure to the medical treatment prescribed. In 1985, Meadow was aware of 90 cases in Britain.

Physical neglect

Neglect is defined in the 1991 guidelines as

The persistent or severe neglect of a child or the failure to protect from exposure to any kind of danger, including cold or starvation, or extreme failure to carry out important aspects of care, resulting in the significant impairment of the child's health or development, including non-organic failure to thrive.

This definition of neglect is as vague as that for physical abuse. Practitioners and lawyers must determine what counts as 'persistent' and 'severe' and they must also define 'important aspects of care'. The only specific forms of abuse referred to are cold, starvation and another medically defined syndrome, that of failure to thrive.

Definitions drawn from the American scene are more specific:

It is presumed that physical, emotional and intellectual growth and welfare are being jeopardised when, for example, the child is:

1 malnourished, ill-clad, dirty, without proper shelter or sleeping arrangements;
2 without supervision, unattended;
3 ill and lacking essential medical care;
4 denied normal experiences that produce feelings of being loved, wanted, secure and worthy (emotional neglect);
5 failing to attend school regularly;
6 exploited, overworked;
7 emotionally disturbed due to constant friction within the home, marital discord, mentally ill parents;
8 exposed to unwholesome and demoralising circumstances. (Polansky et al. 1972)

The specificity of this definition at least demonstrates those areas to which attention should be drawn, but the question of standards is still not resolved. For instance, how ill-clad and dirty does a child have to be to be defined as neglected? At what age can a child be left unsupervised? Terms such as 'exploited', 'emotionally disturbed' and 'unwholesome and demoralising circumstances', far from clarifying matters, pose even more definitional problems. There is no consideration in Polansky's definition of issues such as cultural relativity, material resources and intellectual capacity, which are all important considerations for operational definitions of neglect.[9]

The issue of standards of parental care and behaviour is a major problem for social workers concerned to tackle neglect. The lack of clear definitions makes it problematical to prove neglect in court and may result in such cases being less vigorously pursued than other forms of abuse.[10]

These concerns are particularly pertinent as a result of changes in the 1989 Children Act. Section 31 (10) addresses the issue of how to measure 'significant harm', which is now the sole ground available for the making of a care or supervision order:

Where the question of whether harm suffered by a child is significant turns on the child's health or development, his health or development shall be compared with that which could reasonably be expected of a similar child.

Lyon (1989) points out that the sorts of comparisons being required are 'invidious, if not well nigh impossible, but do raise incredible spectres of class, cultural, racial, religious and ethnic considerations'. There can be little doubt that establishing neglect on these grounds simply will not work.

The 'failure to thrive' syndrome is technically easier to define and prove than general neglect (see Iwaniec et al. 1985). Babies have an expected normal level of growth (weight and length), which is based upon their birth weight and size. Those that fall well below this expectation, with no apparent physical explanation, are considered to be causes for concern, and neglect (both physical and emotional) is thought to be a likely cause of this. Close monitoring of a child's physical growth when placed away from its parents may often show that, with reasonable care and feeding, normal development will take place, thus proving that some form of neglect lies at the source of the problem. The Jasmine Beckford inquiry dealt with this issue in some detail. Jasmine was physically abused and also failing to thrive in terms of physical growth and development. Regular medical checks, had they been arranged, may well have pinpointed the latter as a cause for concern.[11] As a result of this case, there is now more awareness of the need to monitor the physical development of all abused children and greater powers to enforce such monitoring have been created in the 1989 Children Act.

Sexual abuse

Sexual abuse is defined in the 1991 guidelines as 'Actual or likely sexual exploitation of a child or adolescent. The child may be dependent and/or emotionally immature.' Such a definition is again too broad to be of use as a guide to those intervening to protect children. There have been a great number of definitions of child sexual abuse in the past ten years, mainly produced by researchers and clinicians concerned to measure and treat the problem. The following definition comes from a clinical source:

> Any child below the age of consent may be deemed to have been sexually abused when a sexually mature person has, by design or by neglect of their usual societal or specific responsibilities in relation to the child, engaged or permitted the engagement of that child in any activity of a sexual nature which is intended to lead to the sexual gratification of the sexually mature person. This definition pertains whether or not it involves genital contact or physical contact, and whether or not there is discernible harmful outcome in the short-term. (Glaser and Frosh 1988)

As a nominal definition, this one is comprehensive and helpful. It immediately defines a child by reference to the age of consent, 16. It includes both intra-familial and extra-familial abuse. It is unequivocal about the fact that non-contact activities, such as exposure to obscene or pornographic material, constitute abusive behaviour and stresses that the judgement of whether an act is sexually abusive or not should not be influenced by its apparent effects. The only uncertainty in the definition relates to what is meant by a 'sexually mature person'.[12]

The issue of defining sexual abuse in practice is both complex and problematical. There is now general awareness that child sexual abuse is far more common than previously thought and that it affects much younger children than was considered to be the case (see Macfarlane and Waterman 1986). Child health and welfare professionals are now largely agreed that sexual abuse of children is a very serious form of abuse and that intervention to protect children from such abuse of any kind is a very high priority. However, there are major problems in gathering evidence to prove suspicions.

First, there are few clear-cut medical signs of abuse. Thus, most medical examinations of children suspected of having been abused yield little by way of evidence. As was seen in the previous chapter, following Cleveland there is now a good deal of circumspection about certain types of medical evidence that previously were beginning to be considered to be more definite indicators. It is now generally accepted that medical evidence without some form of corroboration from a social and behavioural assessment is not sufficient to prove child sexual abuse in court.

Social and behavioural assessments are hard to be definite about. It is generally thought that sexual abuse of children is a cross-class phenomenon[13] and is as common among more 'respectable' families as it is in families that normally come under the surveillance of welfare agencies. With regard to behavioural indicators, a variety of factors have been identified as associated with sexual abuse of children, e.g. precocious sexual behaviour, withdrawn presentation, parasuicide and suicide, running away from home and anorexia nervosa (see Porter 1984). However, these correlations do not prove connections and can, therefore, only sensitize professionals to the possibility of sexual abuse. They have very little value in terms of the standard of evidence required in courts.

Because of this lack of hard scientific evidence and because of the very secretive nature of sexual abuse of children (Furniss 1991), which makes it unlikely that anyone but the perpetrator and the child know that the abuse is going on, the child's account of events is a crucial factor. It is also, however, a controversial issue. Although there is general acceptance among front-line professional workers that children do not lie about being sexually abused, lawyers, in particular, have pointed to cases and situations in which children can and do make false allegations (see Mantell 1988). The Cleveland report (1988) considered that social workers and clinical psychologists were too uncritical in their adherence to belief in the child, and saw this as contributing to their generally overzealous approach in disclosure interviews (Cleveland 1988: 204–9). A consequence of this has been that social work evidence of child sexual abuse based on such interviews is now treated in court with a good deal of scepticism.

The acceptability of a child's evidence in criminal court is another problematic issue affecting proof of sexual abuse. Until recently, a child's evidence could not be accepted unless it was corroborated by some other evidence, making conviction of alleged offenders far less likely. Now, however, under the 1991 Criminal Justice Act, corroboration of such evidence is no longer a compulsory requirement and videos of children alleging abuse can be used as evidence in court, provided that the child is available for cross-examination (see Cobley 1991). Nevertheless, there is still tremendous pressure placed on children in such proceedings (Flin 1990) and this acts as a deterrent to those deciding whether to prosecute alleged offenders or not.

There is, therefore, currently a good deal of uncertainty about decisions in this field because of the great difficulty associated with proving that the abuse has happened. The general effects of Cleveland have been to create a more cautious approach following a period when there was growing confidence about the way ahead. There now seems to be a good deal of suspected child sexual abuse, but more circumspection about defining it as such and acting on that suspicion without more definite proof.

Emotional abuse

Emotional abuse for the purpose of registration is defined in the Department of Health guidelines as:

> Actual or likely severe adverse effect on the emotional and behavioural development of a child caused by persistent or severe emotional ill-treatment or rejection. This category should be used where it is the main or sole form of abuse.

Defining emotional abuse for practical intervention purposes is extremely difficult. Social workers seem to be particularly aware of and concerned about the emotional ill-treatment of children, but find it extremely hard to pinpoint their concerns. This is because they are tackling areas of major uncertainty and sensitivity, which are both controversial and difficult to prove. Styles of parenting are brought into question by the issue of emotional abuse. For instance, are authoritarian or permissive parenting styles abusive? Is constant criticism of a child an abuse? Can it be proved that such parenting styles have ill effects? Where is the line between acceptable and unacceptable psychological parenting to be drawn? Is it abusive actively to prejudice a child against people of different races and sexes? Some would argue this to be so, but would be hard pressed to prove that such upbringings are actively harmful to those individuals, even though it is likely that society as a whole will be the poorer for such forms of socialization. It is difficult to prove links between causes and effects in this area – Garbarino and Vondra (1987) describe 'stress-resistant' children who despite apparently rejecting parents survive to be reasonably well adjusted adults.

Given these problems, some, like Goldstein et al. (1979) argue that there should be no intervention into this type of case at all on the grounds that it is likely to have more harmful consequences than non-intervention. Wald (1982) supports limited coercive intervention only where

> the minor is suffering serious emotional damage, evidenced by severe anxiety, depression or withdrawal, or untoward aggressive behaviour or hostility towards others, and the parents are unwilling to provide treatment for the child.

Garbarino and Gilliam (1980), on the other hand, use a broad definition that gives professionals a good deal of discretion. They define what they term psychological maltreatment as 'Acts of omission or commission by a parent or guardian that are judged by a mixture of community values and professional expertise to be inappropriate and damaging.' How such a definition could be operationalized is hard to envisage. The most common current view on the issue seems to be that emotional abuse and neglect of children is in itself damaging, but for practical purposes it has to have identifiable serious consequences linked to parenting behaviour before it can be statutorily responded to (see Montgomery 1989).

Factors common to all types of abuse

It has to be stressed that there may be overlaps and connections between the different forms of abuse and the problems associated with their definition. Thus, a child may be physically and sexually abused, physically abused and neglected and so on. Emotional abuse, while theoretically able to occur by itself, is also almost certain to accompany or be a consequence of the other forms of abuse. Until relatively recently, the emotional impact of physical abuse and neglect received little attention. This has been less true in the case of sexual abuse because it was largely the harrowing stories of survivors of such abuse that brought the problem to the public's attention. Currently, the emotional or psychological effects of all forms of abuse are being seen as a unifying factor in identifying and responding to them. Focus on the emotional aspects of abuse is seen as a way of moving forward more positively to improving the quality of life of all children who experience any form of mistreatment. As Garbarino and Vondra (1987: 28) put it,

> Rather than casting psychological maltreatment as an ancillary issue (subordinate to other forms of abuse and neglect) we should place it as the centre-piece of our efforts to understand family functioning and to protect children.

Other forms of abuse

There are other forms of child mistreatment about which concern has been expressed. Psycho-social short stature syndrome, formerly termed deprivation dwarfism, is a syndrome identified by paediatricians whereby growth of children becomes stunted as a result of emotional or physical neglect. It is similar to the failure-to-thrive syndrome, but becomes apparent in older children and can cause physical development to be permanently impaired (Gardner 1972). There has been concern for some time now in the USA about what is termed 'fetal abuse', which relates to behaviours on the part of a pregnant mother, such as tobacco, alcohol and other drug use that can be perceived as harmful to the unborn child (Mackenzie *et al.* 1982). Ritual abuse (see Jones 1991; Jonker and Jonker-Bakker 1991) is a topic of major concern in Britain following allegations in Nottingham, Rochdale and the Orkneys. Such abuse is defined as

> abuse that occurs in the context linked to some symbols or group activities that have a religious, magical or supernatural connotation, and where the invocation of these symbols or activities are repeated

over time and used to frighten and intimidate children. (Finkelhor *et al.* 1988)

Organized abuse is defined in the Department of Health guidelines (1991b: 38) as

a generic term which covers abuse which may involve a number of abusers, a number of abused children and young people and often encompasses different forms of abuse. It involves to a greater or lesser extent, an element of organisation.

Such abuse is sometimes seen as synonymous with ritual abuse. The difference is that while both are clearly pre-planned and involve several adults and children, organized abuse is not centred on magical or religious rites and symbolism.

Institutional abuse is abuse of children that takes place in a school or residential setting. This can encompass any form of abuse, sexual or physical. Finkelhor *et al.* (1988) have written about sexual abuse of children in day nurseries in the USA, following a much publicized case there. In Britain there have been cases of sexual abuse of children in residential care in Leicestershire (see *The Times* 30 November 1990), alleged physical abuse in a home for children with learning difficulties in Lancaster (see *The Times* 11 September 1991) and emotional abuse of children in care in Staffordshire (Staffordshire 1991). Other forms of intra-familial abuse, those associated with divorce and marital conflict (Emery 1982) and working parents who have no time for their children (Garbarino and Gilliam 1980), have been discussed in the child abuse literature. Extra-familial abuse, such as child prostitution and pornography (Ennew 1986), is also a growing concern.

As can be seen, what is defined as child abuse has grown and grown from the battered child of 1962 to a vast range of practices. The field is a very complex one, though it should be stressed that most welfare professionals will tend to focus only on the main forms of abuse outlined in the 1991 Department of Health guidelines. Nevertheless, consideration of the wider issues should put some of the mainstream work into perspective. Abuse of children is now an international issue. Focus is being placed on the quality of life for children across the world. From this perspective the concerns of health and welfare workers in Britain may seem a narrow and specific aspect of a much broader issue. Nevertheless, even at this level, consideration of the issues surrounding child abuse definition should sensitize professionals to the often changing and subjective nature of assessing suspicious cases and to the need to develop criteria that are as clear and objective as possible.

The extent of child abuse

While it may not be of direct relevance to day-to-day decision-making in the fieldwork office or the clinic to know how widespread child abuse is, such

information does have an influence on the policy-maker who determines
resource allocation and the structures for responding to child abuse situations
and, therefore, indirectly on practice. In addition, knowledge gained from
incidence and prevalence studies and official statistics can to some extent
contextualize child protection work by giving a sense of the whole. It can also,
as will be seen, pose important questions about the effects of past and present
policies and practice and point to ways forward.

There are two main sources of statistical knowledge. The first, drawn
largely from government departments, measures the incidence of child abuse
as reported, recorded or registered by official agencies. The second, deriving
from a broader research base, measures the incidence and prevalence of
abuse in a given sample of people.[14] Thus, official statistics tell us more about
the way in which child abuse is defined in practice and responded to over
time, whereas research studies tell us more about the 'hidden' problem, i.e.
abuse that does not come to the attention of those officially authorized to deal
with it.

Official statistics

Any figures relating to child protection work need to be carefully analysed
because of the definitional complications considered in the previous sections.
There are three sets of official statistics that will be referred to here: (a) child
protection register returns; (b) numbers of children in care; and (c) childhood
mortality statistics.

Child protection statistics in Britain

Until 1988, there were no national statistics kept in Great Britain with regard
to the officially known extent of child abuse. To obtain a national picture
before this, use was made of the returns of the NSPCC special unit registers,
which covered approximately 9 per cent of the child population of England
and Wales. From 1988, figures have been available from the Department of
Health, which now annually collates the numbers of children on child
protection registers in England. While there are many problems associated
with interpretation of these statistics because of variations in practice
between local authorities (see Corby 1990), they nevertheless provide at least
some tools with which to assess and monitor trends of practice in general
terms.

Table 4.1 has been devised using extrapolations from the NSPCC figures
and those from the Department of Health. These figures show, first, that
between 1978 and 1984 there was hardly any increase in the overall numbers
of children on child protection registers. By 1986, the numbers had doubled,
coinciding with the publication of the Beckford inquiry report. In the five
years since that time, the figures have again nearly doubled. Whereas,
therefore, between 1978 and 1984 approximately one in every thousand

Table 4.1 Total numbers of children on child protection registers in England and Wales for selected years between 1978 and 1991

Year	Number on register	Source
1978	11,844	Creighton (1984)
1984	12,389	Creighton (1985)
1985	17,622	Creighton (1986)
1986	23,820	Creighton (1987)
1987	29,766	ADSS Survey (1988)
1988	39,200 (England only)	DoH (1989)
1989	41,200 (England only)	DoH (1990)
1990	43,600 (England only)	DoH (1991c)
1991	45,200 (England only)	DoH (1992)

children under the age of 18 was on the child protection register, now there are four per thousand. Another factor to be taken into account is that in the late 1970s and early 1980s children's names remained on registers for longer periods of time than now (in 1990–1 there were 26,600 de-registrations). Thus the relative number of children going on to registers is much greater than the figures at first sight suggest. In 1987–8, 20,900 children's names were added to the register. This figure had risen to 28,200 in 1990–1.

On the face of it, it looks as if parents in these parts of Britain have become increasingly abusive throughout the 1980s. However, such is the magnitude of the rate of increase that this is probably not the case. What is more likely is that there has been growing sensitivity to the issue of the maltreatment of children and the development of ever more elaborate systems to respond to it.

A breakdown of the numbers of children on registers according to different categories of abuse (Table 4.2) provides more detail about the nature of this expansion. The actual number of children registered on account of being

Table 4.2 Numbers of children on child protection registers in England and Wales by category for selected years between 1978 and 1991

Category of abuse	1978	1984	1986	1988	1989	1990	1991
Physical abuse	7944	7856	10,422	11,100	10,000	10,200	9000
Physical neglect	289	933	1888	4900	5300	5600	5600
Sexual abuse	89	1088	5922	5800	5800	5900	5600
Emotional abuse	0	200	455	1700	2000	2200	2600
Grave concern	3522	2312	5133	14,400	16,300	17,900	21,100
Total	11,844	12,389	23,820	39,200	41,200	43,600	45,200

Note: Totals for 1988–91 include small numbers of children registered under joint categories. Figures for these years are for England only. Sources are as for Table 4.1.

physically abused has risen by only approximately 2000 between 1978 and today. In the past four years, the actual numbers have declined by about 2000. In 1978, physical abuse cases accounted for 67 per cent of the total number of registered children. In 1991, they accounted for just under 20 per cent. Thus, for the increase in the numbers of registered children, we have to look elsewhere.

In 1978, neglect cases constituted just under 5 per cent of the whole. In 1991, they constituted 12 per cent, and the rate of increase in absolute numbers between these years was 19-fold. There has been some levelling off of the rate of growth over the past four years.

Child sexual abuse cases were a very minor concern of the authorities in 1978, forming less than 1 per cent of the whole. In 1991, they formed just over 11 per cent of the total – in absolute terms this represents a 58-fold increase. The bulk of this increase had been achieved by 1986. Since then, the numbers have remained at the same level.

Emotional abuse of children did not officially exist in 1978. By 1991, it constituted nearly 6 per cent of the total number of registered children. In contrast to the other categories of abuse so far discussed the numbers of children registered under this category have continued to rise over the past four years.

The grave concern category formed nearly 30 per cent of the whole in 1978 and just under 50 per cent of the whole in 1991. It has been something of a miscellaneous category, incorporating cases where those convicted of offences against children have been living or are about to live in the same household as children, and cases where there have been strong suspicions of physical abuse, sexual abuse or neglect, but no definite evidence. As pointed out earlier, it has now been abandoned and from 1992 all cases will be registered in one of the other categories. As grave concern registered cases come up for review, they will, unless de-registered, be allocated to another category. As a result, the 1992 figures will probably show a substantial increase in all these other categories.

The pattern of events is relatively clear. Over the past 13 years, the focus has shifted from almost exclusive concern with physical abuse of children to a range of forms of child maltreatment. In this process, the actual numbers of children formally registered have increased by more than four times. A quarter of the children so registered are also officially in care and 8 per cent are on supervision orders. This leaves just over 30,000 children living at home with no statutory order imposed, but being monitored and worked with (in theory) according to the guidelines issued by the Department of Health.

Child protection statistics in the USA

The situation presented above, following the same pattern of development, has existed in the USA for some time now.

In 1968, according to Gil (1970), there were 10,931 reports of child abuse, of which 6617 were confirmed cases, i.e. one in every 10,000 children under the age of 18. The bulk of these cases were of physical abuse. In 1980, the American Humane Association found that 788,844 reports of child abuse had been made to the child protective services (a total of 12 per 1000). Only 24 per cent of these reports were about physical child abuse, of which 4 per cent were deemed to be serious. Some 61 per cent of the reports were for child neglect, 13 per cent for emotional maltreatment and 7 per cent for sexual maltreatment. A national incidence study in the USA estimated that in total 1,151,600 cases of all types of abuse and neglect were suspected by professionals for the year May 1979 to April 1980 (18 per 1000). Of these it found that 652,000 (10 per 1000) met stricter criteria for child abuse definition. The breakdown of cases by type of abuse was as follows:

physical assaults	207,600	(3.3 per 1000)
sexual exploitation	44,700	(0.7 per 1000)
emotional abuse	138,400	(2.2 per 1000)
physical neglect	108,000	(1.7 per 1000)
educational neglect	181,500	(2.9 per 1000)
emotional neglect	59,400	(0.9 per 1000)

Twenty per cent of these cases were thought to have serious effects and consequences (National Center on Child Abuse and Neglect 1981).

This national incidence study was repeated in 1986, by which time the number of suspected cases had increased to 1.6 million (approximately 26 per 1000). The diversity of type of abuse remained similar to that of 1980 apart from increases in the sexual exploitation category (National Center on Child Abuse and Neglect 1986). Thus, between 1968 and 1986, the American child protection system mushroomed and diversified.

Comparisons with the British figures are hard to make because some of the American statistics focus on reported, not confirmed, cases of abuse and, even where the focus is on confirmed cases, the standards of confirmation in the USA may well be different from those of registration in Britain. Nevertheless, it is clear that a pattern of expansion has taken place in the USA, similar in type to that in Britain and probably on a far greater scale. If this pattern of events continues in the same way in Britain, the numbers of children coming on to child protection registers is likely to grow much more. There is some reason to believe that the American system incorporates more moderate cases than does the British system. However, even allowing for this, there is still a major gap between the British figure of 4 per 1000 and the 26 per 1000 in the USA.

Numbers of children in care

Children in care statistics give further information about the way in which child protection cases are responded to. In 1989, there were 65,400 children in care, of whom 9500 were on child protection registers. However, not all children who are in care as a result of child mistreatment are placed on child

Table 4.3 Children in care in England and Wales on 31 March 1989 as a result of parental mistreatment (by category)

Reason for being in care	Number
Section 1 (2) (a) CYPA 1969, neglect or ill-treatment	15,859
Section 1 (2) (b) CYPA 1969, neglect or ill-treatment of another child in the household	1767
Section 1 (2) (bb) CYPA 1969, member or likely member of household convicted of offence against children	307
Section 1 (2) (c) CYPA 1969, moral danger	995
Ward of court under section 7 (2) of the Family Law Reform Act 1969	6595
Total	25,523

Note: CYPA, Children and Young Persons Act.
Source: DoH (1991d)

protection registers. Indeed there is a good deal of confusion as to why any children in care should be registered unless they have been placed in the charge and control of a parent or relative and are still considered to be at risk. In fact such children numbered 2700 in 1989. Just over 39,000 children in care (60 per cent of the total) are on some form of court order. It is not easy to be precise about how many of these are in care as a result of mistreatment by their parents. Using the categories in Table 4.3, it is estimated that over 25,000 (39 per cent) children are in care for this reason.

Using these same categories, 3732 children came into care in 1988–9 as a result of parental maltreatment (see Table 4.4 for details). This represents a

Table 4.4 Circumstances in which mistreated children in England and Wales were admitted to care during the year ending 31 March 1989

Reason for admission to care	Number
Section 1 (2) (a) CYPA 1969	1595
Section 1 (2) (b) CYPA 1969	196
Section 1 (2) (bb) CYPA 1969	35
Section 1 (2) (c) CYPA 1969	125
Ward of court under section 7 (2), Family Law Reform Act	1781
Total	3732

Note: See Table 4.3 for definitions.
Source: DoH (1991d)

ratio of between 3 and 4 children per 10,000 coming into care in one year because of some form of maltreatment. Dingwall and Eekelaar (1984) estimated that the rate for the years 1972–82 varied between 1 and 2 per 10,000. It seems, therefore, that abused children are more likely to be committed to care now than in the 1970s and early 1980s. However, the numbers are still very small when compared with the numbers officially investigated.

Child mortality statistics

Another source of information about the extent of child abuse is to be found in child mortality statistics. As a baseline test of effectiveness, it would be useful to know if the number of child deaths attributable to child abuse was reducing over time. Table 4.5 shows statistics for the period between the publication of the Maria Colwell inquiry report and 1989.

On the face of it, there has been a decline in the number of child deaths attributable to violence. The averages for 1974–9, 1980–4 and 1985–9 are 86, 44 and 49 respectively, which is a proportionate reduction even allowing for a fall in numbers of the 0–14 population by over a million during these years. The undetermined child deaths show a slight average increase from 41 for 1974–9 to 53 in 1980–4 and 53 in 1985–9. Taking the two categories together, there has been a decrease from 127 in 1974–9 to 102 in 1985–9.

Table 4.5 Child deaths for children aged from 0 to 14 from homicide and undetermined injuries whether accidentally or purposely inflicted, 1974–1989

Year	No. of homicides	No. of deaths from undetermined causes
1974	106	40
1975	86	43
1976	85	35
1977	78	30
1978	92	35
1979	72	64
1980	47	43
1981	30	70
1982	50	62
1983	45	47
1984	50	46
1985	59	57
1986	53	37
1987	38	51
1988	64	58
1989	33	62

Source: OPCS Mortality Statistics 1974–89, categories E960–969 and E980–989

There are several caveats to be taken into account, however. First, we are dealing with very small numbers and care needs to be taken in assuming trends. Second, we do not know how many of the recorded deaths are the result of intra-familial child maltreatment. A small number of young children are killed by strangers every year. Third, it is highly unlikely that all deaths as a result of child abuse will be recorded as such. The system is not fine-tuned enough to ensure this to be the case. Pritchard (1992) uses these figures to demonstrate that child protection workers are achieving a measure of success despite all the bad publicity that they have been exposed to. Although the trend is mildly encouraging, there is need for great care in using these statistics as definitive proof of the effectiveness of the child protection system.

Incidence and prevalence studies into child abuse

Incidence and prevalence studies are survey-based. Researchers seek by interview and questionnaire to find out how many children in a general population are subjected to maltreatment and how often (see note 14). Definitional issues are very important in the assessment of the value of different studies. So too are methodological concerns, such as the representativeness of the sample and the way in which the research is conducted, e.g. by direct questioning, mailed questionnaire or telephone interview.

Consideration will be given to studies into the incidence and prevalence of physical abuse first and then sexual abuse. One very obvious difference between the research methodologies in these two areas is the fact that, in the case of physical abuse, parents are asked about their use of physical violence against their children, whereas, with regard to sexual abuse, the survivor, not the perpetrator, is the provider of the information. One obvious consequence of this is the expectation that the former will provide a conservative estimate of the true extent of physical abuse.

Physical abuse studies

There have been no large-scale studies into the incidence and prevalence of physical abuse in Britain. Some studies, such as that of Newson (1978), have touched upon the use of violence in child-rearing, but for more focused investigation into the issue we must refer to American surveys. The most influential of these studies have been those conducted by Straus and his colleagues. They completed research studies in 1975 and 1985 and compared the results. The first study was based on face-to-face interviews with 1,146 parents with a referent child between the ages of 3 and 17.[15] They were asked whether they had been physically violent at least once towards this child in the past 12 months. This study was repeated in 1985 with 1,428 parents in similar circumstances. This second study was conducted by telephone interview. The results are set out in Table 4.6.

Table 4.6 Comparison of parent-to-child violence in 1975 and 1985

Type of violence	Rate per 1000 children aged 3 to 17	
	1975	*1985*
Minor violence acts		
1 Threw something	54	27
2 Pushed, grabbed, shoved	318	307
3 Slapped or spanked	582	549
Severe violence acts		
4 Kicked, bit, hit with fist	32	13
5 Hit, tried to hit with something	134	97
6 Beat up	13	6
7 Threatened with gun or knife	1	2
8 Used gun or knife	1	2
Violence indexes		
Overall violence (1–8)	630	620
Severe violence (4–8)	140	107
Very severe violence (4, 6, 8)	36	19

Source: Straus and Gelles (1986)

Straus and Gelles (1986) argue that these studies demonstrate that, between 1975 and 1985, general violence to children has stayed at about the same level. However, the prevalence of severe violence has declined by 24 per cent and that of very severe violence, which the researchers equate with child abuse, by 47 per cent. They attribute this change to a variety of social and economic factors, including the development of child protection strategies and programmes. Stocks (1988) questions the validity of these conclusions, largely on methodological grounds. However, regardless of the issue of the effectiveness of child protection systems, the studies do demonstrate that the annual prevalence of physical child abuse (i.e. 126 per 1000), as measured by direct questioning of parents, far outstrips the rate of official detection in Britain and to a lesser extent that of the USA. Thus, despite the considerable growth of the child protection machinery, there are far more maltreated children going unnoticed than being protected. Studies such as these pose particularly important questions for policy makers, such as whether there is the political will to eliminate all child abuse. If there is, then considerably more resources will be required to achieve that goal than are currently available. Primary prevention schemes will need to be implemented. Incidence and prevalence studies demonstrate the enormity of the problem to be tackled.

It should be noted that there are other studies of physical child abuse prevalence. Birchall (1989) lists 19 British and American studies between 1952 and 1986. However, many of these are extrapolations from small samples and many are also now somewhat dated.

Considering the publicity that physical abuse of children has received since the early 1970s, it is surprising that there has been so little detailed research into its general incidence in Britain. Currently we are having to guess the total size of the problem and are reliant on data from another country to give us a rough idea. There can be little doubt, therefore, that there is a particular need for much more information on this topic.

Sexual abuse prevalence studies

Studies of the prevalence of sexual abuse have been abundant over the past ten years or so. This has been more evident in the USA again, but there are at least some British studies and there is more work being done in this field since Cleveland (Kelly *et al.* 1991). The American studies are generally more sophisticated methodologically and broader in scope. These will be considered first.

The results of these studies are very wide-ranging and at first sight somewhat confusing. Finkelhor *et al.* (1986), in a summary of studies found that prevalence of child sexual abuse varied from 6 to 62 per cent for females and 3 to 31 per cent for males. He attributes this variation to several factors. These include:

1 The lack of standard definitions of child sexual abuse. (Some studies adopt broad definitions, others narrow definitions. For instance, some studies incorporate non-contact sexual abuse in their definition, others do not. Some studies include extra-familial abuse in their definitions whereas others do not.)
2 The lack of a standard upper age limit. (Some studies adopt an upper age limit of 15, others 18.)
3 The lack of agreement about the age difference between the abused child and the perpetrator. (Some studies do not consider this a factor at all. Others use five and ten year age gaps as defining factors.)
4 Different sample selections. (Some studies are drawn from college students only, while others are drawn from a more diverse background in terms of class and age.)
5 Different forms of data collection. (Some studies use face-to-face interviews with trained interviewers, which seem to elicit higher incidences than do more impersonal approaches.)

Finkelhor's own survey study in the late 1970s was of 796 college students (Finkelhor 1979). It was a questionnaire study, included non-contact and extra-familial abuse, set the upper age limit for abuse at 16 and specified age gaps between abusers and perpetrators. He found that 19 per cent of women and 9 per cent of men had experienced some kind of sexual abuse during childhood.

Russell (1984) surveyed a community sample of 930 women in San

Francisco. In total, 647 incidents of child sexual abuse were disclosed to her interviewers. The definitions she used were as follows:

Extrafamilial child sexual abuse: one or more unwanted sexual experiences with persons unrelated by blood or marriage, ranging from attempted petting (touching of breasts or genitals, or attempts at such touching) to rape, before the victim turned 14 years, and attempted forcible rape experiences from the ages of 14 to 17 years inclusive.

Incestuous child abuse: any kind of exploitive sexual contact or attempted sexual contact, that occurred between relatives, no matter how distant the relationship, before the victim turned 18 years old. (Russell 1984: 180–1)

One hundred and fifty-two women (16 per cent) reported at least one experience of incestuous abuse before the age of 18 years. Of these, 108 (12 per cent) had been sexually abused before the age of 14, 290 women (31 per cent) had experienced extrafamilial abuse before the age of 18 and 189 (20 per cent) before the age of 14. In all, these 290 abused women had 461 experiences of being abused. These results are seen to be at the high end of the spectrum. Russell's interviewers (all female) certainly probed further and more persistently than was the case in other studies. On the other hand, she points out that many cases of non-contact abuse were recounted, which were not included in the figures. The inclusion of these incidents raised the overall rate of abuse to 54 per cent. Russell also rated the seriousness of the incestuous child abuse incidents. She found that 23 per cent of the cases were very serious (genital–genital and oral–genital contact), 40 per cent serious and 36 per cent less serious. The ratios for extra-familial abuse were 53 per cent very serious, 27 per cent serious and 20 per cent less serious.

Finkelhor and his associates (1990) reported on a national survey carried out in 1985. A total of 1481 women and 1145 men were interviewed by telephone. The definitions used included contact and non-contact abuse by any person. Twenty-seven per cent of the women had a history of sexual abuse and 16 per cent of the men; 19 per cent of the female victims and 62 per cent of the male victims had experienced actual or attempted sexual intercourse; 29 per cent of the girl victims were abused by family members compared with 11 per cent of the boys; the latter were more likely to be abused by strangers (40 per cent compared with 21 per cent for girls).

It is hard to generalize about these studies. However, one fact that they all emphasize is that child sexual abuse is far more prevalent than would have been considered possible 15 years ago. Most commentators argue that studies are likely to produce an under-estimate of the real incidence of sexual abuse of children because of the shame attached to it and the fact that survivors are likely to have repressed the memory of it. A second commonly emphasised finding is that girls are more vulnerable than boys. Finkelhor et al. (1986) in their study of studies found that the overall ratio was 79 : 21, but felt that for various social reasons men were less likely to disclose incidents of sexual abuse than women and, therefore, that the true ratios were closer than this figure suggests. Russell's study shows that over half of all women are subjected to some form of sexual abuse before the age of 18. Clearly social work intervention would be inappropriate in all such cases. Nevertheless, figures of 16 per cent of all women experiencing some form of incestuous abuse, two-thirds of which is deemed very serious or serious, is a sobering thought for both young females and agencies mandated to provide them with some protection. The later Finkelhor study (Finkelhor *et al*. 1990) points to 10 per cent intrafamilial abuse which, given the lower rate of abuse of boys (who in contrast to girls are just as likely to be abused by strangers as in the home), lends support to the rate found by Russell.

On the British scene, Birchall (1989) lists six studies since 1978. Mrazek *et al*. (1983) surveyed medical professions to get an estimate of the prevalence of child sexual abuse. They found a rate of 0.3 per cent, which is generally accepted as being a vast under-estimate of the total size of the problem. Nash and West (1985) carried out a study of 315 young women and students in Cambridge and found that 48 per cent had experienced some form of abuse. Approximately 25 per cent reported non-contact abuse and 82 per cent were abused in the first instance by non-family abusers. Thus, there is evidence in this study that half of all women are subjected to some form of sexual abuse as children, but it is largely of a kind that may not require the sort of intra-familial intervention traditionally carried out by social work agencies.

Of the other studies, the MORI poll survey (Baker and Duncan 1985) is probably the most comprehensive. This study took a representative sample of 2019 people of all ages over 15 and using the following definition of child sexual abuse asked them if they had ever had such an experience before the age of 16:

A child (i.e. under sixteen) is sexually abused when another person, who is sexually mature, involves the child in other activities which the other person expects to lead to their sexual arousal. This might involve intercourse, touching, exposure of the sexual organs, showing porno-graphic material or talking about sexual things in an erotic way.

One hundred and five of those questioned said that they had been sexually abused (12 per cent of women and 8 per cent of men); 14 per cent of those who said that they had been abused said that they had been sexually abused within their own families (1.3 per cent of the whole sample); 51 per cent (4.8 per cent of the whole sample) said that they had been abused by strangers and 35 per cent by someone they knew who was not a relation. Just over half of those abused said that the abuse they had experienced involved no physical contact. Nine people (0.45 per cent of the sample) said they had been subjected to incest involving sexual intercourse with a relative.

These findings are much more conservative than those of the American studies. Lafontaine's review of studies (1988) in Britain and the USA comes to the conclusion that the best estimate of the overall extra- and intra-familial prevalence rate of abuse is 10 per cent and this refers to contact abuse only.

The search for a better estimate of the size of the problem goes on. Nevertheless, Lafontaine feels that prevalence and incidence studies have achieved some important goals:

> There has been enough research to show that the sexual abuse of children is not a negligible issue or a question of public hysteria but a serious social problem. Even the lowest estimate of its prevalence indicates a large number of children are involved. (Lafontaine 1990: 68)

This is undeniably true. The prevalence rate of intra-familial abuse pointed to by the MORI poll survey is 13 per 1000 and the rate of incest is 4 per 1000.[16] Currently the number of children on child protection registers as a result of sexual abuse is 0.5 per 1000. Thus there is still a lot of work for child protection agencies to do.

Concluding comments

Prevalence and incidence studies of child abuse, while riddled with methodological and definitional problems, can, if carefully interpreted, add to our understanding of the problem. It is important to disentangle from them what is valid and relevant to the concerns of different sectors in society. For instance, Straus and Gelles in their 1975 study (see Gelles and Cornell 1985) found that 75 per cent of children in their sample had been subjected to physical violence at least once in the previous twelve months. Clearly not all these cases are the concern of child protection agencies. Violence to children (within limits) is not yet culturally disapproved of in American and British societies. Child protection agencies are mandated to deal with cases considered to be beyond the norm. Society as a whole may wish to tackle the broader issue of child correction and child care by developing primary prevention programmes that aim to discourage the use of physical punishment of children. For these purposes, the findings of the Straus and Gelles study are important. Child protection agencies need to sort out the aspects that are relevant to them, such as the abusive violence, and organize their resources accordingly.

The position is similar with regard to child sexual abuse. Children are clearly subjected to far more sexual abuse than was previously imagined possible. Nevertheless, not all the abuse is relevant to the particular concerns of child protection agencies. The findings, especially those of the American studies, point to the need for a major cultural change regarding sexual behaviour. Child protection agencies, unless they are much better resourced and given a broader remit, will inevitably continue to focus on intra-familial abuse. Even so, prevalence studies point to the need for a major rethink about the size of this aspect of the problem and the associated resource implications.

5

Who abuses whom

There has been a vast quantity of research, largely American, conducted into the questions of who is most likely to abuse children, and which children are most likely to be on the receiving end of that abuse. The goal of this research has largely been prediction and, therefore, prevention.

With regard to the who abuses question, the thinking is that if it is possible to identify those parents (and others) who are most likely to abuse or continue to be dangerous to children, then early and decisive intervention is likely to afford those children greater protection. With regard to the question of who is most likely to be at the receiving end of abuse, it is clear that there is a close association between this and the question of who abuses. Children in close proximity to those with a likelihood of abusing are obviously those who are most at risk. However, not all children in this situation seem to be equally at risk. Some children seem to be singled out for mistreatment and researchers have looked into this aspect of child abuse in some detail.

There is a third related issue, that of why child abuse happens. The question of causation is very closely linked to the question of who abuses and who is abused. Indeed, the interrelatedness of these three aspects of the problem of child abuse cannot be sufficiently emphasized. However, for the purposes of analysis, these issues will be looked at separately. In this chapter answers to the questions of who abuses and who is abused will be considered. Theories of causation will be the subject of Chapter 6.

Who abuses

Researchers into the issue of who abuses children have looked at a wide range of variables that they have felt likely to be associated with abusive behaviour. Inevitably, given the amount of research that has been carried out, this summary will be a selective one. The factors selected for closer inspection are as follows:

1 The gender of those who abuse.
2 The age of those who abuse.
3 The association between poverty, race and child abuse.
4 Parents who have been abused themselves.
5 Family structure and child abuse.
6 The psychological capacities of those who abuse.
7 Miscellaneous research.

The gender of those who abuse

It is generally thought that mothers are mainly responsible for mistreating children in cases of neglect and physical abuse, especially those at the younger end of the spectrum, and that fathers, or father substitutes, are responsible for nearly all acts of sexual abuse of children. Common assumptions about parenting roles and the nature of sexuality probably account for both these views. First, child care is seen to be the responsibility of women and, therefore, when things go wrong the fault is thought to lie with them. This is seen to hold true even in cases where it has been established that a male has been the perpetrator of physical abuse.[1] Second, women's sexual nature is seen to be such that they are thought highly unlikely to abuse children sexually. It is notable that, despite this view, women are still held to be partly responsible for what happens – hence the term 'collusive mothers'.[2]

Physical abusive and neglect

With regard to physical abuse and neglect, research findings are not as helpful as they might be. Many researchers make the assumption that women are the key figures with regard to these forms of abuse. Often they do not clarify who has abused or neglected the child when there are both male and female carers living in the family. In lone-parent families (see below), it is usually assumed that abuse is the responsibility of the lone carer, unless there is evidence to the contrary. In both these situations, there is a likelihood that women might well be over-represented in the abuser category because of beliefs about their roles, responsibilities and natures. In this way researchers replicate the views and practices of social workers and other professionals, who carry out much of their work in such cases almost exclusively with women.[3]

Creighton and Noyes (1989) analysed data on the perpetrators of all forms of abuse reported to the NSPCC between 1983 and 1987. They found that natural mothers were only slightly more frequently implicated as abusers than fathers in cases of physical abuse, much more frequently implicated as abusers in neglect and emotional abuse cases, and considered to play a negligible part in sexual abuse. However, with regard to physical abuse they point out that 'If the data is analysed by who the child was living with at the time then natural mothers were implicated in 36% and natural fathers in 61% of the injury cases where the child was living with them' (Creighton and Noyes 1989: 21). This suggests that children in two-parent families are more likely to be physically abused by their fathers than by their mothers. In addition there is some support for the view that men living with children are more likely than women to abuse them seriously. Creighton (1984), using register returns for 1977–82, found that mothers were implicated in 41.4 per cent of serious injuries to children and fathers in 32.9 per cent, but where there were two parents living together fathers were implicated in 49.1 per cent of cases and mothers in 36.1 per cent. Thus it can be concluded that for a variety of reasons, associated largely with male gender-biased assumptions, women are thought to be more implicated in the physical abuse and neglect of children than is in fact the case.[4]

Sexual abuse

The evidence for the sexual abuse of children is more clear-cut. Finkelhor (1984) estimates that 95 per cent of girls and 80 per cent of boys are sexually abused by males. Of 114 women who reported that they had been sexually abused in Nash and West's (1985) study, only one had been abused by a woman. Of 411 sexually abused children referred to the Great Ormond Street Hospital for Sick Children between 1980 and 1986, 2 per cent had been abused by females (Ben-Tovim et al. 1988).

There are studies of female sex abusers. Krug (1989) studied eight cases in detail and came to the conclusion that female sexual abuse of children mirrored that of male sexual abuse:

> The sexual abuse typically involved the mother satisfying her own emotional and physical needs for intimacy, security and perhaps power by actively seeking out the son, either on a nightly basis, or when she and her living partner were in conflict. (p. 112)

Banning (1989) considered such abuse to be on the increase and attributed this development to the blurring of roles between men and women. However, there is a need for some degree of perspective when considering these accounts. While it is wrong to assume that women do not sexually abuse children, one should not fall into the trap of seeing such abuse as perpetrated equally by men and women. As Finkelhor (1984: 184) points out, 'to take the appearance of some forms of sexual abuse by women to mean that sexual abuse is not primarily committed by men is also wrong and has no support in any of the data.'

The age of those who abuse

Physical abuse

Traditionally, physical abuse and neglect of children has been associated with young and immature parents. Baldwin and Oliver (1975) and Greenland

(1987), in their studies of serious and fatal child abuse cases, both confirmed such an association.

Smith *et al.* (1974: 576) assert that 'Child abuse is associated with both illegitimacy and prematurity of parenthood.' Fifty-four per cent of mothers in their study had had their first child before the age of 20. Lynch (1975) in another study found the same in 40 per cent of her sample. Hyman (1978) found that the mean age of 85 mothers with children aged under five referred to the NSPCC was 23 compared with the national average of 28. These studies, however, are all of small scale. Some were carried out without control groups and different definitions of abuse have been used. These factors make comparisons and generalizations very difficult. By contrast, Gil's sample of 1380 cases of reported abuse in the USA in the late 1960s (Gil 1970) led him to state that the age distribution of parents did 'not support the observation of many earlier studies of physically abused children and their families, according to which the parents tend to be extremely young' (Gil 1970: 110). Current figures from the NSPCC suggest that such a view is still valid (see Creighton and Noyes 1989: 16). The findings about age and physical abuse are not, therefore, consistent enough to provide clear connections and there is, as a result, need for care with their interpretation.[5] It may be convenient to associate child abuse with young parenthood. However, the evidence is not nearly strong enough to have much predictive value, even in association with other factors considered indicative of risk.

Sexual abuse
There has been little emphasis placed on the age of sexual abuse perpetrators. By and large, fathers (and father substitutes) who sexually abuse children within the family are likely to be older than physically abusing parents because in most cases the age of the victim is higher (see below). However, the age of the abuser is not generally considered to be an important issue in sexual abuse, except where the perpetrator is a child or adolescent.

Abuse by children
Abuse of younger children by adolescents has recently become a focus of concern for researchers. Straus *et al.* (1980), in their study, estimated that over 19 million children a year (nearly a third of the total child population of the USA) engaged in abusively violent acts against a sibling. They found that the violence was usually inflicted by older children on younger, that it decreased with age and, surprisingly, that aggression of this kind was only slightly more characteristic of boys (83 per cent) than girls (73 per cent).

Davis and Leitenberg (1987) estimate that 20 per cent of all child sexual abuse incidents in the USA are attributable to adolescent offenders. Indeed, many adult sex offenders report that their first sexual offences occurred during adolescence. Fehrenbach and his colleagues (1986) estimated from a study of adolescent sex offenders that 95 per cent were male, that 19 per cent had been sexually abused themselves and that the bulk of their victims were known to them and a third were relatives. Johnson (1989) carried out a study of 13 female child perpetrators, aged between 4 and 12. Her main findings were, first, that these girls had all been severely sexually abused over long periods of time and, second, that most of their victims (77 per cent) were members of their own families. Fehrenbach and Monastersky (1988) studied 28 female adolescents charged with rape or indecent liberties. They found that 20 of these had been either physically or sexually abused themselves and that most of the abuse they perpetrated took place when they were baby-sitting. While these two studies should remind us that girls sexually abuse children as well as boys, such abuse is primarily perpetrated by males.

Poverty, race and child abuse

Physical abuse

Partly because of a traditional focus on individual and psychological factors in the understanding of child abuse, there has been less direct attention paid to the association between broader social factors, such as poverty, class and race, and such abuse. Yet, nearly all studies of official reports and most research surveys demonstrate a strong correlation between poverty and physical abuse and neglect. Gil (1970) found that between 80 and 90 per cent of parents of 1380 children who were officially reported to have been physically abused in the USA were in the lower social classes, with high dependency on public assistance benefits. Straus *et al.* (1980) in their survey found that blue collar workers were more likely to punish physically and abuse their children. In Britain, Becker and Macpherson (1988) found that 90 per cent of referrals for child abuse in Strathclyde in the late 1980s involved children in families dependent on state benefits.

It has been argued that child abuse is a cross-class phenomenon and that the high proportions of lower class families being suspected of such abuse result from the fact that they are more open to state surveillance. This is because of their need for state resources, application for which is at the cost of reduced privacy and independence. From this point of view, the official figures merely demonstrate that the children of the poor who are being abused are more likely to be spotted than those in the higher social classes.

Children from non-white families are over-represented in official reports of child abuse in the USA. Gil (1970) found that a third of all his sample cases were children from non-white families. At the time such families constituted 15 per cent of the total population. Lauderdale *et al.* (1980) found that black families were also most likely to be reported for child abuse in the state of Texas. Incidence studies provide a mixed picture. Straus *et al.* (1980) found no difference between the rates of severe violence employed in black and white families in 1975. However, Hampton *et al.* (1989) found that such violence had increased in black families in the period between then and 1985, whereas for white families there had been a decline in its incidence. Burgdorff (1981) found that, compared with poor white families, poor black families were less abusive to their children.

Data regarding race and child protection have not yet been collected by government departments in Britain and very few studies check their samples for ethnicity. Hyman (1978) reported that 14 per cent of her sample of cases referred to the NSPCC had black fathers. Creighton and Noyes (1989), however, stress that the overwhelming majority of the children registered by the NSPCC between 1983 and 1987 were from white European ethnic backgrounds. Generally the amount of hard information is meagre. One would expect black children to be over-represented in child abuse statistics, partly because their families are more open to surveillance as a result of figuring highly among indices of deprivation (Brown 1984) and partly because, until recently, cultural misunderstanding and the operation of both institutional and direct racism may have increased the chances of suspicions of abuse in black families being confirmed.[6]

Sexual abuse

Most incidence studies of child sexual abuse point to its existence among all strata of society. Finkelhor *et al.* (1986) argue that class, ethnic and regional factors do not seem to affect the incidence of sexual abuse of children in the USA. In a national survey held in 1985, the only exceptions to this were boys of English or Scandinavian heritage, who were at higher risk than those from other ethnic groupings (Finkelhor *et al.* 1990). The MORI Poll survey in Britain found that 'there are no significant differences between the abused, non-abused and refused-to-answer groups with regard to social class and area of residence' (Baker and Duncan 1985: 459).

There is little clear-cut data about the social class composition of families where child sexual abuse is officially reported. Ben-Tovim and his colleagues (1988) kept rough figures on families seen at Great Ormond Street Hospital between 1982 and 1986. Only 8 per cent of the fathers were employed in non-manual occupations. The bulk of families coming to the notice of the NSPCC as a result of child sexual abuse are from the poorer classes (Creighton and Noyes 1989: 18–19). The arguments that apply to physical abuse and neglect regarding state surveillance of the poorer classes could also apply to sexual abuse.

There is little in the way of relevant information on ethnicity and officially reported sexual abuse. It is unlikely that black families will be over-represented in this category. As was stressed in Chapter 4, there is a probability that cultural ignorance and stereotyping may lead to less intervention in this area rather than more (Stubbs 1989).

Parents who have been abused themselves

The issue of the intergenerational transmission of abuse is a thorny one indeed (see Kaufman and Zigler 1987; 1989). There are considerable methodological problems in demonstrating linkages between behaviours over generations. At the level of common sense, the argument that an abused parent is more likely than a non-abused parent to harm his or her own children seems to have some credibility. However, it is important to know whether this view is supported by empirical evidence and, if it is, then to what extent. Attention needs to be paid to the discontinuities as well as the continuities. Knowledge of the circumstances in which abused parents do not abuse their own children is of as much importance to child protection professionals as that of the circumstances in which they do.

Physical abuse

Steele and Pollock (1974) interviewed 60 parents who had physically maltreated their children and found that they had all been abused themselves as children. Their definition of what constituted abuse for these parents was, however, very wide-ranging and included being subjected to 'intensive, pervasive and continual demands' from their own parents.

Oliver (1985), using official records, uncovered 147 families out of a population of 200,000 in north Wiltshire where abuse of children had happened in successive generations. However, the potential usefulness of this study is diminished by the fact that we are not told how many of the parents who were abused themselves in the first generation did not go on to abuse their own children.

Jayaratne (1977), using Gil's (1970) relatively low transmission rate findings (14 per cent in the case of mothers and 7 per cent in the case of fathers), argues against the intergenerational hypothesis. Cicchetti and Aber (1980) argue that the hypothesis has been overstated and that situational and interactional factors within the family are more telling indicators than the history of the parents.

Hunter and Kilstrom (1979) conducted an important study on this subject (particularly with respect to methodological issues). They interviewed 282 parents of newborn children admitted to a regional intensive care nursery for premature and ill infants. Forty-nine of these parents had themselves been abused. At follow-up a year later, nine of these had abused their children. Only one child from the rest of the sample had been abused. Thus the intergenerational rate in this prospective study was 18 per cent. If a retrospective study had been carried out on the ten abused children, the rate would have been 90 per cent. This study clearly demonstrates how a retrospective approach can give an exaggerated impression of the extent of intergenerational abuse.

Egeland (1988) followed up over a period of 12 years 267 women considered before the birth of their first child to be at some risk of abuse, and found that there was an intergenerational transmission rate of abuse of about one-third. Perhaps more importantly, he also looked for factors that improved parents' chances of avoiding repetition of the abuse that they had experienced, and identified two: the development of satisfying personal relationships and social networks; and an ability to verbalize and be open about their own experiences.

The findings of this study are supported by those of an earlier study by Straus (1979). Making an estimate from the 1975 intra-familial violence incidence study, carried out by him and his colleagues, he concluded that the rate of all types of intergenerational abuse varied between 25 and 35 per cent. He found that there was more risk for the child if the parents had been ill-treated, but that the majority of ill-treated children do not become abusive parents.

It is worth noting an issue raised earlier: that all these studies focus almost entirely on transmission of violence and abuse through mothers whereas, to the best of our knowledge, men are responsible for at least half of all physical abuse. There is very little research into the antecedents of male adults who physically abuse.

Sexual abuse
The picture is only slightly better in this respect with regard to sexual abuse. Despite the fact that males are responsible for nearly all such abuse, there is still considerable focus on women as the key link between sexual abuse over two generations. Goodwin *et al*. (1981) found that 24 per cent of mothers of abused children had had prior incest experiences compared with 3 per cent of a control group. Faller (1989) found that nearly half the mothers of a sample of 154 sexually abused children either had experienced or knew of sexual abuse in their own families of origin. This study is particularly useful in that it also checked the experiences of the male offenders in these cases – nearly 40 per cent of them had also experienced or knew of sexual abuse in their families as children.

Studies of male perpetrators of sexual abuse who have been imprisoned show relatively high proportions of these men having been sexually abused themselves as children. Groth and Burgess (1979) found that 32 per cent of a group of 106 child molesters reported some form of sexual trauma in childhood. Yet of the 274 cases seen by Ben-Tovim *et al*. (1988), only five of the perpetrators had been abused themselves. This leads to speculation as to whether there are two types of abuser: the persistent offender who is a danger to many children outside their families and the intra-familial abuser, the latter being less traumatized as a child than the former.[7] Fehrenbach *et al*. (1986) estimated that 19 per cent of largely male adolescent sex offenders had themselves been sexually abused. Johnson (1988) found that 49 per cent of child perpetrators of sexual abuse had themselves been abused and, as has been already stated, young female sexual offenders also studied by her were all found to have been sexually abused. Many of the children in both these studies were physically abused as well.

There is clearly some intergenerational linking between sexual abuse. It seems to be roughly in the same proportions as for physical abuse and neglect. However, the form of transmission is complex. This is partly due to the focus of the research studies. There is little attention paid to intra-familial male adult abusers and, therefore, little information about them. Faller's study is an exception to this. However, there is more information about persistent child abusers and about the abuse experienced by mothers of children who are sexually abused. The focus on the latter seems to implicate such women in the abuse of their children. It is interesting to note the rarity of sexual abuse by women given the extent of abuse they experience, whereas the opposite seems to be true of men.

The topic of intergenerational transmission of abuse is clearly a problematic one. It has been argued that focus on this issue is pessimistic as far as those who have been abused are concerned. It can also, from another point of view, be seen to be over-deterministic, taking away individuals' responsibilities for their own actions. That continuities exist is not in dispute but, as Straus points out, there are now more pertinent questions to be asked:

> The time has come for the intergenerational myth to be put aside and for researchers to cease arguing 'Do abused children become abusive parents?' and ask, instead, 'Under what conditions is the transmission of abuse likely to occur?' (Straus 1979: 191)

Family structure and child abuse

There is considerable current concern about the changing shape of the family and the effect that it may be having on child care practices and children's behaviour. Official statistics show that lone parenthood is on the increase, one-third of all marriages end in divorce and large numbers of children live in reconstituted families.[8] Two facets of family structure have been looked at by child abuse researchers: lone parenthood and stepparenting (particularly with regard to sexual abuse).

Lone parent families and child abuse

American official figures in 1981 showed that 43 per cent of children reported for all kinds of abuse came from single-female household heads and 5 per cent from single-male household heads, the national percentage for all such households being 17 (National Center on Child Abuse and Neglect 1981). Creighton and Noyes (1989) found that a quarter of all children registered for physical abuse by the NSPCC in England and Wales between 1983 and 1987 lived in lone-parent families. Nearly half of those registered for neglect, over half of those registered for failure to thrive and a third of those registered for emotional abuse also lived in one-parent households.

With regard to physical abuse and neglect, Sack et al. (1985) carried out a study of 802 adults in Oregon and found the prevalence of abuse to be twice as high in single-parent households as in those with two parents. Gelles (1989), using data from two national incidence studies of violence in the family, came to the conclusion that lone-parent families were no more likely than two-parent families to use violence overall, but that they were more likely to use severe and very severe violence, particularly in the case of the single male parent. Creighton and Noyes (1989) found somewhat surprisingly that a fifth of children registered for sexual abuse came from lone-female headed homes. On the face of it, one would expect such children to be safer from abuse by males in such situations.

Overall both official reports and survey findings concur: children in lone-parent families are more at risk of all forms of abuse and neglect than their counterparts in two-parent families. To what extent this is the case is not clear – Gelles's estimate is much lower than that of Sack and his colleagues. In addition, these rather bald statistics do not tell us anything about the dynamics or processes that might help to account for why there should be this variation in abuse rates between these two family types. Clearly economic stress is likely to be an important factor. The high percentage of neglect cases among lone-parent families shown up in the NSPCC figures could also point to this. Issues surrounding the control of children and social isolation could also play a part. With regard to sexual abuse, Finkelhor (1986) argues that children in lone-female headed households could be exposed to a greater number of male adult figures than those in two-parent households and that this could place them at statistically greater risk of being sexually abused.

All this paints a rather negative picture of lone-parenting. The advantages of such families should also be taken into account, such as the potential for less interpersonal conflict between parents. There is need for much more research into the impact of lone-parenting (benefits and costs) on child-rearing in general.

Stepparents and child abuse
There is not a great deal of available information on the impact of stepparenting on physical abuse and neglect. Creighton and Noyes (1989) found that 32 per cent of physically abused children lived with one natural parent (mainly female) and one substitute parent (mainly male). The percentages for other forms of abuse were as follows: neglect 15 per cent, failure to thrive 11 per cent and emotional abuse 36 per cent. Reconstituted families are thus well over-represented in these abuse statistics, but there has been little follow-up research as to why this is the case or into the process of abuse in such families.

On the other hand, there seems to be much fascination with the issue of whether blood-tie parents are more likely to abuse their children sexually than non-blood-tie relatives and more research into this topic as a result. Of the cases seen by Ben-Tovim *et al*. (1988) between 1982 and 1986, 46 per cent of the perpetrators were natural parents and 27 per cent stepparents (nearly all male). Of 198 paternal offenders studied by Gordon and Creighton (1988), 46 per cent were non-natal fathers and 54 per cent were natal fathers. Russell (1984) found from her sample of 930 women that 17 per cent (1 in 6) of those who had had a stepfather as a principal figure during their childhood had been sexually abused by him and that the comparable figures for biological fathers was 2 per cent (1 in 40). In addition she found that stepfathers were more likely to commit seriously abusive acts. It seems to be the case, therefore, that children are more at risk of being sexually abused by a stepparent, or parent-substitute, than by their natural parents.

Two caveats need to be borne in mind. First, there is a danger of assuming that all stepparents present a risk to children. This is clearly not true. Even using Russell's high figures of stepfather abuse, five out of six stepfathers do

...heir children. Second, as Russell herself comments, there ...hatsoever for considering sexual abuse by step-fathers as ...exual abuse by biological fathers' (Russell 1986: 16). There is ...or more broad-based research into the impact of family ...ildren in reconstituted families and, as with lone-parent ...is need for attention to be paid to positive features and ...well as to negative consequences.

The psychological capacities of those who abuse

In this section attention will be paid, first, to whether mental illness plays a part in the causation of physical child abuse and, second, to the association between such abuse and the intellectual capacities of parents. Research into the psychological make-up of child sexual abusers will then be considered.

Physical abuse and mental illness

Mainstream thinking about linkages between physical child abuse and neglect and mental health issues has been fairly limited. The generally held view is that, in the main, women (there is very little reference to men) who abuse their children are not mentally ill. They are considered to have problems with parenting linked to psychological incapacities to nurture and care for their babies and children.

There is an acceptance that mental illness plays a small part in the aetiology of physical abuse, but this view is based on mental illness being equated with severe psychotic states. Thus, Greenland (1987) found that less than 10 per cent of 100 parents from families where child deaths had occurred in Ontario were suffering from mental illnesses, but they were all of a severe psychotic nature. Straus et al. (1980) attribute less than 10 per cent of all types of family violence to mental illness. However, there are some studies that have taken a broader definition of mental illness and, as a result, have demonstrated a closer association between such illness and physical child abuse. Hyman (1978) found that, in 25 per cent of the 85 cases she studied, psychiatric illness had been diagnosed in the mothers. Oliver (1985) found that 34 per cent of 147 mothers had been treated psychiatrically for depression, as had 5 per cent of the fathers. Smith (1975) found that three-quarters of the mothers and two-thirds of the fathers in his study had 'abnormal personalities', but only a very few had been formally diagnosed as mentally ill.

It may be the case that there are some forms of psychological state, such as depression, whose effects and influence are under-estimated as contributory factors to the physical abuse and neglect of children. Brown and Harris (1978) associated depression in working class women with a variety of poor environmental factors. There are also links between men's violence to women and depression (see Kelly 1988). The role of depression seems to have been underplayed in thought about and research into child abuse. The female carers of several children who have been the subject of public inquiries, such as Christine Mason (Doreen Aston), Beatrice Henry (Tyra Henry) and

Rosemary Koseda (Heidi Koseda), have all been described as showing symptoms of depression.[9]

This is a very problematic issue. Some family violence researchers are very keen to dissociate forms of abuse from mental illness on the grounds that such violence should not be seen to be the product of abnormal behavioural states, but rather the acts of sane people (Gelles and Cornell 1985). Roberts (1988: 46) epitomizes this view: 'psychiatric labels seem unjustified when so many practitioners are convinced that the potential for child abuse is within us all, given a sufficient number of stressful circumstances.' There is also a danger that focusing on the role of depression in child abuse could serve to place even more emphasis on women. Nevertheless, this seems to be an area that merits further consideration.

The intellectual capacities of parents who physically abuse
There has been only a small amount of research into the intellectual capacities of parents who abuse their children. Some early studies pointed to a very strong connection between low intelligence and child abuse. Rates drawn from samples by Smith (1975) and Young (1964) were as high as 50 per cent. Such findings have not, however, been replicated in more recent studies. Creighton and Noyes (1989) found that 10 per cent of mothers and 5 per cent of fathers of children on registers had attended special schools. While this is a much lower rate than those suggested by the earlier studies, it is still well above the national level. Thus there is evidence of a significant correlation between low intelligence and officially reported child abuse.

There are, however, several factors that could account for this association, the most obvious being that the heightened concern that exists with regard to people with learning difficulties bringing up their own children results in their child care practices being exposed to greater scrutiny than those of parents of normal intelligence. Care should be taken not to see all people with learning difficulties as a homogeneous group with similar characteristics. They do share some common problems, but these stem mainly from their potential for being undervalued and exploited by others.

Research that demonstrates the circumstances in which parents with learning difficulties abuse their children is more useful than research that simply demonstrates correlation rates between low intelligence and child abuse. The study by Tymchuk and Andron (1990) is a good example of this. They compared two small groups of low IQ mothers, half of whom had a history of abuse or neglect of their own children and half who had not. The former in fact had higher IQs than the latter. The important difference seemed to be the degree of support they had received as pregnant women and parents. The women who had neglected their children had had far less support than the non-neglecters.

Sexual abuse
In recent times, there has been little linkage between particular psychological characteristics and child sexual abuse. There has been much more emphasis on interactive rather than individualistic factors than in the case of physical

abuse and neglect. There has been no research linking mental illness with sexual abuse. Traditionally, incest has been linked to families of low intelligence, but there is little research evidence to show this to be the case. Finkelhor *et al.* (1986) raise several important questions about the personality characteristics of those who sexually abuse children, such as: why a person would find relating to a child sexually gratifying and congruent; why a person would be sexually aroused by a child; why he would be blocked in efforts to obtain sexual and emotional gratification from more normally approved sources; and, finally, why he would not be affected by societal taboos. Research into these questions and others relating to the psychological make-up of those who sexually abuse children is urgently needed.

Other factors associated with those who abuse children

There are many other factors associated with those who abuse children. In this section, five other areas will be briefly addressed: alcohol; social isolation; marital or partner problems; criminality; and pregnancy, bonding or neo-natal difficulties.[10]

Alcohol

Alcohol has been closely linked with child abuse from the early days of the NSPCC at the time when the Temperance movement had a high profile. It is still cited as a contributory factor to child abuse (Browne and Saqi 1988). However, Orme and Rimmer (1981) in their review of research into the connection between alcoholism and physical child abuse up to that date point out that assessing the value of the different studies is difficult because of the problems of achieving common definitions of the two phenomena. They come to the conclusion that 'The most striking finding that emerged from our study was that there was not adequate empirical evidence to support an association between alcoholism and child abuse.' (Orme and Rimmer 1981: 285). There has been little empirical research into the connection between sexual abuse and alcoholism. Lafontaine (1990: 100), quotes Maisch (1973): 'It would be a mistake to deduce from suitable cases a direct, specific causal connection between alcohol and incest.'

There is also little hard information about the connection between drug misuse and child ill-treatment. There has recently been a tendency to see such misuse as a risk factor in terms of the care of children (Murphy *et al.* 1991) and current concerns about foetal abuse are likely to intensify the focus on parents taking drugs and consuming alcohol (Parker *et al.* 1988). More information on this subject is clearly needed. The research pointing to the dubious connection between alcohol misuse and child abuse suggests that it would also probably be wrong automatically to assume a close linkage between drug misuse and abuse of children.

Social isolation

The connection between social isolation and child abuse has been per-suasively argued by Garbarino (1982) and Polansky *et al.* (1979), among others. This topic will be discussed as a causal explanation of child abuse in the next chapter. Smith (1975) found that 49 per cent of his sample of abusing parents had no opportunities for having a break from the child, as opposed to 26 per cent in his control group. They had no contact with parents, relatives, neighbours or friends. Several studies of physical abuse and neglect report similar findings (Skinner and Castle 1969; Giovannoni and Billingsley 1970). Seagull (1987), in a helpful review of studies, argues that social isolation is more closely linked to neglect than to physical abuse.

The value of these studies is limited. First, they do not employ common definitions of social isolation. Second, they do not measure the quality of contacts. An individual may have many familial and social contacts, but these may not be supportive or alleviate the stresses of child care. Third, they assume that social isolation causes abuse, whereas the reverse may be true. Families may isolate themselves to prevent the discovery of abuse or become isolated because they are neglecting their children. Therefore, although there is a rough association between certain forms of abuse and social isolation, there is a need for more detailed research into the way in which these variables interact.

Marital or partner problems

Lukianowicz (1971), in an early study, pointed to an association between physically abusive parents and poor marital relationships. Ben-Tovim et al. (1988) found that half the perpetrators of child sexual abuse and two-thirds of their partners considered that they had relationship problems. Creighton and Noyes (1989) found that the stress factor that was ranked as most severe for all registered children was the 'marital problems' of their parents. The usefulness of this aspect of knowledge is open to question. First, there are problems involved in assessing the quality of relationships. Second, there are many adults with children who have relationship problems and do not abuse their children. Third, abuse of children may take place with no apparent conflict between its adult carers.[11] Fourth, the term 'marital or partner problems' could include a whole host of behaviours that may not be equally important – for instance, it could include constant verbal rows and violent physical assaults. Certainly, as a predictive tool, this aspect of knowledge is fairly useless. A more fruitful area of study is the connection between violence to women and violence to children. Brekke (1987) has pointed to such connections with regard to physical abuse and Truesdell et al. (1986) in relation to sexual abuse.

Criminality

Previous history of child ill-treatment on the part of an adult is considered to be an important indicator of risk with regard to children living with them. Creighton and Noyes (1989) demonstrate that there has been an increase in numbers of parents with records for offences against children figuring in child protection registrations between 1983 and 1987. In many of the cases that were the subject of public inquiries, parents, particularly fathers, had been previously convicted of offences against children. However, there has been little systematic research into recidivism rates with regard to physical abuse of children.

Somewhat more attention has been paid to recidivism rates among child sexual abusers. Furby *et al*. (1989) in a review of studies found the rate to be as high as 56 per cent in some and that this was regardless of whether offenders receive specific treatment or not. Care has to be taken not to extrapolate this finding to all those who have sexually abused children, in that the studies reviewed focus largely on what is probably the worst type of offender. It would be useful to know, if there are sexual offenders who do not reoffend, what their characteristics are and the circumstances of their offending.

Some studies have pointed to correlations between general criminality and child abuse. Oliver (1985), in his study of 147 families who had abused children over two generations, found a considerable degree of general criminality among his sample, but only a small amount of such criminality was associated with child abuse. Correlations of this kind tell us little other than about the type of family whose children come under closest scrutiny from the state. There seems to be no logical reason why general criminality should have any particular connection with child abuse.

There is a need for a good deal of caution in using previous history of child abuse on the part of adults as an indicator of their children being at risk. Our current state of knowledge is very limited. At present it suggests: (a) that there is a need to investigate such circumstances, and (b) that care should be taken not to assume that 'once an offender, always an offender'.

Pregnancy, prematurity, bonding and other neo-natal problems
Greenland (1987) points out that several studies in the 1960s and 1970s found a correlation between child abuse and pregnancy. Elmer (1977) found that nine of her sample of twenty abusive mothers were pregnant at the time the abuse was referred. It should not be construed from this that all pregnant women are a threat to their other children. This is clearly not the case. The message of findings such as these is that pregnancy can create extra stress on parents, knowledge of which may be crucial to ongoing work with families where children are already considered to be at risk.[12]

Peri- and neo-natal difficulties have received arguably more attention than any other potential causal factor in the study of child abuse. The general view adopted by researchers in this field is that where there are problems at birth, such as prematurity, that result in early separation of mother and child, there is a potential for poor mother–child relationships, rejection and abuse. Lynch and Roberts (1977) reported that use of a checklist, including significant separation from the child after birth and concerns reported by midwives about mothers' early responses to their babies, was an effective predictor of future care and potential abuse. Murphy *et al*. (1981) retrospectively studied 80 cases of children abused in the Cardiff area and found that, compared with controls, more had been born pre-term and were of lower birth weight. In the USA, Benedict and White (1985) studied over 500 cases in a similar way and also associated prematurity, low birth weights and longer stays in hospital around birth with children who were later abused. On the other hand, Leventhal *et al.* (1984) found no relationship between prematurity, low birth weight and abuse in a study of 117 abused children (with controls). There was a much closer correlation with young maternal age than with any other factor.

Most of the evidence, despite Leventhal's findings, points to a correlation between birth problems and later abuse and neglect. This does not mean, of course, that wherever these types of birth difficulties occur abuse will result. It means that the chances are higher. The research findings demonstrate the connections, but do not necessarily explain why they exist or the process whereby abuse results. Bonding difficulties have been most often cited as potential causal factors, i.e. mothers and children miss out on a crucial time for attachment to each other, which can set in train a set of events such as uncertain handling, problems in feeding and lack of mutual pleasure, leading ultimately to abuse. However, doubts have been raised about the crucial importance attached to immediate post-birth bonding (see Sluckin *et al.* 1983). Other factors could account for the correlation between neo-natal difficulties and child abuse. First, looking after prematurely born and/or low birth weight children who generally require more attention and care is likely to put carers under extreme stress. Second, it is probable that the majority of the mothers in these studies who were experiencing peri-natal difficulties were from poor backgrounds.[13] Inadequate material resources for looking after young babies are probably an additional major factor in the quality of care that is provided.[14] Much medical-based research tends to underplay such social concerns.

As with most of the other research in this chapter, the focus of studies of neo-natal bonding problems is on the mother. This is a major weakness. There needs to be more attention paid to the involvement (or lack of involvement) of fathers in early child care. Some studies have suggested that the lack of early bonding between fathers and children could be a contributory factor in the causation of child sexual abuse (see Parker and Parker 1986).

Who is abused

All children are potentially vulnerable to abuse by those adults who look after them through childhood because they are dependent on them for all aspects of physical and emotional protection and care. Most children are not mistreated by their parents because protective behaviour is considered natural and instinctive (Bowlby 1971). However, a great deal of effort has been expended on trying to predict where breakdowns in this normal protective behaviour are likely to occur, by focusing on the characteristics and circumstances of children who are abused as well as on those of their parents. Clearly there are factors common to both, and in the section on who abuses, those associated with parents, such as their own experiences of abuse, their psychological state and the quality of their marital or partner relationships, have been considered and do not need to be reviewed again here.

Finkelhor and Korbin (1988), writing from an international perspective, but with an eye to poorer countries in the southern hemisphere, point out that the following children are most vulnerable to abuse and neglect: (a) those with inferior health status; (b) children who are deformed or handicapped (though in a few societies they are protected by a special status); (c) female children; (d) children born in unusual, stigmatized or difficult conditions; (e) excess or unwanted children; (f) children with disvalued traits and behaviours; (g) illegitimate children; (h) children born in situations of rapid economic change. While such children are less obviously at risk in northern industrialized societies, they are still more vulnerable to abuse within these societies than those who do not share these characteristics. Many of the factors listed above have been considered in the first section of this chapter. The factors that remain to be discussed are: age; gender; parent–child relationship problems; physical and mental disability; family size.

Age

Using Department of Health statistics for 1989 (DoH 1990), the age breakdown of children on child protection registers is set out in Table 5.1. What this table shows is that children are most likely to be officially considered to be at risk in their first year of life and, thereafter, less at risk the older the age. This pattern holds true for physical child abuse, neglect and grave concern. The reverse is true for sexual abuse until the age of 16, and emotional abuse provides a mixed picture. With regard to physical abuse and failure to thrive, there is particular concern about very young children because of their greater vulnerability and dependence (and also the stress on young parents created by this dependence).

Table 5.1 The age of children placed on child protection registers during the year ending 31 March 1989 by category of abuse

Category of abuse	Age on 31 March 1989				
	Under 1	1–4	5–9	10–15	16 and over
Physical abuse	1.10	0.83	0.51	0.40	0.10
Neglect	0.61	0.45	0.25	0.10	0.01
Emotional abuse	0.09	0.12	0.11	0.06	0.02
Sexual abuse	0.07	0.24	0.36	0.46	0.20
Grave concern	2.70	1.29	0.79	0.49	0.10
Total	4.57	2.93	2.02	1.51	0.43

Note: Figures are rates per 1000 in each age group.

In the case of sexual abuse, the official figures show that the peak ages for registration are between 10 and 15 years. Finkelhor *et al*. (1986) found that the most common age for the onset of sexual abuse for both boys and girls was between the ages of 8 and 12. This fits with the generally accepted view that in many cases where abuse of this kind is reported, it may have a long prior history.

It must be stressed that these age estimates only provide general pointers. There is evidence of child sexual abuse occurring at much younger ages in children (see Macfarlane *et al*. 1988; Hobbs and Wynne 1986) and of physical abuse at relatively late ages, as in the case of Stephen Menheniott.[15]

Gender

Again the Department of Health statistics provide a useful starting point. Table 5.2 shows a breakdown of children on registers in 1989 by gender. Overall official reporting figures suggest that girls are more subject to abuse than boys. Finkelhor and Korbin (1988) argue that in many societies throughout the world (India, for example) girls are more subjected to abuse because they are less valued for their economic utility. In our society, these economic factors do not apply. Yet girls are as a whole still more vulnerable. The reason for this is the difference in sexual abuse rates.

Although the difference is not great, it is worth noting that boys are more exposed to physical abuse, neglect and emotional abuse than girls, as far as official intervention is concerned. Creighton and Noyes (1989) reported similar findings from the NSPCC register returns between 1983 and 1987. There seem to be no obvious reasons why this is the case. It could be speculated that, in the case of physical abuse, physical punishment of boys is more generally sanctioned as a means of control in our society than of girls and that this cultural norm leads to more excessive violence in their case.

Table 5.2 Estimated rates of child protection registrations during the year ending 31 March 1989 by sex and category of abuse

Category of abuse	Boys	Girls
Physical abuse	0.58	0.48
Neglect	0.25	0.23
Emotional abuse	0.09	0.08
Sexual abuse	0.15	0.55
Grave concern	0.81	0.86
Total	1.94	2.28

Note: Figures are rates per 1000. Totals include small numbers of children registered under joint categories.

Parent–child relationship problems

There has been a good deal written about the contribution of the child to his or her own abuse. This seems a strange and, on the face of it, somewhat offensive concept. However, there is some evidence to suggest that particular children are singled out for abuse. Family therapists, in particular, and behaviourists are interested in the dynamics of child abuse and why particular children are 'selected' for such abuse and not others. Children who are not wanted or who are considered to be the wrong sex by their parents are seen to be at greater risk (see Roberts *et al*. 1980). Friedrich and Boriskin (1976) list a variety of factors associated with the child that may contribute to abuse taking place. These include prematurity and genetic differences, which make some children cuddlers and some not. The latter are seen to be more at risk because they do not 'reward' their parents. They write:

> It would be fanciful to conclude that the special child is the sole contributor to abuse. But the opposite extreme, the all too prevalent notion that abuse is exclusively a function of a parental defect, seems equally specious. (Friedrich and Boriskin 1976: 288)

Once again, the dynamics of the situation need to be stressed. Much depends on the parent–child mix. As Belsky and Vondra (1989: 188) so clearly put it,

> The undermining effect of a difficult child on parental functioning will be lessened when the parent has an abundance of personal psychological resources. Conversely, an easy-to-rear child can compensate for limited personal resources on the part of the parent in maintaining parental effectiveness.

Physical and mental disability

There is no doubt that children with physical and mental disabilities place additional child-rearing strains on families. It might be expected, therefore, that such children are more likely to be exposed to abuse and neglect. A recent review of American studies (White *et al*. 1987) came to the conclusion that there were linkages between children with physical disabilities and child abuse, but that the nature of the linkages was not clear (see also Westcott 1991).

Jaudes and Diamond (1985), using data from a study of 37 children with cerebral palsy, argue that it is necessary to disentangle abuse that causes disability from that inflicted on already disabled children. They conclude that as many as a tenth of mental disabilities may be caused by abuse and that abuse of disabled children is relatively higher than abuse of the non-disabled population. Ammerman *et al*.'s study (1989) supports this view. Theringer *et al*. (1990) point out that children with mental handicaps are particularly vulnerable to sexual abuse and exploitation because of their relatively powerless position.

These studies, therefore, all affirm that disabled children are more vulnerable to abuse than their non-disabled counterparts. However, there are still questions to be answered about which disabled children in which situations are most at risk. Friedrich (1979), in a general study of parents with children with disabilities, found that marital satisfaction was the best overall predictor of coping. Such a finding obviously does not take into account the situation of lone parents. Nevertheless, the gist of the message is clear, namely that close support and help are important ingredients in bringing up all children and particularly those with disabilities.

Family size

Creighton (1984) and Creighton and Noyes (1989) found that families with four or more children figured disproportionately in cases registered by the NSPCC between 1977 and 1987. Just over a quarter of all registrations involved such families, yet they make up only 10 per cent of families with children in social classes IV and V. Creighton and Noyes broke down the registrations by category of type of abuse for the years 1983 to 1987 and found that families with four or more children constituted just over a third of all sexual abuse registrations and just under a third of all neglect registrations. Small-scale studies (Hyman 1978; Corby 1987) have not found a connection between family size and referral for child abuse. A related issue is that of the age gap between children. Some studies have found that there is a correlation between abuse and families with several children close in age (see Browne and Saqi 1988: 59–60). It must be concluded, therefore, that children in larger families with siblings close in age are statistically more at risk of abuse.

Concluding comments

The research studies considered in this chapter have all sought to answer the two questions of who abuses and who is abused, with the aim of pinpointing targets of prevention and intervention. As has been seen, there are weaknesses and biases in most of the research studies that to a large degree reduce their usefulness for practice. The main weaknesses of these studies have been repeatedly stressed.

They are, first, that they have focused too much on general correlations and not enough on particular details, so that we know, for example, that children living in reconstituted families are overall more at risk than those living with both natural parents. Yet we know little about the degree of risk, what factors exacerbate the risk or in what conditions reconstituted families do a good job of rearing children. These sorts of criticism apply to almost all of the factors that have been associated in the research studies with child abuse. The reason for this weakness lies in the mislaid emphasis on predicting and targeting the problem. There is a need to consider the hows and whys of child abuse as well. Second, many of the studies demonstrate gender-blindness and slip into the easy assumption that the mother is the key figure in the child abuse process. Again such a view does not do justice to the hows and whys of child abuse.

This does not completely invalidate the work that has been done, but stresses that it needs to be used in a careful and critical manner. Such research can, if used carefully, sensitize professionals to risk potential, but so far it provides a basic starting-point only.

6

The causation of child abuse

Social workers and other professionals involved in the field of child abuse have generally been less concerned about why such abuse happens than they have about the type of person who abuses and the type of child who is most vulnerable to abuse. This is probably because the latter two questions seem to have a more direct impact on prediction and prevention (if we can identify those most likely to be at risk, then we can do something about it). The question of why child abuse happens is not considered as so directly significant to the day-to-day practicalities of child protection work. Such an enquiry has traditionally been seen to be more the province of theorists than of practitioners. This state of affairs is understandable, given the increased volume of child protection work and the pressures on front-line workers not to make mistakes.[1] However, endeavouring to understand why abuse of children takes place serves three main functions. It gives a greater sense of control to the worker over events that may otherwise seem inexplicable, it gives a sense of direction for ongoing work or treatment (whichever term is preferred) and it informs those responsible for policy-making in this field. For these reasons, understanding why abuse has happened has a very important contribution to make to child protection work.

A broad range of theoretical perspectives has been brought to bear on the aetiology of child abuse. They derive from diverse sources, survey the problem at different levels and, as a consequence, do not necessarily complement each other. Indeed there is a good deal of conflict and disagreement between adherents of different approaches, creating problems that until recently have not been constructively addressed. There is evidence of a move towards a resolution of these issues with the development of integrative approaches, which go some way towards combining the various perspectives to provide more comprehensive but also, inevitably, more complex explanatory accounts (see Garbarino 1977; Belsky 1980).

Overviews of causation theories tend to categorize them in different ways (see Sweet and Resick 1979; Ostbloom and Crase 1980; Smith 1984). However, there seem to be three main groups of perspective: those that focus on the instinctive and psychological qualities of individuals who abuse; those that focus on the dynamics of the interaction between abuser, child and immediate environment; and those that emphasize social and political conditions as the most important reason for the existence of child abuse. This categorization will be used as the structure for this chapter. In addition, consideration will be given to attempts to combine these perspectives to provide a more holistic picture.

Psychological theories

In this section consideration will be given to the contribution of the discipline of biology, attachment theory, the psychodynamic perspective and learning theory.

Biology and child abuse

There has been little direct application of principles drawn from the biological sciences to the understanding of child abuse among humans. Nevertheless, biological theory does underlie some approaches, particularly those of attachment theory and the psychodynamic perspective, and it is has been argued, notably by sociobiologists,[2] that Darwinian theories, such as natural selection and the survival of the fittest, have something to offer to our understanding of child abuse. Reite (1987) puts forward the view that there are many factors common to human child care and neglect and that of animals:

> Human and non-human primates share a substantial common evolutionary history, and many of the behavioral systems we are talking about, including perhaps much of that underlying social attachment are likely biologically determined to a significant degree. (Reite 1987: 354)

He points out that animals abuse their young in circumstances where there are aberrations or disturbances in early mother–infant attachment, and where environmental stresses such as over-crowding or lack of social support prevail. In a similar vein, other writers have drawn some comparisons between certain types of child abuse and what is termed 'the culling process' among animals, whereby the weakest in the litter are neglected in times of food shortage (Barash 1981).

Sociobiologists have in a very general way applied these principles to the issue of step- and substitute-parenting and child abuse. Some non-genetic parents in the animal world have been noted to be very cruel to infants. Hrdy (1977) found that in one species of monkey, males seeking to mate with females already with litters, but with no male protector, killed the young. The explanation for this behaviour, according to sociobiological theory, is simply that as these monkeys have no investment in the genes of these infants, the sooner the infants are out of the way the quicker the adults can produce offspring of their own. On the other hand, sociobiologists point to examples of non-genetic inspired altruism where infant birds and animals are nurtured and protected by non-relatives. Such behaviour is attributed to a species survival instinct and, it is argued, takes place only where there are benefits for the giver (Barash 1981: 132–69).

It is hard to know what weight to give to such ideas. While much of the theorizing of sociobiologists seems to be reductionist and over-stated, it does remind us of the part that instinct can play in certain behaviours and that it is a variable not to be overlooked or completely dismissed. Unthinking and indiscriminate use of such theory could, however, fuel prejudice and lead to over-reliance on common sense (and instinct!) as a tool for understanding the way in which people behave.

Attachment theory and child abuse

Attachment theory is described by Crittenden and Ainsworth (1989: 435) as:

> a relatively new, open-ended theory with eclectic underpinnings. Intended as a revision of psychoanalytic theory, particularly Freudian instinct theory and metapsychology, it has been infused by present-day biological principles with an emphasis on ethology and evolutionary theory, as well as by control-systems theory and cognitive psychology.

The main theoretical tenets of attachment theory are derived from the work of one person, John Bowlby (1971). In the period immediately after the Second World War, he carried out studies into the nature and effects of maternal deprivation on young children (Bowlby 1951). He initially theorized that any significant separation of a child from its mother in the first five years of life could have deleterious effects on its emotional development and could lead to a variety of psychological and social difficulties in later life, such as the development of an affectionless personality and becoming a juvenile delinquent. Originally, the reasoning for this process was derived from psychodynamic theory, i.e. that the child developed a psychologically healthy sense of self through consistently rewarding contact with its mother. As his work developed, Bowlby drew more and more from the biological sciences and animal behaviour and placed more emphasis on the physical aspects of mother–child bonding and attachment. In the final outcome he argued that a child properly attached to its mother gains the dual benefit of physical protection and psychological security. He saw the process of attachment as an instinctive, two-way, symbiotic process.

Bowlby's early theorizing was criticized by Rutter (1978) for not taking into account the fact that the child could become attached to other significant figures as well as the mother. What was important, according to his argument, was the consistency and the positive nature of the relationship.

Thus the roles of the father and other relatives in the emotional development of the child needed to be given more consideration.

Feminists have criticized attachment theory on the grounds that it has limiting and restrictive implications for women, because of its prescription that mothers should be in close proximity to their children for the whole of their infancy. Most attachment theorists now concede that children at around the age of three can cope with separation because they can by use of language and reasoning understand and accept explanations of what is happening.

Until fairly recently, attachment theory was not directly applied to the problem of child abuse, though it has had a major influence on general child care policy and practice. Currently, poor attachment experiences are seen to be both a cause and a consequence of child abuse. Crittenden and Ainsworth (1989) argue that repeated consistent and rewarding interactions between a mother and child lead to high self-esteem and the capacity to trust. Non-responsive, rejecting and inconsistent responses from the mother lead to anxiety, insecurity, a lack of self-worth and an inability to relate to others. This problematic interaction is considered to lessen the child's chances of making satisfying peer relationships later on because a sense of self and trust of others, which are essential to this process, do not exist. The pattern may then be repeated with the child's own children, thus providing some explanation of how abuse is transmitted from one generation to the next (see Chapter 5). This process is not considered inevitable because the effects of poor early attachment experiences are thought to be remediable by attachment to a surrogate figure or by successful counselling.

Various studies of different kinds have been carried out to test attachment theory in relation to physical abuse and neglect (see Egeland and Vaughan 1981; Main and Goldwyn 1984; Frodi and Lamb 1980). All demonstrate connections between poor parent–child relationships and child abuse. Frodi and Lamb, for instance, found that adults known to have abused children were both more aroused by children's crying and less responsive to their smiles than adults with no known record of abuse. Other studies (Browne and Saqi 1988; Gray et al. 1977) have produced evidence to support this connection between parental non-responsiveness and later abuse and neglect.

What are the strengths and weaknesses of this theoretical approach? The strengths lie in its convincing and detailed explanation of the process whereby abuse and neglect potential can be derived from poor adult–child relationships and be transmitted through them (see Argles 1980). The weaknesses lie, first, in the theory's failure to account more fully for the fact that the majority of parents who have been abused themselves do not go on to abuse their own children and, second, in the fact that insufficient account is taken of the total dynamics of the family – the focus is almost exclusively on the mother–child dyad. One could also argue that the theory does not take into account social stress factors, such as poverty and unemployment. However, Crittenden and Ainsworth do not totally ignore these factors. They acknowledge the high incidence of abuse among poor families and the impact of environmental stress, but point out that

> Knowing the nature of family attachment relationships and the individuals' associated representational models should enable one to specify more precisely which families and/or individuals will be the most vulnerable to external stressors. (Crittenden and Ainsworth 1989: 458)

It should be noted that attachment theory has not been specifically used to explain sexual abuse of children, though, as was noted in Chapter 5, it has been argued that where men are involved early on in the care of children there is reason to believe that such abuse is less likely to occur (Parker and Parker 1986).

Psychodynamic theory and physical child abuse and neglect

There is considerable overlap between psychodynamic theorizing about parent–child relationships and that of attachment theory and it is not easy to disentangle these two approaches. The main difference is that attachment theorists consider that these relationships are governed by instinct, whereas psychodynamic theory emphasizes the importance of internal mental processes in the way in which these relationships unfold.

Freud's work forms the kernel of psychodynamic thought, but it has been subjected to considerable variation by his followers. There are several good overviews of Freudian theory.[3] The key arguments of this perspective are that human beings mentally adapt their instinctive drives to the demands and requirements of their social circumstances. In the process of so doing, they develop personality traits that persist throughout life and influence their relationships with others. Freud's belief was that the dominant human instinctual drive was libidinal or sexual. He also theorized that very young children had such sexual drives and he devised an elaborate explanation of how these were moulded into pro-social behaviours and internalized to shape an individual's character.

Summarized very briefly, Freud postulated that in the first five years of life infants went through three psycho-sexual stages: the oral, the anal and the genital. These stages of development were linked to sources of physical pleasure – the oral stage to feeding, the anal stage to elimination and the genital stage to sexual stimulation. For Freud, socialization meant the suppression of these pleasures in order to function as a responsible person in society. Parents carried out this repressive/socializing task. As a result, childhood sexuality went through a latency stage only to reassert itself in adolescence, by which time individuals were considered to be more able to manage their libido for themselves. As a result of this process, the psyche of each individual was made up of the id (libidinal drive), the superego (the conscience or voice of the parent, which repressed the id) and the ego (the integrating element that balanced the id and superego and formed the visible or social aspect of the personality). The personality was also made up of different levels of consciousness as a result of this socializing process – the conscious (that part of the mind used in everyday life), the preconscious (that part of the mind from which past material could be summoned with prompting) and the unconscious (that part of the mind to which libidinal drives and urges had been exiled; these were normally unavailable to consciousness).

How does this relate to child abuse? With regard to physical abuse, Freudian or psychodynamic theory has been the most dominant explanatory model since its rediscovery in 1962. Yet this has rarely been made fully explicit. Sweet and Resick (1979) comment: 'Although most of the literature on child maltreatment has been influenced by psychodynamic concepts there have been few comprehensive attempts to construct a psychodynamic theory of child abuse.' Steele and Pollock's (1974) account of child abuse causation is still probably the best example of a psychodynamic explanation (see also Green et al. 1974). They considered that physical abuse was associated with a breakdown in motherliness. In terms of Freudian psychodynamics, they hypothesized that from the very early stages the children of abusing parents are not responded to in a way that helps them to progress through all the necessary psycho-sexual stages. They are frustrated by lack of adequate response almost from the first contact and, therefore, are unlikely to develop the sort of integrated personality that enables them to relate responsively to others:

> Stimulation of the aggressive drive with its accompanying anger toward the frustrating caretaker, coupled with the parallel development of strict superego rudiments, inevitably leads to a strong sense of guilt. This guilt, largely unconscious, predominantly in relation to the mother, persists throughout the patient's life and leads to turning much of the aggression inward towards the self. When the parent misidentifies the infant as the embodiment of his own bad self, the full aggression of his punitive superego can be directed outward toward the child. (Steele and Pollock 1974: 122)

Thus, put simply, child abuse is seen to be the result of excessive superego demands.

The role of the non-abusing parent was not ignored by Steele and Pollock, nor was the contribution that a child might make.[4] However, as in the case of attachment theory, the main focus is on the mother–child dyad. From the psychodynamic perspective, all other factors are secondary. The mother's psychological make-up (and occasionally the father's as well) is the key to the issue.

Psychological treatment, focusing on improving the parent's ability to relate to other people, is seen to be the solution to the problem. Such treatment is to be achieved by insight development (through a psychotherapist) and by the effects of a rewarding relationship with a social worker over a period of time. This model of response remained a major influence on both

American and British child protection work until relatively recent times (see Halston and Richards 1982; Letourneau 1981).

The strengths of this approach, as with attachment theory, are that it can help professionals to understand the intra- and inter-personal dynamics of child abuse and point to intervention aims and strategies. It is still hard for many in the child protection field to comprehend and tolerate violence to children – the psychodynamic approach provides a tool for this purpose. The weaknesses lie in the very heavy focus placed on women as the key carers without sufficient consideration of the circumstances in which they are operating and in the lack of attention to social and environmental factors.[5]

Psychodynamic theory and child sexual abuse

With regard to the sexual abuse of children, psychodynamic thought has rather a mixed history. According to Masson (1984), Freud, before his development of the psycho-sexual personality theories outlined above, hypothesized that hysteria in women may have been caused by their being sexually abused as children. This hypothesis was based on disclosures to him by women whom he was treating. He relayed his ideas to fellow doctors in Vienna, but they rejected his hypothesis mainly because, since hysteria was such a commonly diagnosed illness, the implication was that incestuous abuse was of epidemic proportions. Freud's response was to go away and look at his material again. Soon after, he lay the foundations of the theory of psycho-sexual development. Reference has already been made to the oral, anal and genital stages. With regard to the last, Freud hypothesized that, as part of their normal development, boys and girls at this stage 'desired' their parents of the opposite sex. This desire was repressed and the repression led to modelling along the lines of the same sex parent. When this process was disturbed, this led to developmental problems and the possibility of neurosis. Thus Freud argued that when he dealt with adults with such neuroses and tried to help them unlock these childhood repressions, it was not surprising that a lot of sexual material should arise. However, contrary to his original view, he saw these accounts as fantasies or wish-fulfilments rather than as recollections of fact.

Such theorizing was highly influential in psychoanalytic circles and was one factor in predisposing psychotherapists and psychiatrists for many years to disbelieve accounts of sexual abuse. In the past decade or so, as a result of increased general awareness of the problem, there is now a strong 'believing' school among psychoanalysts, the most famous example being Alice Miller (1985).

Psychoanalysts as a whole, however, have still not theorized about why child sexual abuse happens. Most would consider such abuse to have a very damaging effect on personality development, particularly if it took place in the first five years of a child's life, because of its distorting effect on the process of psycho-sexual development, but little has been written from this point of view about the causation of sexual abuse. Finkelhor et al. (1986), reviewing research on child sexual abusers, find two main views among psychoanalytic writing on this subject: first, that they have arrested psychosexual development and choose to relate at a child's emotional level; second, that they have general low self-esteem and, therefore, that they gain a sense of dominance and control by victimizing children. Neither explanation properly explains, however, why such people resort to sexual abuse in response to these emotional difficulties.

Learning theory and child abuse

Learning theory, while embracing many different approaches, is based on the deceptively simple view that behaviour is shaped, or learned, by the interaction of an individual with the environment. The internal processes described by psychoanalysts are completely rejected. Classical learning theorists (Pavlov 1927; Skinner 1953) see behaviour as a response conditioned by external stimuli or reinforcers and dismiss the notion of any internal functioning at all. From this point of view, what is not observable does not exist. However, since this early theorizing, learning theorists such as Bandura (1965) and Michenbaum (1977) have incorporated social modelling and the notion of internal cognitive reasoning processes into their analyses of how behaviour operates, and these more complex theories are generally accepted by most learning theorists now.

From this general perspective, child abuse is a problem resulting neither from personality traits nor from lack of attachment. Rather it is largely the result of having learned dysfunctional child-care practices or, alternatively, of not having learned functional child-care practices. The issue of punishment looms large here. Adults who have themselves experienced punitive treatment may well rely on such methods to discipline their own children. Most learning theorists see punishment as effective in the short term, but less so in the long term. It also has unwanted side-effects for both the punisher and the punished. Positive reinforcement of pro-social behaviours and negative reinforcement (e.g. ignoring) of anti-social behaviours are seen as more effective and enduring influences on behaviour.

Dubanoski et al. (1978) describe a set of behavioural explanations of why children are physically abused. First, parents may lack effective child management techniques; second, they may deliberately use punitive child-rearing practices; third, the abuse may result from explosive acts triggered by the child; fourth, there may be a high level of stress; fifth, parents may have seriously negative attitudes towards the child. Each of these problems might lead to the need for a variety of responses, including teaching new techniques, teaching self-control, and focusing on attitude change.

Learning theorists have been applying their ideas to child abuse cases in the USA and Britain since the mid-1970s (see Isaacs 1982). In Britain, Reavley and Gilbert (1979), McAuley and McAuley (1977) and Smith and Rachman (1984) have all reported on interventions using learning theory approaches to modify parenting behaviours in families where physical abuse has occurred.

The general finding has been that simply teaching new child management techniques is in many cases inadequate. There is need for attitudinal change on the part of parents as well, particularly where problems have been well established over a long period of time and motivation for change is low. Generally the results of behavioural interventions into child abuse have not been impressive.[6]

In the USA, there are more positive reports of behavioural interventions (see Crozier and Katz 1979; Denicola and Sandler 1980; Wolfe *et al*. 1981). The numbers in the samples are, however, small. Smith (1984) attributes the relative success of these interventions to the fact that therapeutic change is more embedded in the American culture and that intervention programmes there are frequently enforced with the full backing of the courts.

The strengths of the learning theory perspective lie to some extent in its clarity and specificity. The learning theorist intervening in a case of child abuse would, for instance, focus on the actuality of the abuse, the situational factors, the antecedents and the consequences of the event, the attributions placed on the child by the parents, and their attitudes towards punishment and control. The personality of the parents and their developmental history would not be a major concern. There is also more potential for change than with the psychodynamic perspective, in that early experiences are not considered to be as deterministic.

Learning theory suffers from the same weaknesses as those of other psychological theories so far reviewed, namely that it often focuses on the individual abuser to the exclusion of the impact of wider networks. It may be that the strength of learning theory with regard to child abuse is also its weakness – it runs the risk of over-simplifying the problem in its search for clarity. In addition, it has so far paid little direct attention to the issue of child sexual abuse.

Cognitive approaches to child abuse

Cognitive approaches merge to a large extent with modern learning theory approaches. However, there is a growing interest, particularly in the USA (Newberger and White 1989), in the application of cognitive theory principles to the understanding of child abuse. The essential feature of this approach is that the way people perceive, order, construct and think about the world is an important key to their behaviour. In the previous section, it was noted that parental attitudes were perceived to be important, as well as their actual behaviour. Cognitive theorists point to the value of finding out how parents who have abused children perceive that child's behaviour. Larrance and Twentyman (1983) argue that attribution theory could help to explain why parents who have not been abused as children do abuse as adults. Their argument is that they may have developed a 'frame' or view on a child and/or on themselves that leads on to child abuse.

Newberger and White put forward a useful model of levels of parental awareness. At the first level, the child is seen by the parents purely as an extension of themselves. At the second level, the parents ascribe conventional roles to the child. At the third level, the child is seen by the parents as an individual with its own changing needs. They argue that abuse is more likely to take place when parents are at the first level. Although most parents progress to the highest level with time and experience and without outside help or intervention, this is not true in all cases. According to this view, intervention must be focused on helping parents to perceive their children differently, and such activity can help to prevent recurrence of abuse.

There is not much information about the use of cognitive approaches in child protection practice. In Britain, Scott (1989) has developed such work with general child care problems with some success, but, as with the behavioural approach, such success has been achieved with the less complex and less well-established problems.

Social psychological theories

In this section attention will be paid to theories that consider behaviour (a) to be a product of interaction between individuals, (b) to be determined by family dynamics and (c) to be influenced by social networks and supports. These approaches may be termed middle-range in that they fall between focus on the individual and focus on broader social factors. Essentially the relationships between individuals and their immediate environments are seen as key determinants from these perspectives. The three areas of interaction have been separated from each other for analytic purposes, but many theorists of these persuasions see close linkages between them.

Individual interactionist perspectives and child abuse

The key defining factor of the individual interactionist approach is that behaviour is seen to be determined less by intra-personal factors such as prior experiences, or by learning, and more by interactions between people. From this perspective, greater attention is placed on the dynamics of current relationships than on parental background or characteristics. Thus, inter-actionists take the child's contribution to situations of abuse much more into account, and also that of the spouse or partner (Kadushin and Martin 1981).

A climate of abuse can result from parents lacking skills to cope with difficult behaviour and from certain children continually exposing that inadequacy. From this perspective, the combination of factors is as important as the weight of them, if not more so. Thus, a difficult crying baby with two parents with low tolerance of stress and high aggression levels is particularly at risk, whereas a more easily comforted and responsive child with parents who have the same characteristics may not be. The child can, from this perspective, reward the parents and enhance their skills or further deskill them and lower their self-esteem. Similarly the parents' responses will affect the responses of the child in a circular process. Wolfe (1985) argues in similar vein to Larrance and Twentyman (1983) that parents do not have to have been abused themselves as children for them to abuse their own children. His explanation is different, however, in that he sees violence as a product of interactional events rather than of internal attribution processes. He argues that it is possible for a frame of violence to develop within families. Similarly, Dibble and Straus (1980) point out that violence to children can and does take place in families where parental attitudes are disapproving of such violence. This, they argue, is because such violence is often situational, not a product of attitudes. Their study involved only families with two parents and they found that violent behaviour on the part of one parent was likely to influence the other parent to be violent even if he or she was personally opposed to using violence against children. These studies lend support to the view that violence breeds violence.

This perspective on violence in the family offers another dimension with regard to the dynamics of why and how physical abuse of children occurs and persists. However, as is true of all the perspectives so far considered, a major weakness is that individuals are seen in isolation from wider social influences and stresses.

Family dysfunction theory and child abuse

Family dysfunction theory broadens the focus a little more in that its concern is with the impact of family dynamics on the behaviour of its members. This theory and family therapy, the treatment method derived from it, are of relatively recent origin. They originated within the field of psychiatry and the aetiology of mental illness.

Family therapy is a theoretically eclectic discipline. Initially it drew mainly from psychodynamic theory and concentrated on the impact of family life on the psychological development of the individual. However, most current practitioners adopt a systems perspective based on the work of Minuchin (1974), which theorizes that there are two main sub-systems within the family, that of the parents and that of children, and emphasizes the need for boundaries (with some degree of permeability) to be maintained between the two in order to ensure a healthy climate for all family members. Therapy is focused on examining the nature of current boundaries and on improving communication between family members. Another family therapy approach is termed 'strategic'. Family therapists of this school see the family as a powerful system that resists attempts to change it from the outside (Dale et al. 1983). Carefully worked out tactics and strategies are needed to break down this resistance to create the best conditions for change.

With regard to physical child abuse, dysfunctional family theory has not had widespread influence as an explanatory theory. However, family therapy techniques as a mode of intervention have more recently attracted attention. Asen et al. (1989) focus on how family dynamics contribute to abuse. They refer to the notion of stand-in abuse where the child is subjected to violence by its parent as a means of 'getting at' the other parent. The notion of a child as 'scapegoat', the bad one in the family and the reason for all the family's ills, is another example of a family dysfunction explanation of child mistreatment. There is a general lack of focus on causes of behaviour among family therapists. Their concern is with the here-and-now dynamics of family life and how to break or change patterns of behaviour. From this point of view, the notion of 'cause' in the linear cause-and-effect sense is seen to be less relevant than the process.

In contrast to its limited impact on the physical abuse field in Britain, family therapy thinking has, until recently, played a major role in the explanation of the cause of child sexual abuse. This is largely owing to the pioneering work of Ben-Tovim and his associates at the Great Ormond Street Hospital referred to in Chapter 3 (Ben-Tovim *et al.* 1988). Their approach, which incorporates both psychodynamic and systems theories, is broadly based on the hypothesis that child sexual abuse serves the function of keeping together families that would otherwise collapse. The classic scenario is that of the abuse of a teenage daughter by her father, who is considered to be seeking emotional and sexual gratification because communication and sexual relations with his wife have broken down. It is believed in many cases that the wife/mother knows (whether consciously or subconsciously is not made clear) what is happening and passively colludes in the continuance of this situation. This collusion is thought to serve the function of freeing her from responsibility without sacrificing the unity of the family. The solution to the problem is seen to be one of opening up the secret to all family members, disentangling the knotted relationships and freeing individuals to decide on their futures. The means for achieving this is by family meetings and the use of family therapy techniques.

The strengths of the family dysfunction approach are that it heightens awareness of the powerful nexus of relationships that the family can be sheltering and demonstrates how it can sustain unacceptable forms of abuse. However, it suffers from the problem of many systems-based theories in that although it describes well how dysfunctional families operate, it is much more limited in explaining the reason why they function in the way that they do. The Great Ormond Street team explain sexual abuse by reference to the emotional need of the perpetrator and the structural dependence on adults of the child victim. Feminist critiques of family dysfunction theory have stressed the lack of attention paid to gender power relations (see below). Family therapy thinking has also been criticized for focusing too much on the family as a closed system cut off from wider systems and social influences. There is evidence of the development of more flexible family dysfunction approaches that take into account both these issues (Treacher and Carpenter 1984; Masson and O'Byrne 1990; Barratt *et al.* 1990; Jenkins and Asen 1992). A final criticism is that the explanatory value of the family dysfunction approach is limited to the types of abuse situation outlined above. It does not help to explain the wide range of forms of sexual abuse that can take place in families, e.g. abuse of infants and abuse by siblings.

Social ecological approaches

General systems theory has been adapted by social work theorists in both the USA and Britain to broaden traditional emphasis on personal problems and to move away from concentration on personal pathology (Pincus and Minahan 1973). This development has been evident over the past 15 years or so in Britain and for a slightly longer time in the United States. Such thinking has not been directly and specifically applied to child abuse in Britain except in a general way with regard to social isolation. In the USA, however, direct attention has been paid to the way in which the interrelationship between human beings and their social environment can have an impact on the incidence of child maltreatment. The influence of systems theory there seems to have grown in the 1980s with the development of general concerns about the environment.

Germain and Gitterman (1980) provide a good example of the thinking behind this model:

> The ecological perspective provides an adaptive, evolutionary view of human beings in constant interchange with all elements of their environment. Human beings change their physical and social environments and are changed by them through a process of continuous reciprocal adaptation. . . . Like all living systems, human beings must maintain a goodness-of-fit with the environment. The Darwinian concept of 'fit' applies both to organisms and their environments: to the fitness of the environment and the fitness of the organism, each with the other and through which both prosper. (Germain and Gitterman 1980: 5–6)

From this perspective, human behaviour is more influenced, or determined, by the context in which a person lives rather than purely by intra- or inter-personal factors. In the particular case of child abuse, it is hypothesized that where environmental conditions are unfavourable to families, the incidence of abuse is likely to be higher. In the USA, Garbarino has been particularly active in exploring these connections. He found in both rural and urban areas that officially reported abuse was higher in those neighbourhoods where indicators of social stress, population mobility and poverty were highest (Garbarino and Crouter 1978). A major factor was seen to be isolation from possible support systems (Garbarino and Sherman 1980), be they the extended family or community-based systems such as neighbourhood centres and day-care facilities: 'A strong pro-social neighbourhood climate can have a beneficial impact – by increasing participation – on persons whose individual predilection is to be isolated' (Garbarino and Sherman 1980: 606).

Garbarino links this theoretical approach to others in that he does not preclude individual history as an additional causative factor and he acknowledges that culture plays a part, in that, if there were not cultural justification for the use of force against children (see below), then it would not happen, however deprived the conditions in which families were living (Garbarino 1977). Nevertheless, given these factors, stress, created from living in environments that are not conducive to psychological health and development, is seen to be a major contributory factor to child mistreatment and points to solutions other than focus on the individual, most notably community-based initiatives to break down isolation and to create a sense of belonging and shared problems. In Britain, examples of this type of approach are to be found in Holman (1988).

There are difficulties with 'proving' the validity of this theory, not least because of the fact that poorer communities are more likely to come under the close surveillance of public authorities and, therefore, produce higher official rates of abuse. There is also a need for closer attention to be paid to which particular deficits in what circumstances contribute to child maltreatment and the process by which this happens (see Seagull 1987). Cohen and Adler (1986), looking more broadly at social network interventions, are opposed to the use of community-based initiatives as the solution to all social problems. They are concerned that they could be used as cheap-option cure-alls, mirroring the current debate in Britain about community care packages for the mentally ill and elderly.

The main strength of the social ecological approach lies in the way in which it broadens the scope of thinking about why abuse of children occurs. It shifts the focus from individual pathology to the influence of the immediate environment and the need to tackle the problem at that level. At the same time many exponents of this approach pay little attention to political factors that contribute to the deterioration of neighbourhoods and the disorganiz-ation and break-up of social networks. Attention to these issues might well lead to quite different solutions to the problem.

Sociological perspectives and child abuse

Sociological perspectives on child abuse have not had a major influence on child protection thinking and work in Britain, except in the case of sexual abuse and gender issues. The reason for this is two-fold. First, such perspectives do not provide clear indicators for practice in that they look broadly at the conditions that create the climate for child abuse rather than at how this works out in individual cases (Corby 1991). Second, many sociological perspectives provide a challenge to those who are intervening into families to protect children, in that they question the ethics and politics of mainstream assumptions (Howe 1991). Thus, they have an unsettling quality in that they locate the 'cause' of the problem outside the sphere of influence of the professional worker and they consequently pose uncomfortable questions about the validity of that professional intervention.

The main sociological perspectives to be considered in this section are those that have been articulated by researchers and others involved in the child abuse field, namely the social cultural perspective, which draws linkages between child abuse and general social approval of the use of violence to maintain control and order, the social structural perspective, which relates child abuse to the maintenance of general inequality in northern industrialized societies, and perspectives that link child abuse to gender and generational inequality.

The social cultural perspective

The work of Straus and Gelles in the USA has already been referred to several times in relation to their national surveys into the incidence of physical child abuse (see Chapter 4). In these studies, they and their colleagues reported high levels of intra-familial violence of all kinds. They came to the conclusion that such violence was the norm and that individuals were more likely to be subjected to violent acts within families than outside them. In an attempt to explain these high rates, they argued that violence is a socially sanctioned general form of maintaining order and that it is approved of as a form of child control by most people in American society. It can be argued from this perspective that a society that approves of the corporal punishment of children in schools and endorses the old adage 'spare the rod and spoil the child' sets the scene for a variety of unwanted forms of violence, of which physical child abuse is one. Thus, child abuse is seen to be on the same spectrum as socially approved forms of violence rather than as a separate pathological phenomenon.

Goode (1971) examines the process whereby such culturally approved violence takes hold. The family is seen as a power system mirroring that of the wider society (see also Wolff 1981). Conformity and compliance with rules are seen as desirable and are ultimately enforced by the use of violence (or the threat of it). Both children and parents are socialized into believing that this type of rule enforcement is legitimate and ultimately beneficial. Goode goes on to explain why it is that use of violent force is more common among poorer families. Parents with more resources at their disposal are less likely to resort to overt use of force. Normally they will be able to maintain control by other means. Poorer parents with less resources have fewer alternatives to violence for asserting their wills.

Gelles and Cornell (1985) argue that an important contributory factor to child and other forms of intra-familial abuse is the likelihood that the perpetrator will get away with it, partly because it takes place within the confines of the family and is, therefore, difficult to prove in the world outside (i.e. in a court of law) and partly because of the state's traditional reluctance to interfere in family affairs. From this perspective, it is clear that there is a need for change at a broad societal level to the way in which we treat and control children. There is a need to encourage non-violent means of ensuring pro-social behaviour. There have been moves in this direction in Britain, with the banning of corporal punishment in state schools in the late 1980s. Scandinavian countries have outlawed the use of physical punishment by parents, with some degree of success in terms of rates of reported child abuse.[7] Freeman (1988), among others, has argued for the implementation of similar legislation in Britain.

The same sort of analysis can be applied to sexual abuse: that because sexual exploitation of women and, to a less extent, of children, is societally tolerated in, for instance, art, cinema, advertising and prostitution, a climate is set whereby sexual abuse results. Again, from this perspective, it is seen as part of a continuum rather than as an act of a totally different quality or dimension.

The strengths of the social cultural perspective are that it broadens the focus in comparison with psychological and social psychological theories and helps in the understanding of how societal influences can contribute to the incidence and form of child mistreatment despite the fact that society officially sets out to reduce and prevent such occurrences. The implications for social policy are that there is a need to tackle the issue on a broader front and that intervention into individual cases alone is not sufficient for dealing with the problem. The major weakness of this perspective lies in the fact that it does not help to explain why some people within our flawed culture abuse and others do not.

The social structural perspective in relation to child abuse

Gil's research and writing, already frequently referred to, form the corner-stone of this perspective. His early work (1970) convinced him that child abuse was class-related and that 'psychological' explanations of abuse by themselves were too narrow and grossly underestimated the contribution of stress, caused by poverty and material deprivation, to the causation of child abuse.

He developed his ideas further to lay some of the blame for child abuse on the policies of the state (Gil 1975, 1978). He put forward a broad definition of abuse (see Chapter 4), which included all children whose developmental needs could not be met, whatever the reason. This definition lays the blame for child abuse at the door of the state over and above the person who actually abuses, because it sanctions inequality and low standards of housing, health, education and leisure for the children of the poor. From this point of view, the state, far from being the benign rescuer of children when parents ill-treat them, is actually the villain of the piece because it abuses children directly by its failure to provide adequate facilities for them to lead a fulfilling life, and it also creates stresses for parents that increase the likelihood of their committing acts of abuse or neglect. Parton (1985) has lent support to this perspective in Britain:

> Child abuse is strongly related to class, inequality and poverty both in terms of prevalence and severity. . . . Locating the problem in terms of social structural factors has important implications for the way we define the problem, the way we explain it and the best way of doing something about it. For solving the problem requires a realignment in social policy

which recognises the necessity of attacking the social, economic and cultural conditions associated with the abuse. (Parton 1985: 175–6)

The strength of the social structural approach is that it does justice to the accepted fact that physical child abuse has a close association with deprivation. As has already been seen, this is particularly so with regard to neglect (see Wolock and Horowitz 1984). Its weakness lies in the fact that not all poor people abuse their children and, therefore, it is not a sufficient explanation. This perspective has so far not taken into account structural factors other than class and poverty. In particular it has been silent on the issue of gender and generational inequalities (Parton 1990). Finally, it does not address the issue of the aetiology of child sexual abuse, which is generally considered not to be linked to class and poverty.

The social structural approach has not had a great deal of support in child abuse circles. Pelton (1978) has pointed to the fact that structural inequality explanations pose a threat to those who espouse clinical and medical approaches to child abuse. Other writers have seen Gil's views as 'idealistic' (Greenland 1987) or beyond the scope of the helping professions and, therefore, not applicable to day-to-day practice.

The feminist perspective and child abuse

Most of the perspectives so far outlined are considered by feminist thinkers to be gender-blind. As has been pointed out, all of the psychological perspectives assume that women are the key carers of children and that, if things go wrong, then the focus must fall on their behaviour. The interactionist perspectives broaden the focus, but assume an equal power base between men and women. Neither of the two sociological perspectives discussed above pays much attention to the issue of gender.

A radical feminist perspective on the issue of child abuse has only recently begun to emerge. The stimulus for this has come from the 'discovery' of child sexual abuse, because it is an act committed predominantly by males and feminist explanations seem highly relevant to it. From this starting-point, the feminist perspective is now being usefully applied to all forms of abuse.

The feminist perspective on child sexual abuse has been articulated by several writers in the USA and Britain (Rush 1980; Herman 1981; Dominelli 1986; Nelson 1987; Macleod and Saraga 1988; Driver and Droisen 1989). There is little equivocation about the reason for the existence of child sexual abuse and the form that it takes:

Generally boys and men learn to experience their sexuality as an overwhelming and uncontrollable force; they learn to focus their sexual feelings on submissive objects, and they learn the assertion of their sexual desires, the expectation of having them serviced. (Macleod and Saraga 1988: 41)

Abuse in the form of violence against women is a normal feature of patriarchal relations. It is a major vehicle men use in controlling women.

As such it is the norm not an aberration. The rising incidence of child sexual abuse reveals the extent to which men are prepared to wield sexual violence as a major weapon in asserting their authority over women. (Dominelli 1986: 12)

The attention of these writers is not on individual males. Individual pathology is discounted as a cause of child abuse (as is family pathology). Rather, abuse is seen as an extreme example of institutionalized male power over females. The implications for policy of this perspective are similar in kind, if not focus, to those of the other sociological perspectives. Sexual abuse is an issue that needs tackling at a societal level as well as at the individual level. Men abuse children because of the general power imbalance between the sexes and the different forms of socialization that they experience as a result, not because of psychiatric illness or emotional deficits.

With regard to physical abuse and neglect, the issues for the feminist perspective are less clear-cut. As has already been seen, women are as implicated in the physical abuse and neglect of children as men. Thus the argument that such abuse is created by the conditions of patriarchy does not sit as easily in this case as in that of sexual abuse. However, as was argued in Chapter 5, women spend far more time with children than do men and cope with the stresses of child care, often with little support. Under such conditions, it is surprising that the numbers of women who abuse and neglect children do not vastly exceed those of men. From this point of view, men are disproportionately violent to children. The implication is that women's violence to children is much more likely to be stress-related than that of men.

From this perspective, the patriarchal nature of our society does, therefore, have a role to play in the causation of physical abuse and neglect of children. The argument is taken further by some feminists in that they see the notion of motherhood, a product of patriarchy, exacerbating the already existing stresses placed on women looking after children.

The strength of the feminist perspective on child abuse as a whole is that it opens up a dimension that until relatively recently has been missing from explanations about why child abuse occurs. Reference was made in Chapter 5 to the way in which (in the case of physical abuse and neglect) men seem to have been overlooked in terms of intervention. The feminist perspective points to the error in this in that understanding and challenging the nature of male–female power relations, at an institutional and individual level, is of major importance in the theory and practice of child protection work. The challenge should be both to the impositions placed on women within the family and to the way in which males are socialized (Hearn 1990). The weakness of the feminist perspective is that there is a danger that it can be used in a reductionist and exclusive way, attributing every ill to patriarchy and overriding all other explanatory accounts.

The children's rights perspective

Freeman (1983) has identified two main schools of thought on children's rights, the protectionist and the liberationist.

Protectionist thinking about children has been applied to child care issues through legislation since the late nineteenth century (see Chapter 3) and still underlies much of current policy and practice in the field of child abuse. Essentially the argument from this viewpoint is that children have the right to protection from their parents by outside bodies in circumstances where their health and welfare are at risk. In the absence of these conditions, parents have the responsibility of determining their children's rights up to prescribed ages.

The liberationist perspective is of more recent origin and derives mainly from the field of education. Holt (1974) provides a good example of the extreme end of this type of thinking. His argument is that childhood is an oppressed status and that the current state of affairs in which parents grant concessions to children who have little redress against their actions and decisions is unjust and reinforces their oppression. He proposes a series of rights that children should have, such as the right to choose where to live, the right to vote and the right to have the same financial status as adults. In short, his view is that children should have exactly the same rights as adults. Age is seen as irrelevant and self-determination as paramount. Scarre (1980) has pointed out some of the obvious weaknesses in this approach, most notably that children are both physically and emotionally dependent on their parents for several years. Paternalism is, from his viewpoint, a largely beneficial protective mechanism for children until they can reach maturity.

Recently, there has been a shift in official thinking about children's rights away from a traditional protectionist perspective towards viewing children in a more independent light. This is largely due to events in Cleveland. The traditional view that children are either the responsibility of the family or, where abuse occurs, that of the state has been thrown into question by what happened there. The Cleveland Report (Cleveland 1988) was highly critical of the way in which children were treated during investigations. It pointed out that 'There is a danger that in looking to the welfare of children believed to be the victims of sexual abuse the children themselves may be overlooked. The child is a person not an object of concern' (p. 245). The 1989 Children Act also takes children's rights of this kind more closely into consideration.[8] However, neither the Cleveland Report nor the Children Act could possibly be seen as liberationist in the way in which Holt proposes. In fact they reflect a half-way house position between the protectionist and liberationist viewpoints. Children's views are to be taken into account, but there is no suggestion that they should prevail.

In respect of physical abuse, the development of anti-corporal punishment legislation and policy reflects the influence of liberationist views. The thinking is clear – if children had the same rights in society as adults and, therefore, similar individual status (one that was not prescribed by family relations), they would be less likely to be the object of physical abuse and neglect. For instance, we do not consider it proper to smack adults for misbehaving. Were children to have individual rights without reference to their parents we would not consider such treatment to be acceptable in their case either.

The main strength of the children's rights perspective is that it compels us to consider matters from the child's point of view as an individual rather than purely as a family member and points to changes in the status of children at a societal level as a solution to the widespread problem of child abuse. Its weakness lies in the fact that most children cannot be seen in isolation from their parents because of their dependence on them. Children's rights protagonists tend to ignore this fact and also the fact that many parents do not have the means to achieve the high standards that the children's rights perspective properly demands.

Concluding comments

Virtually all researchers into the field of child abuse point to the dangers of adopting single-cause explanations of the phenomenon. While some explanations may seem to be particularly useful for the understanding of certain forms of abuse (e.g. attachment theory appears to have particular relevance in the case of physical abuse or emotional rejection of young babies), they are unlikely to be sufficient in themselves.

There has been (and still is) a polarization between different perspectives on why child abuse occurs, with single explanations dominating in different camps. The most obvious example is the clash between the feminist perspective and that of family therapists over the aetiology of child sexual abuse. In the field of physical abuse, the case of Jasmine Beckford highlights the clash between psychological and sociological perspectives. The social workers in this case focused on improving the social circumstances of the parents of Jasmine by helping them find more suitable accommodation, by providing Jasmine's mother with supportive help at home and by obtaining nursery school provision for Jasmine. The focus was on external factors – improving the quality of life, thereby reducing stress and enhancing parent–child relationships. The report criticized the social workers on a variety of grounds, including not taking into account the psychological background of the parents. With the value of hindsight, this criticism was justified and greater attention to inter- and intra-personal factors may have led to greater caution in decision-making.

It is clear that social workers and other professional workers in this field need to be open to a wide range of explanations of child abuse in order to intervene effectively into families where children are thought to be at risk, even though this approach may be more complex than that of following a single theory. Attempts to integrate the different approaches to child abuse are being made. Belsky (1980), using an ecological framework, has pointed to a four-level approach: ontogenic development, the microsystem, the exosystem and the macrosystem. The first is concerned with what the individual parents bring to the situation, their developmental background and experiences; the microsystem is concerned with the interaction of individuals within the family; the exosystem is concerned with the immediate social environment within which the family functions; the macrosystem takes into account broader structural factors, such as cultural attitudes to violence. The way in which these different systems interact is the key to the likelihood of abuse occurring or not[9] (see also Ostbloom and Crase 1980; Wiehe 1989). All these integrative models have been devised with physical abuse in mind. Finkelhor *et al.* (1986) provide a similar type of model for child sexual abuse.

The way forward is clearly in the direction of further attempts at integrating ongoing research into the aetiology of child abuse. While practitioners may be more concerned with what is directly relevant to practice, it should be borne in mind that a broad range of integrated knowledge provides a strong base from which to operate. As Gordon (1989: 298) persuasively argues, on the basis of her historical research into child protection agency records,

> The most helpful social workers were those who understood family-violence problems to be simultaneously social/structural and personal in origin, and who therefore offered help in both dimensions. Good caseworkers might help a family get relief, or medical care, or a better apartment, and build a woman's or a child's self-esteem by legitimating their claims and aspirations.

7

The consequences of child abuse

Although it could be argued that paying close attention to the consequences or effects on a child of being abused is less important than focusing on ways of preventing such abuse happening in the first place, there are many good reasons for such careful scrutiny.

First, while there is no doubt that all abuse of children is likely to have harmful consequences, some forms of abuse may be more harmful than others and have different implications for intervention. There is the constant concern that some forms of intervention may add to the harm already created by the abuse that the child has suffered rather than alleviate it. Knowing about the consequences of different forms and levels of abuse can contribute to decisions about the best way to respond to it.

Second, there is a preventive aspect to focusing on the consequences of abuse. The issue of intergenerational transmission of abuse was discussed in Chapter 5. Greater focus on the effects of abuse can lead to better treatment measures, which will reduce the likelihood of abuse being repeated in the next generation.

Third, there is the issue of abuse survival. This again was discussed to some extent in Chapter 5. There are children who, despite experiencing forms and degrees of abuse that would lead us to expect that they would be severely damaged as a result, appear to cope well and without apparent psychological ill-effects. Studying how these children successfully survive also has implications for intervention and treatment.

Research into the effects of child abuse suffers from similar problems and limitations to research considered in previous chapters. First, there are the same methodological issues with regard to sampling and the use of controls. Some studies use small clinical samples while others select their samples from a broader range of cases. Some studies do not use controls and those that do go to different lengths to match them with their samples. Second, there are the same problems about agreed definitions of what constitutes abuse. Lack of definitional clarity makes comparability between different studies difficult – it is not always possible to be sure that you are comparing like with like. Some studies are careful to differentiate between types of abuse and degrees of severity, while others are not.

In addition there are some problems that are particular to research into the consequences of abuse. These are, first, the difficulty of deciding on the length of time to be allowed for follow-up of cases and, second, the difficulty of establishing causal connections between abuse events and later behaviour. These problems are closely linked. Research that is carried out soon after the abuse has occurred will obviously miss out on evaluating longer-term effects. On the other hand, the greater the gap between the abuse event and the later behaviour the less chance there is of causally linking the two because of the existence of more intervening variables. The following example demonstrates some of these issues.

Prostitution has been seen to be a consequence of sexual abuse. Silbert and Pines (1981) interviewed 200 juvenile and adult prostitutes in San Francisco. They found that 60 per cent had been sexually abused as children. On the face of it, this seems reasonable proof that there is a direct connection between being sexually abused as a child and becoming a prostitute. However, as far as we know, the vast majority of sexually abused women do not become prostitutes and, therefore, this uncritical reading of these findings is not acceptable. More information is needed to find out in more detail why and in what circumstances the abused women in this study turned to prostitution. Silbert and Pines do provide more details about the type of sexual abuse experienced by their sample: 60 per cent were abused by an average of two people over a period of 20 months; two-thirds of these were abused by father figures and 82 per cent said that their abuse had been accompanied by some degree of force. Thus, these variables – length of time of abuse, the close relationship between abuser and abused and the use of violence or threats of violence – could be linked with the outcome of prostitution. However, despite this attempt to be more specific, the account is still deficient. There are many social, cultural, economic and interpersonal factors that may also have been important determinants of the later behaviour of these women, in addition to the fact that they were victims of serious sexual assault early in their lives. The latter may have a predisposing effect, but to reach the conclusion that prostitution is a direct consequence of sexual abuse is simplistic and misleading.

Most studies of the consequences of child abuse differentiate between short-term and long-term effects. In what follows, focus will be placed on the short- and long-term consequences of, first, physical abuse and neglect, with some reference to the impact of emotional abuse, and then on those relating to sexual abuse.

The consequences of physical abuse and neglect

Short- and medium-term effects on emotional development

Calam and Franchi (1987) provide a good overview of psychological characteristics displayed in the short term by children who are physically abused or neglected. Many of these characteristics can be seen as survival tactics adopted by the powerless in the face of harsh or neglectful treatment. Such abused children develop a form of pseudo-maturity that manifests itself in behaviour aimed at keeping their parents happy. Generally they have a lack of appetite for, or confidence in, play. Such children become self-critical and lacking in self-esteem. 'Frozen watchfulness' is another response, usually to more extreme forms of deprivation, i.e. the child seems to be wary of human contact and to lack emotional reaction. Hyperactivity and inability to settle for any substantial length of time have also been seen as typical of the behaviour of abused children. These initial responses may or may not persist. Calam and Franchi studied a small number of abused/neglected children attending an NSPCC day centre with their mothers and came to the conclusion that 'severity of injury was not the major determinant of the degree of disturbances that they showed; the family environment that they were continuing to experience was likely to play a more significant part' (Calam and Franchi 1987: 191). From this viewpoint, this early negative psychological development is caused not so much by the actual physical abuse as by the way in which parents relate emotionally to their children, and it is maintained by the way in which they continue to interact with them regardless of whether they use physical violence again or not.

Steele (1986), along similar lines, stresses that the main feature of being an abused child is inconsistent care, which in general terms leads to a sense of insecurity. This evidences itself in low self-esteem, problems in developing a sense of self-identity, a diminution in the ability to cope with life and its stresses, a lack of ability to take pleasure in things and to make lasting attachments, depression, delinquency and masochism. For Steele, as for Calam and Franchi, physical abuse *per se* is not the issue. It is the emotional quality of parenting that is the key:

> Physical abuse does not necessarily cause trouble. Most people have had physical injuries, fractures or burns during childhood due to purely accidental causes and they have not been harmed by it because they have been comforted and cared for by good caregivers at the time of the incident. Damage comes when the injuries are inflicted by those to whom one looks for love and protection and there is no relief from the trauma (Steele 1986: 283–4)

For Steele, the emotionally incapacitating effects of this type of early mistreatment can only be alleviated by positive interpersonal experiences.

Many researchers have found a correlation between physical abuse and negative emotional consequences without being specific about the dynamics of the process. Kinard (1980) reviewed nine studies carried out between 1971 and 1978 and found that, although the samples were small in size and there were methodological differences, 'these investigations are remarkably consistent in the findings that abused children show substantial deficits in emotional development' (p. 452). He comments further: 'The results corroborate reports of case histories depicting the abused child as having a negative self-concept' (p. 452). Toro (1982), Lamphear (1985) and Augoustinos (1987) have carried out similar reviews of studies and Kinard's conclusions are largely confirmed.

Erickson et al. (1989) carried out a series of studies to discover the effects of different types of abuse on children. They studied four 'abused' groups of children over the first six years of their lives. These groups consisted of children: (a) who were physically abused; (b) whose parents were hostile and verbally abusive; (c) who were neglected; and (d) whose parents were psychologically unavailable (i.e. they were emotionally abusive). Overall there were 84 'abused' children and they were compared with a control group of 85 'non-abused' children from similar socio-economic backgrounds. Children from all the 'abused' groups were generally rated as having less confidence and lower self-esteem than those in the control group. Differences between the groups, while not as clear-cut as in the comparison between abused and non-abused, were nevertheless apparent. At age four the neglected and emotionally abused children were the cause of most concern. With regard to the latter, the researchers write:

The sharp decline in the intellectual functioning of these children, in their attachment disturbances and subsequent lack of social/emotional competence in a variety of situations is cause for great concern. The consequences of this form of maltreatment are particularly disturbing when considered in light of the fact that it is probably the least likely pattern of maltreatment to be detected. (Erickson et al. 1989: 667)

However, at age six these children, whose parents were described as psychologically unavailable, fared as well as the other groups of abused children. The group giving most cause for concern at this stage was the neglected children, who were very low achievers in school. Other studies have also pointed to the fact that neglected children seem to be lower in self-esteem than children who have been physically abused (Oates et al. 1985).

In Britain, the main study in this field is that of Lynch and Roberts (1982). They followed up 39 physically abused children four years after investigation and treatment. They compared the progress of these children with a similar number of their non-abused siblings. Their findings were in line with the American studies referred to so far, namely that generally the abused group were developmentally, emotionally, educationally and socially below the norms for children of their age. This was regardless of whether they had been removed from home or whether they remained with their parents receiving

supportive help from outside agencies. With regard to psychological development only, these abused children were commonly described as
showing signs of anxiety, extreme shyness and fear of failure.

One study has reached different conclusions to the rest, that of Elmer
(1977). She compared 17 abused children with 17 children matched in most
aspects except for the fact that they had been referred to hospital because they
had experienced accidents rather than abuse. These children were followed
up at one year and eight years after the incident (in the second follow-up they
were also compared with 24 children who had been neither abused nor
hospitalized as a result of accidents but were otherwise matched). Elmer
found no differences between the children in any of the groups with regard to
emotional development. She also found no significant difference between the
eight abused children who had been removed from home following the abuse
incident and the nine who had remained at home.

This study has raised some controversy in that the implication of its
findings is that the effects of abuse of children by their parents are no worse
than the effects of living in stressful and impoverished circumstances without
being so abused. It has been criticized because of its small sample size and
ironically because the control group used was too closely matched to the
'abused' group:

> if an attempt was made to match for all the factors, apart from confirmed,
> inflicted injuries, as Elmer did in her study (1977), one might simply
> obtain a control group of children who were abused but not actually
> identified as such. (Lynch and Roberts 1982: 5)

Generally, however, it is clear that physical ill-treatment, neglect and
impoverished parenting all have negative consequences on psychological
development over the short- and medium-term period. As will be seen in the
next section, which considers social and intellectual functioning, these
consequences lay the foundation for other forms of negative responses on the
part of mistreated and deprived children, which in turn can create further
negative responses from those with whom they interact, and so on. The
implications for practice are, among other things, the need to pay close
attention to the emotional needs of the child as well as to his or her physical
safety. Oates *et al*. (1985: 162–3) argue the point convincingly:

> Although considerable emphasis is placed on supporting abusive
> parents to prevent further episodes from occurring, it is essential that the
> future emotional development of the abused child should be em-
> phasized. As the majority of abused children remain in their natural
> families, they also require treatment while support is being given to their
> parents. This should first include a careful assessment of the child's
> developmental and emotional status followed by a long-term program
> for the child which aims at improving the child's skills in interpersonal
> relationships and in building up self-esteem.

Effects on social and intellectual functioning

The consequences considered in this section need to be seen as following on from the emotional problems outlined above. The consequences of abuse seem to have cumulative effects unless they are responded to early on.

Relationships with peers

Mueller and Silverman (1989: 538) argue that the way in which children manage peer relationships and the experiences that they derive from them have important implications for relating to others in later life and for future mental health: 'Contemporaries increasingly seek one another as the primary sources of support, security and intimacy.' Children who have been mistreated seem to fare badly in peer relationships according to research findings (see George and Main 1979; Reidy 1977; Hoffman-Plotkin and Twentyman 1984; Jacobson and Straker 1982; Howes and Espinosa 1985). All these studies find that physically abused and neglected children are both more aggressive and more withdrawn than their peers in play and general interaction with them. Lewis and Schaeffer (1981) concur with these findings, but hypothesize from their study that the reason for poor social functioning on the part of abused children may not be the result of the psychologically incapacitating effects of being poorly cared for or ill-treated. An alternative explanation could be that their parents are themselves socially isolated and do not provide, or value, peer contacts for their children.

There could be other factors than these that mark out ill-treated children for poor peer relationships. They could be disruptive in school (see below), poorly dressed by the standards of the rest of the neighbourhood and avoided by their peers for these reasons. The effects of these experiences could be for them to react in an aggressive way or to withdraw. Most of the research in these areas has been carried out by developmental psychologists and their focus points them more in the direction of explanations based on the effects of parent–child relationships than towards social factors. Bearing this in mind, however, there can be little doubt that abused and deprived children do not generally enjoy good peer relationships and this, therefore, can add to the difficulties they may already be experiencing in their intra-familial relationships.

School performance

Most studies of the early school performance of mistreated children point to under-achievement. Lynch and Roberts (1982) found that most of their sample performed below their IQ potential at school, the most notable deficiency being in use of language. Other studies confirm this finding (Oates *et al.* 1984; Egeland *et al.* 1983). Martin (1972) hypothesized that language delay is characteristic of the abused child because of lack of trust in his or her environment, which in turn results in being afraid of risk-taking and acquiring little practice in speech and expressive language (see also Allen and Oliver 1982). However, as in the case of peer relationships, broader social factors may come into play. Ill-treated children may be less attractive to teachers and more demanding in terms of time. If they are aggressive or avoidant in class, they may be seen as troublesome or pass unnoticed. Knowledge of family backgrounds may lead to low expectations in terms of intellectual performance. Although most ill-treated children underperform at school, there is some suggestion that abused children of high intelligence do reasonably well. It is argued that generally such children avoid the worst effects of abuse because they are able to understand and meet parental expectations more easily than children of lower intelligence (Frodi and Smetana 1984).

Two important messages come across from research into the short- and medium-term effects of physical abuse and neglect so far reviewed. The first is that early depriving experiences can set up a cycle of events that can reinforce the ill-effects of those early events. The second, linked to the first, is that incidents of abuse, while traumatic and occasionally causing lasting physical damage and death (see below), are not *per se* the major determinants of negative consequences. The ongoing climate within the family seems to be of prime importance in determining whether or not such consequences persist.

Resilient children

It seems that not all children are similarly affected by similar experiences. Some children are more resilient to traumatic events and cope better than others. Mrazek and Mrazek (1987) list 12 factors that can account for resilient survival behaviours.[1] Most of these are associated with the child's personality and intelligence (see above), but some are linked to situational circumstances, such as the formation of positive relationships with people outside the family and access to good educational and health facilities. Lynch (1988) points out that although most of the children in her 1982 study with Roberts fared badly as a result of their ill-treatment, 23 per cent showed no obvious adverse effects. She drew up a profile of these survivors:

> We saw a trend for the children who were problem-free to have been identified as abused when they were young but to have escaped long-term neurological deficit. They were unlikely to have experienced perinatal problems or to have accumulated both developmental and behavioural normalities before intervention. Following intervention, although they may have been the subject of legal proceedings, these were unlikely to have been protracted or recurrent and placement changes were few. One possible protective factor identified among the abused children was the possession of above-average intelligence.
> (Lynch 1988: 210)

In essence, Lynch is saying that abuse identified early and responded to in a definite fashion is likely to result in the best outcomes, particularly if the children concerned are intelligent. Augoustinos (1987: 25) argues that these factors are important provided the abuse is not too severe and prolonged:

It is possible that the more severe and frequent the neglect and abuse, the less significant other factors become in affecting developmental outcome. In less severe cases, however, these factors may be better predictors of outcome than the maltreatment itself.

Clearly there is an implication that the responses of professionals can influence the consequences of abuse in some circumstances for better or for worse. These issues will be considered more fully in Chapter 8.

Severe mental and physical delay as a result of child abuse
These consequences of abuse clearly have both short-term and long-term effects and usually result from severe deprivation. Mental retardation as an outcome of abuse can happen in two ways: as a direct consequence of physical injury and as a result of gross understimulation. Reference was made in Chapter 5 to the difficulty of disentangling the web of events with regard to physical abuse and mental retardation, it not always being clear which comes first (Jaudes and Diamond 1985). Kempe *et al.* (1962) found that 28 per cent of physically abused children suffered permanent brain damage. Lynch and Roberts (1982) found that 19 per cent of their sample were mentally retarded. Lynch (1988) reviews six American studies that show an average rate of mental retardation among their samples of abused children of 38 per cent compared with national rates of between 10 and 15 per cent. These figures all seem to be very high. They are derived largely from hospital samples, which suggests they are at the extreme end of the spectrum. Samples drawn from child protection registers would most probably produce much lower rates.

   Another consequence of severe physical and emotional deprivation of children is the failure to grow properly. This can be a result of the failure-to-thrive syndrome (see Chapter 4) and for the most part permanent damage does not occur provided that intervention takes place at an early stage (King and Taitz 1985). Failure to grow in older children has also been attributed to emotional and physical ill-treatment. Until recently this syndrome was termed 'emotional dwarfism' and is now called psycho-social short stature syndrome (Ps4). This results from very severe neglect, and successful treatment is long and protracted.[2]

Longer-term pathological effects of child abuse

As was stressed in the introduction to this chapter, the longer the gap between the abusive incident and the behaviour associated with it, the greater the uncertainty about the linkage. This has already been demonstrated in the case of child sexual abuse and prostitution and should be borne in mind throughout this section, in which the following long-term effects, which have been linked with physical abuse and neglect, will be considered: mental illness, drug-taking, delinquency and violent crime, and general life experiences and outlook.[3]

Mental illness

Surprisingly little attention has been paid to the connection between child abuse and later mental illness. This issue was considered briefly in Chapter 5 in the context of whether there is a link between the mental health of abusing parents and their behaviour. Here the issue is whether being abused or neglected as a child can lead to mental illness.

Carmen *et al.* (1984) analysed the case-records of 188 inpatients in an American psychiatric hospital to see if there was evidence of abuse (as children and wives) in their backgrounds. They found that 80 (43 per cent) of these patients had histories of some form of abuse; 80 per cent of these had been physically abused and half sexually abused; 90 per cent had been victimized by family members; 65 per cent were female. They argue that these figures are probably an under-estimation of the real incidence of abuse in this population because they included only those cases for whom there was unequivocal evidence that abuse had occurred.

Comparisons between abused and non-abused patients showed that the former presented with more and greater problems. They generally remained in hospital for longer periods, were more likely to be alcohol abusers and were more likely to inflict injuries on themselves.[4] They lacked self-esteem and the ability to trust, and found it hard to cope with their own aggressive impulses. Abused male patients were more outwardly aggressive, whereas abused female patients were more passive and directed their anger inwards. The authors stressed that there was a need to spend more time focusing on the abuse these patients had suffered as children than directly on the psychiatric illness itself.

There are many possible intervening variables that could account for these illnesses, and by no means all physically and sexually abused children develop psychiatric illnesses. There are also issues relating to the definition and diagnosis of psychiatric illness. Nevertheless, many people who are treated as psychiatric patients are likely to have been ill-treated in childhood. Sensitization to this issue, along the lines suggested by Carmen and her colleagues, can only be of benefit to them.

Drug-taking

Cohen and Densen-Gerber (1982) studied social histories of 178 American and Australian patients being treated for drug or alcohol addiction and found that 84 per cent of them had been physically abused and neglected as children. Again one must be careful in causally linking these two phenomena. Several studies of drug abuse have emphasized the cultural supports for such behaviour, rather than seeing it as a product of personal pathology (Parker *et al.* 1988).

Delinquency and violent crime

Lewis *et al.* (1989) summarize American research into the links between delinquency and child abuse. Most prospective studies show that about 20 per cent of abused children go on to commit crimes as juveniles. Retro-spective studies show a variation of rates, ranging between 9 and 84 per cent. Lewis *et al.* report on a longitudinal study of 411 boys conducted in Britain by West and Farrington (1977), which shows a link between harsh parental discipline and violent crime. However, as with other research into the long-term consequences of physical abuse and neglect, making causal connections is highly problematic.

Lewis and her colleagues have carried out extensive research into violent juvenile and adult offenders and find that many have been violently assaulted themselves, frequently suffering from neurological impairments as a result, and that many have witnessed extreme violence to others in the family home. Furthermore, they argue that there is a high rate of psychiatric disturbance in the parents of violent offenders:

> Many subsequently violent individuals are raised in conditions of extreme irrationality as well as violence. . . . Abuse alone does not usually create violent youngsters. It would seem that abuse, family violence and neuropsychiatric vulnerabilities in the child engender violence. (Lewis *et al.* 1989: 717, 718)

These studies may be dealing with individuals at the extreme end of the spectrum and there are competing views about the generation of violence and aggression. Nevertheless, what is known about serious abuse cases in Britain suggests that some, particularly male, abusers experienced similar types of upbringing to those depicted here.[5]

General life experiences and outlook
There are very few prospective longitudinal studies of what happens to a cohort of abused children in adulthood. Nearly all the studies considered so far have been retrospective. As has been seen in Chapter 5 (see Hunter and Kilstrom 1979), such studies tend to exaggerate the connections between the behaviours being focused on and abuse.

There are two American studies that have followed up abused children many years later, both of which have methodological problems. McCord (1983) carried out a record-based follow-up of children known to welfare agencies between 1939 and 1945. He traced 85 per cent of an original sample of 131 abused and 101 non-abused boys and found significantly higher degrees of alcoholism, divorce and occupational stress among the former. Those that did best from this group were those that achieved better educational performances. This study, therefore, points to the effects of abuse negatively affecting adult life. However, the study suffers from the lack of qualitative data to fill out the details of the bare facts, making it hard to know what weight to attribute to the findings.

This deficit is made up by the second study, which provides a good deal of qualitative interview-based information, but suffers from the weakness of not having a control group. Martin and Elmer (1992) followed up after 20 years a sample of 19 children who had been physically abused in the early 1960s

(Elmer 1977). They found them all to be unemployed or in poor jobs, but stress that this probably reflected the economic state of the USA at this time. Their employment situation was, however, the only factor common to the whole sample. The rest of the findings present the picture of a very mixed bag. Some had poor coping skills and had undertaken very few responsibilities in their adult life; others were happily married with families. There was little evidence of aggressive interpersonal relationships, but more of general resentment to and suspicion of outsiders and authority. Overall, there was no consistent pattern of linkage between current behaviour and early abuse.

Concluding comments

The amount of research material into the consequences of physical abuse and neglect is relatively limited compared with that related to the prediction of abuse. The studies reviewed here suffer from the problems of causally linking abuse and outcome, from weak and vague definitions of abuse and from a lack of attention to social factors as influences on behaviour, e.g. the differential impact of abuse on women and black people.[6]

Having referred to these problems, the following general picture of the consequences of physical abuse and neglect emerges from the research that exists. Many physically abused children suffer considerable emotional and psychological problems in their early childhood, leading them to have problems in trusting other people and to suffer from a sense of personal worthlessness. Socially and intellectually they do not perform well because of this. Many physically abused children tend to be both aggressive and withdrawn; neglected children as a whole seem to be less aggressive, but are more likely to exhibit withdrawn behaviour. A relatively small number of children suffer permanently from the physical effects of injury and severe neglect. Some children seem to survive well and cope despite all the odds. Much depends on the quality of their relationships with members of their family and others during childhood and also on the individual personality and intelligence of the child in question. In the longer term, there are more tenuous links between being physically abused and mental illness, drug abuse, delinquency and violent criminality and general adjustment to life.

The consequences of child sexual abuse

Research into the impact of sexual abuse on victims seems to be more abundant than that into physical abuse and neglect. This stems to a large extent from the way in which sexual abuse has been rediscovered in recent times; that is, as a result of women recounting their childhood experiences and the effects these continued to have in their adult lives. Such accounts have led to greater sensitivity to the consequences of such abuse, particularly with regard to its long-term effects.

Generally, although there are the same methodological problems as in studies of the consequences of physical abuse, particularly in relation to definitional issues and the use of control groups, research into the effects of child sexual abuse seems to be more systematic and detailed. Nevertheless, there are still major difficulties in sifting out the direct impact of the abuse from that which may be attributed to other variables, such as pre-existing problems, responses to the abuse by significant adults (including professionals) and later depriving experiences.

The main overviews to be found in the literature are those by Browne and Finkelhor (1986) and Beitchman *et al*. (1991, 1992). The studies reviewed by these writers differentiate between short- and long-term effects and this is the structure used here. After a review of the main findings of research into these two types of effects, consideration will be given to key variables that are thought to have an important influence on the extent and severity of the consequences.

Short-term effects of child sexual abuse

The research on the short-term effects of sexual abuse is not as well developed as that in relation to the long-term effects. Beitchman *et al*. (1991) point out that only one of the 49 studies reviewed by Browne and Finkelhor is an empirical study of children with a control group. Studies making up this deficiency since 1986 have been in greater supply, but the net result of the findings is disappointing for those who would like to build intervention and short-term treatment approaches on the basis of research information.

Browne and Finkelhor (1986) prefer the term 'initial effects' to 'short-term effects' because the latter suggests that such effects do not persist, which may or may not be the case. They define 'initial effects' as those which become evident in the first two years after the known onset of the abuse. Beitchman *et al*. (1992) make the important point that there may be long-term effects without short-term effects first having been apparent.

The following behavioural and emotional responses have been found to be evident in the short term.

General psychopathology
Gomes-Schwartz *et al*. (1990) studied 156 sexually abused children treated by a family crisis programme in New England. They assessed these children on a variety of emotional and behavioural criteria, and compared them with children referred to them for reasons other than sexual abuse and also with similar aged children in the general population. On overall ratings, severe psychopathology was higher for children of all ages who had been sexually abused than it was for children living in the community. For the 7- to 13-year-old group, who were generally more vulnerable than abused pre-school children and older adolescents, the degree of difference was as great as 40 per cent. However, in comparison with other patients at the centre, the degree of overall psychopathology was slightly less.

Fearfulness
Browne and Finkelhor (1986: 149) stress that 'the most common initial effect noted in empirical studies is fear.' Gomes-Schwartz *et al*. (1990) found that 45 per cent of their most vulnerable group of children (the 7 to 13 year olds) were experiencing fearful reactions to what had happened to them within the first six months following the onset of abuse. Browne and Finkelhor found rates as high as 83 per cent in a study by De Francis (1969). However, Beitchman *et al*. (1991) point out that similar degrees of fear and depression (see next section) are to be found in general psychiatric populations and, therefore, the emotions attributed in these studies specifically to sexual abuse could be linked to other stress-inducing factors.

Depression, withdrawal and suicide
Friedrich *et al*. (1986) found from a sample of 61 sexually abused females that 46 per cent were experiencing a range of internalized emotions including depression within two years of being abused. They also found that a withdrawn reaction was more common in younger victims. Anderson *et al*. (1981) found that 25 per cent females who had been sexually abused showed symptoms of depression afterwards. Other studies have also pointed to an internalizing response by school-age sexual abuse victims (Goldston *et al*. 1989; Kolko *et al*. 1988). Lindberg and Distad (1985) found that one-third of their clinical sample of 27 adolescents with incest histories had attempted suicide.

Hostility and aggression
On the other hand, some victims of child sexual abuse respond by directing anger and aggression outwards. This response is more common among adolescents. Gomes-Schwartz *et al*. (1990) identified such a response in between 45 and 50 per cent of the 7 to 13 year olds in their sample, and Friedrich *et al*. (1986) found that children aged from 6 to 12 were more likely to externalize their feelings than younger children. Gomes-Schwartz *et al*. point out that there are problems associating aggressive reactions purely with sexual abuse because many of the children in their sample were also subjected to physical violence or the threat of it. Thus the aggression they displayed could have been a result of this rather than of the sexual abuse they experienced.

Low self-esteem, guilt and shame
The findings with regard to low self-esteem as a short-term consequence of sexual abuse are rather mixed. De Francis (1969) reported that 58 per cent of victims expressed feelings of inferiority. However, Gomes-Schwartz *et al*. (1990) found that their pre-school age sample of sexually abused children 'exhibited a more positive self-concept than the normative population' (p. 88). This finding held true for the older age groups as well. Conte and Schuerman (1987) report on the adverse effect that guilt can have as victims mature, but there is no evidence of such guilt among pre-school age children

(Lusk and Waterman 1986), which is as we would expect given the social nature of this emotion.

Physical symptoms
Browne and Finkelhor (1986) report on clinical studies that find an association between sexual abuse and subsequent sleeping and eating disorders. However, Gomes-Schwartz *et al.* (1990) report that relatively few school age children in their sample exhibited serious somatic complaints. Beitchman *et al.* (1991) argue that such behaviours are as common in general psychiatric populations and, therefore, could be associated with factors other than sexual abuse.

Running away and other 'acting-out' behaviours
Running away from home has been associated with sexual abuse of adolescents in several research studies (Meiselman 1978; Herman 1981) Silbert and Pines (1981) found that 96 per cent of female prostitutes who had been sexually abused as children were runaways. Other 'acting-out' behaviours associated with sexual abuse are truanting, drug and alcohol abuse and promiscuity. Not all studies, however, support such connections (Johnston 1979; Goldston *et al.* 1989).

Cognitive disability, developmental delay and school performance
Gomes-Schwartz *et al.* (1990) found relatively high rates of both cognitive disability and developmental delay in their pre-school sample. They are careful not to see these problems as consequences of sexual abuse, speculating that they may have existed before abuse took place and may have contributed to these children's vulnerability to such abuse. The school performance of the abused 7 to 13 year olds was significantly worse than for the general population, a finding supported by Tong *et al.* (1987), but again there are problems in linking this specifically to sexual abuse.

Inappropriate sexual behaviour
Precocious and excessive sexual behaviour in sexually abused children is widely reported on by both parents and professionals and confirmed by studies of children playing with anatomically correct dolls (Jampole and Weber 1987; Sivan *et al.* 1988). Gomes-Schwartz *et al.* (1990) report that 27 per cent of 4 to 6 year olds who had been abused exhibited excessive sexual behaviour and 36 per cent of 7 to 13 year olds. Deblinger *et al.* (1989) found high rates of sexually inappropriate behaviour in a sample of 155 children, as did Friedrich *et al.* (1986). Beitchman *et al.* (1991) feel that the variation in rates should lead to caution in making assumptions that sexual abuse is necessarily a precursor to inappropriate sexual behaviour in children. Nevertheless, this linkage is clearer and stronger than that between sexual abuse and any of the other factors so far considered.[7]

Summary

Two conclusions can be drawn from this brief review. The first is that while an appreciable number of sexually abused children do experience behavioural and emotional problems in the two years following abuse compared with children who have not been abused, the linkage between these behaviours and sexual abuse is weak and other factors could account for them. As Beitchman *et al.* stress:

> We do not know whether many of the symptoms reported in the literature are specific to sexual abuse or whether they are attributable to other factors such as the child's pre-morbid level of functioning or a disturbed home environment. The contribution of these preexisting constitutional and familial factors to observed psychopathology needs to be more carefully examined. (Beitchman *et al.* 1991: 552)

The only clear direct outcome is that of inappropriately sexualized behaviour, which occurs in between a quarter and a third of all sexually abused children.

The second conclusion is that sexual abuse *per se* does not have an incapacitating effect in the short term for most children. Browne and Finkelhor (1986: 164) point out that 'In the immediate aftermath of sexual abuse one-fifth to two-fifths of abused children seen by clinicians manifest some noticeable disturbance.' It should be stressed that this apparently strange conclusion may result from the fact that a broad definition of sexual abuse is used in most of the studies including, for instance, various degrees of seriousness and both intra- and extra-familial abuse. Which children do suffer most will become clearer when consideration is given later in this chapter to variables such as violent abuse and abuse by a close and trusted relative. It has to be stressed that research into this area is still new and experimental and it is important, therefore, to interpret the findings carefully and not to draw hasty conclusions from them at this stage.

Long-term effects of child sexual abuse

Many of the behaviours and emotions discussed in relation to short-term effects of sexual abuse are also to be found in studies of long-term effects. As stressed at the start of this chapter, the linkages, seen to be problematic in the case of short-term effects, are even more problematic with regard to long-term effects because of the greater length of time between the abuse and the observed behaviour and because of the possible effect of a much wider range of intervening variables.

Fear and anxiety

Briere (1984) is reported in Browne and Finkelhor (1986) to have found that women sexually abused as children were twice as likely as non-abused women to experience fear, anxiety and nightmares and three times as likely to experience difficulties sleeping. However, a complicating factor in terms of a specific linkage with sexual abuse is that 49 per cent of his sample had also experienced physical violence as children and women. Beitchman *et al.* (1992: 106) came to the following conclusion on this linkage: 'While anxiety symptoms among adult women appear to be associated with CSA, it is not clear that this effect is independent of force or the threat of it.'

Depression and suicide

Beitchman *et al.* (1992) review eight studies and find that six report an association between child sexual abuse and depression as measured by either self-rating or psychiatric diagnosis. Fromuth (1986) did not find a connection, but the average age of her sample was 19.4 years whereas most of the other studies involved older women. With regard to suicide, studies are more equivocal in their findings. Disentangling cause and effect is again a problem and suicide attempts and thoughts seem to be most closely linked to women who have experienced physical violence as well as sexual abuse as children.

Self-esteem

Browne and Finkelhor (1986: 156) point out that, 'Although a negative self-concept was not confirmed as an intitial effect, evidence for it as a long-term effect was much stronger.' Bagley and Ramsay (1986) report a low self-esteem rate of 19 per cent among women sexually abused as children and 5 per cent among their control group. Herman (1981) reported that 60 per cent of her clinical sample of 40 female victims of incest had negative self-images compared to 10 per cent of her control group.

Likelihood of revictimization

Russell (1986) found that 65 per cent of women sexually abused as children were victims of subsequent or attempted rape, compared with 36 per cent of non-abused women. She also found that between 38 and 48 per cent had been subjected to physical violence by husbands and partners compared with 18 per cent of the control group. Briere (1984), as already stated, found that 49 per cent of his sample of women abused as children had been violently assaulted by men as adults. Various reasons have been put forward for the association of child sexual abuse and subsequent abuse, ranging from increased vulnerability in the case of girls leaving home as a result of their abuse experiences, to psychological needs to have their feelings of low self-esteem reinforced by further ill-treatment.

Sexual disturbance

As has been seen, sexualized behaviour was the short-term effect most closely related to child sexual abuse. Consideration has already been given to the questionable link between prostitution and child sexual abuse. Research shows there is a connection between being abused as a child and problems with sexual behaviour in adult life. There are difficulties in evaluating the validity of this research in that sexual problems are not clearly defined and there may well be high levels of sexual dysfunction or dissatisfaction in the general non-abused population. However, clinical studies such as those of

Meiselman (1978) produce very high rates of sexual difficulties (87 per cent), and non-clinical studies, with the exception of Fromuth (1986), all find significantly higher rates among their abused samples than among non-abused controls.

Other long-term consequences of sexual abuse
Eating disorders such as anorexia nervosa and bulimia nervosa have been linked to sexual abuse. Oppenheimer *et al.* (1984) reported that a third of their sample of women with eating disorders had been sexually abused before the age of 15. Alcohol and drug abuse have also been associated with child sexual abuse (Peters 1976; Herman 1981; Briere 1984).

There is some evidence to link child sexual abuse with personality disorder in adults (see Beitchman *et al.* 1992: 109), but as yet the link is weak. The link between child sexual abuse and mental illness has already been referred to in the section on physical abuse (Carmen *et al.* 1984). Clearly there is room for much more exploration of this connection. Finally, it should not be forgotten that there are physical consequences of sexual abuse. Jaudes and Morris (1990) collected data from a sample of 138 sexually abused children referred to hospital between 1979 and 1987 and found that one-third of them had a sexually transmitted disease. Their average age was just over six years old. Although, despite their name, it is possible for sexually transmitted diseases to be passed on in non-sexual ways, the chances of this are very small (Neursten *et al.* 1984). Some deaths are also closely linked to sexual abuse. Most of these are extra-familial, but there are cases of deaths being associated with intra-familial abuse as well (O'Hagan 1989: 72–3).

Summary
During the 'rediscovery' of child sexual abuse in the 1980s, considerable emphasis was placed on its long-term incapacitating effects, based on individual studies and case accounts. The findings of research into the general long-term effects confirm that women who have been sexually abused are more likely than women who have not been sexually abused to have problems in later life with regard to fear, anxiety, self-esteem, depression and sexual satisfaction, and to be vulnerable to further abuse. However, such consequences are not inevitable. Browne and Finkelhor (1986) estimate that less than one-fifth evidence serious psychopathology, but stress that this fact should not be used to minimize the seriousness of child sexual abuse. Long-term mental health can be seriously affected. In the section that follows, the focus will be on factors that can be influential in creating the worst outcomes.

Variables affecting both short- and long-term consequences

Seven variables have been associated in the literature with influence on the harmful effects of child sexual abuse: age at onset of abuse; the sex of the abused child; the degree of seriousness of the abuse; the duration of the abuse; the relationship of the abuser to the abused; whether the abuse was accompanied by violence; and the way in which the abused child was helped and responded to at and after the time of disclosure.

Age at onset of abuse

Throughout the preceding sections, the age of the child at the onset of abuse has been referred to because clearly some reactions are age- or development-specific. It is generally believed that both the short- and long-term consequences of sexual abuse are less harmful the younger the children, because of their lack of awareness of the social stigma attached to sexual abuse. Gomes-Schwartz et al. (1990) (see section on general psychopathology) found that their 7 to 13 years age group experienced more adverse reaction than did children in their 4 to 6 years and 14 to 18 years groups. Adams-Tucker (1981) found that children first abused after the age of 10 experienced worse short-term symptoms than did those first abused before this age. By contrast, Russell (1986) found that longer-term ill-effects were more likely to be experienced by those first abused in pre-puberty rather than in adolescence. Beitchman et al. (1991) suggest that age needs to be considered in conjunction with other variables. It could be that many children discovered to have been abused in early childhood may not have suffered the adverse effects of a long period of abuse or have been subjected to as much violence (see below), as they are unlikely to resist as strongly as older children, and that these factors could account for the less traumatic effect rather than age per se.

Sex of child

Overall, there is not enough research in this area to come to definite conclusions. Abuse of girls and boys can take different forms and this may account for different outcomes rather than the fact that the victims are boys or girls. Pierce and Pierce (1985) report that boys are more likely to be subjected to violence when being sexually abused and, therefore, more likely to suffer negative effects. On the other hand, girls are more likely to be abused by their natural fathers and to be removed from home following abuse, both factors being associated to some extent with negative outcomes (see below). It is possible that sexually abused boys are more socially stigmatized than sexually abused girls because of the relative rarity of such abuse and its threat to masculine assumptions. This too could increase negative effects.

The degree of seriousness of the abuse

The research findings linking severity of abuse (measured by type of abuse, e.g. whether it was penetrative or not) with harmful consequences are not consistent. Browne and Finkelhor (1986) refer to ten studies that considered both long- and short-term effects of abuse of different degrees of severity. Six of these found that there was a link between harmful outcomes and the severity of the abuse; four found no significant link. They conclude: 'Thus it is premature to conclude that molestation involving more intimate contact is necessarily more traumatic than less intimate contact' (p. 169). Beitchman *et al*. (1992) argue that the studies quoted by Browne and Finkelhor as not proving an association did not include enough serious abuse on which to make a proper judgement. They look at some additional studies and conclude that there is a linkage between serious abuse and trauma as perceived by the victim, but a less strong association between such abuse and objectively measured mental health.

Duration of abuse

Browne and Finkelhor (1986) reviewed 11 studies that measured the link between duration of abuse and trauma. They found that six confirmed that the longer abuse went on the more traumatic was the effect on the victim and five did not. They did not differentiate between short- and long-term effects. One might expect there to be similar short-term responses to abuse of long and brief duration, and Gomes-Schwartz *et al*. (1990) confirm this. Beitchman *et al*. (1992) argue that abuse of longer duration is associated with longer-term lasting harm. They stress that the picture can be distorted by the impact of violence. There are many instances of one-off abuse accompanied by violence, which can have traumatic effects on victims. If this is allowed for, then the link between duration of abuse and long-term harmful effects is stronger than Browne and Finkelhor suggest.[8]

The relationship of the abuser to the abused

Clinical accounts suggest that the more closely related the abused child is to the abuser the greater is the degree of harm likely to result. Thus intra-familial abuse is likely to have a more harmful effect than extra-familial abuse, and abuse perpetrated by a natural father more than that perpetrated by an uncle. Browne and Finkelhor (1986) found that several studies that compared all intra-familial abuse with all extra-familial abuse concluded that the harmful effects were the same. They attribute this unexpected finding to the fact that extra-familial abuse is more likely to be accompanied by fear and that some relatives who abuse may be less trusted than, say, a neighbour with whom the abused child might normally have more interaction. However, abuse by father figures compared with that by all other perpetrators was considered to result in greater trauma. Beitchman *et al*. (1992) concur with this finding, pointing to gross betrayal of trust as the reason for the degree of trauma or lasting harm created. They also point out that such abuse is likely to be of longer duration and to reflect and create considerable family dysfunction (see below).

Abuse accompanied by violence

Browne and Finkelhor (1986) consider the use of violence or the threat of it as the most important factor contributing to both short- and long-term distress and harm. The study by Russell (1986) provides a good example of the closeness of the association between these two variables. All those who reported violent abuse experienced extreme or considerable trauma, as did 74 per cent of those who experienced forceful abuse. Of those who experienced non-forceful abuse, 47 per cent experienced lasting harm.

Response to abuse

Gomes-Schwartz *et al.* (1990) found that a negative (e.g. non-believing) response by a parent or parents to a child's allegation of sexual abuse was associated with greater short-term psychopathology on the part of the child. It exacerbated the already existing problems. Conte and Schuerman (1987) found that a supportive response from the family was an important factor in reducing the extent of long-term problems following sexual abuse. Beitchman *et al.* (1991, 1992) refer to several other studies that confirm the influence of family response on both short- and long-term harm. Their view is that victims of child sexual abuse are more likely than non-victims to come from disturbed families and, therefore, that they are particularly likely to be responded to by their families in a negative way. Clearly this argument is more relevant to intra-familial abuse. Also of importance in this area is the response of professionals to allegations of sexual abuse. Elwell and Ephloss (1987) found that bad handling of intervention by the police and other professionals was associated with increased short-term trauma. Gomes-Schwartz *et al.* (1990) found that children removed from their families showed the most short-term problems but, as Browne and Finkelhor (1986) comment, these might have been the most problematic cases in the first place.

There seems, therefore, to be reasonable evidence to suggest that sexual abuse is likely to be most harmful in the following instances:

1 Where the abusive act involves penetration.
2 Where the abuse has persisted for some time.
3 Where the abuser is a father-figure.
4 Where the abuse is accompanied by violence, force and/or the threat of it.
5 Where the response of the family is negative.

While the age and sex of the abused child has some impact on the outcome, the research does not provide clear indications of the direction of these variables' effects. There is not sufficient information on the impact of professional intervention to evaluate conclusively its effect for good or ill.

Concluding comments

For some health and welfare practitioners, the degree of detail of all this research may seem unnecessary, in that child sexual abuse of the type in which they frequently become involved – largely intra-familial and often of a very serious nature – clearly has harmful effects on the child. It can seem to be somewhat hair-splitting to separate which element of abuse in a generally abusive situation causes the most harm. Similarly, research which suggests that children who are removed from families do less well than those who remain can be frustrating when it is apparent that removal is the only feasible course of action. Nevertheless, there are some important and relevant findings, namely that sexual abuse of children is not necessarily incapacitating for them in later life. There is a tendency among professionals to make this assumption, which can in itself have negative effects.[9] In particular, awareness of the impact of the variables just discussed is an important starting-point for assessing the consequences for the child and how to organize a response. Such knowledge provides a framework for intervention, not a blueprint. Children whom one would expect to suffer less harmful effects on the basis of known research findings may in fact experience considerable trauma. As has been repeatedly stressed, there are weaknesses in the research, and findings need to be carefully interpreted. Nevertheless, despite its limitations, this is the best formal available knowledge and it should, therefore, have relevance for policy and practice in this field.

8 Research into child protection practice

What does research tell us about the way in which health and welfare professionals respond to child abuse and the effectiveness of this response? These are the questions that will be addressed in this chapter.

The amount of research into British child protection practice is limited. There are very few studies of the work of mainstream statutory agencies (see Dingwall *et al*. 1983; Corby 1987; Waterhouse and Carnie 1992). Child protection public inquiry reports give glimpses of practice approaches, but there is no way of knowing how typical they are. Frankly, we have very little formal knowledge about how child protection work is carried out in these agencies.

There are more, but still relatively few, accounts and evaluations of intervention into physical abuse and sexual abuse cases by voluntary agencies and in hospital settings (e.g. Baher *et al*. 1976; Lynch and Roberts 1982; Dale *et al*. 1986; Ben-Tovim *et al*. 1988), and a few accounts of action research projects (e.g. Smith and Rachman 1984; Browne and Saqi 1988).

There have been very few studies of the effectiveness of child protection interventions. As will be seen, there has been much greater emphasis on this type of evaluation in the USA. There is only a very small amount of research into the consumer end with regard to parents (Brown 1986; Corby 1987) and no formal research data about the views of children.

Some of these research gaps can be filled by the findings of research into general child care practice. Parton (1989) points to the considerable overlap between child abuse and general child care problems and stresses that much of the recent research into statutory child care practice (see DHSS 1985a for an overview) includes child protection practice as well. Clearly findings from these studies have much relevance to our concerns.

Studies and accounts of practice will be considered in the following way. First, those relating to prevention and prediction will be examined. Second, the focus will be on studies and accounts relating to assessment and decision-making at the early intervention stage and later in the process, when important long-term plans are being considered. Third, effectiveness studies and related issues will be analysed.

Prevention and prediction

Prevention

There is little reference to preventive practice in the child abuse literature. While many commentators agree that prevention is the most constructive approach to the problem, there are few examples of ways of achieving this. Gough (1988) considers this issue and finds that there are three types of preventive strategies: those targeted at the whole population, such as community education programmes; those targeted at certain communities, usually those afflicted by poverty and deprivation; and those targeted at certain groups of families in which children are considered to be at risk.

With regard to the first type of preventive strategy, Gough finds little evidence of abuse awareness campaigns in Britain. The main exceptions to this are educational programmes in schools aimed at equipping children to protect themselves against sexual abuse. Gillham (1991: 48–63) provides a useful overview of such programmes and research related to them. He questions their effectiveness, which has generally not been rigorously tested. Most programmes of this kind tend to focus on extra-familial abuse and one study has demonstrated that they have only limited impact (Kelly *et al*. 1991).

The second strategy involves lay and professional people operating in community centres to provide general help and support with parenting for any family in a particular geographical area. Such projects are often headed by voluntary societies, but also by social services departments. The focus is on general child care problems rather than specifically on child abuse (see Holman 1988).

The third strategy involves selecting out certain types of parents who are considered to be potentially abusive to their children for extra support from nursing or medical staff. This type of selective or predictive approach has received a good deal of attention, particularly by the medical profession. Some reference has already been made to predictive studies in Chapter 5, but they will now be considered in greater detail.

Predicting child abuse

The idea of predicting abuse is an attractive one because of its preventive potential. It also has financial appeal because it raises the possibility of targeting limited resources on those areas where they are most needed and most likely to be effective. However, there are considerable problems associated with the predictive approach in practice, as the following studies and critiques of them show.

In the USA, Kempe and Kempe (1978) reported on a study in which 350 mothers and their new-born babies were screened for child-abuse potential. On the basis of interviews and observations around the period of giving birth, 100 mothers were rated as 'high-risk' and 50 as 'low-risk'. Fifty of the 'high-risk' mothers were followed up after two years and it was found that eight of their children had been placed on child protection registers compared with none of the low-risk group. Five of these eight children had been hospitalized with serious injuries. In addition, the high-risk children were significantly more likely to have undergone accidents in the two years and their parents were more likely to be considered 'abnormal'. On the basis of these findings, the authors claimed to have successfully predicted 79 per cent of all incidents of abuse that took place during this period, i.e. 75 out of 95.

Both Parton (1985) and Montgomery (1982) have subjected this study to close scrutiny and are critical on three main accounts. The first is that the definitions used for abusive behaviour are very loose and wide-ranging. As we have seen, they included accidents in the home and 'abnormal parenting'. Montgomery points out that only the eight cases that were registered should properly have been considered abusive, a view which, if accepted, drastically reduces the high rate of accurate prediction claimed by Kempe and Kempe. The second issue is that even if one uncritically accepts this 79 per cent positive prediction rate, this still means that 21 per cent of parents were wrongly suspected of abusing their children, the implications of which will be considered below. Third, 20 of the 95 cases of abuse were missed.

Half the 'high-risk' parents in the Kempe and Kempe study had been offered differential support services in an attempt to evaluate which of these were most effective. Twenty-five were given normal services and 25 received additional therapeutic input from psychiatrists. Gray et al. (1977) evaluated the impact of these services. Although they found no significant differences in parenting quality between the two groups, all the seriously injured children (five in total) came from the group that did not receive psychiatric help, thus pointing to some degree of effectiveness resulting from this process of prediction and targeting of special services.

Parton (1985) reports on a study in Bradford by Lealman et al. (1983), who used maternity records to predict the likelihood of abuse (measured by the much narrower criterion of child protection registration). In all, 28 children out of a total of 2802 were registered, of whom 17 were predicted. However, although the researchers predicted nearly two-thirds of the eventual abusers, in so doing they wrongly predicted 483 others, a false positive rate of 28 to 1! With regard to intervention, Lealman et al. found that specialist social work input did not significantly affect family functioning or, in contrast to the findings of Gray et al., influence the rate of serious abuse.

Dingwall (1989) subjects prediction studies carried out at the Park Hospital in Oxford to close scrutiny (see Lynch and Roberts 1977, 1978; Ounsted et al. 1982). He finds that these studies all have weaknesses because they employed vague definitions of child abuse and because the criteria on which the predictions were based are questionable. Dingwall's view is that parents from lower social classes are more likely to be predicted as potential abusers because they are more likely to be seen as troublesome at an early stage by health professionals. In addition, he points out that the fact that the definitions of abuse used by the researchers are very general and include concerns linked to parental non-cooperativeness means that all that is being predicted is that families originally perceived as troublesome continue to be seen as such:

> There may be a simple circularity here: the record of non-compliance predicts future non-compliance which is likely to precipitate the labelling of a child as abused, but which has no established relationship to the actual treatment of the child. (Dingwall 1989: 40)

Browne and Saqi (1988) report on a series of predictive studies carried out with health professionals in the Surrey area. Using a 12-item checklist (see Appendix) at birth and after one month on a population of 14,238 families, they identified 949 of these as high-risk. However, the results after two years were disappointing in terms of successful prediction – only 1 in 17 (6 per cent) had abused their children (no definition of abuse given). They concluded from this that: (a) the items used focused too much on background influences and stress, and not enough on ongoing family interaction patterns that were deemed to be important regardless of stress; and (b) that these should be measured not at birth or in the period immediately after, but at a later date. On the basis of further research, Browne and Saqi propose a programme of secondary screening. Families initially assessed as being at high risk using the 12-item checklist should in their view be further screened at between three and six months by health professionals with a focus on the quality of the parent–child interactions. Assessment of these interactions should give a much more accurate picture of where to target resources. They do not prescribe what form these interventions should take other than that they should be carried out by health visitors.

In summary, these studies demonstrate that it is possible to predict between two-thirds and four-fifths of known future abuse. On the debit side, however, is the fact that in this process at least 20 per cent of any sample are likely to be wrongly thought to be likely to abuse or neglect their children, and if one uses an official narrower definition of child abuse the rate of false prediction soars to a much higher level. Therefore, these studies fail in their aims of accurately targeting those families who might benefit from specialist help. In addition, they provide little in the way of information about the best way to prevent the abuse they predict.

It is not only the effectiveness of the predictive approach that is in question. There are also major questions about the ethics of this sort of activity. Is it, for instance, ethical to make an assessment of potential parental care without informing parents of what is happening? Is it ethical not to inform parents about concerns resulting from this assessment? It is not clear from these studies whether parents had any awareness of the fact that they were being assessed in this way. The only justification for this lack of openness can be that secrecy is essential in order to ensure the well-being of the child. There is, however, no evidence that lack of candour is likely to improve the safety of the child. Working with parents on the basis of shared concerns may be a more effective strategy in achieving this goal.

In concluding this section on prediction, it should be stressed that there is little evidence of maternity screening and service targeting of this kind taking place in mainstream practice. Only in exceptional cases where parents have previous histories of child abuse or where there are obvious signs of problems on maternity wards are families subjected to special scrutiny at the time of the birth of a child. Otherwise screening is left to the wit, experience and training of community health professionals. This system can be both effective and non-stigmatic because of its universalist base. However, to work well, such services need to be well resourced and workers need to be well trained in the issues surrounding child abuse and well integrated with other, particularly welfare, services.[1]

A final point to be made about predictive work is that it has been used almost exclusively in the area of physical abuse and neglect. Predicting the likelihood of sexual abuse in this way has so far not figured so highly on the agenda.[2]

Assessment and decision-making

The practice of assessment in child protection work clearly has some links with the preceding section on prediction, in that its function is to make plans for the future on the basis of what is known about a family's past and present in the light of available research knowledge. There are two key assessment points in child protection work: (a) when abuse first comes to light and there is a need for short-term decision-making; and (b) when there is a need to decide on the action required to ensure the longer-term future protection and well-being of the child. The former will be considered in this section and the latter in the next.

Short-term decision-making at child protection case conferences

The lack of detailed research into short-term assessment and decision-making in child protection cases makes it hard to know how it is actually carried out. Officially such assessments take place at inter-disciplinary case conference settings. However, there are important decisions reached before this stage, particularly those about whether allegations or suspicions of abuse are of sufficient seriousness to warrant case conferences. There has been hardly any research into which child abuse referrals result in case conferences and why. This major gap in our knowledge is made worse by the fact that pre-conference consultations and assessments have probably increased since the Cleveland inquiry which, as was pointed out in Chapter 3, advocated greater use of such preliminary discussions where sexual abuse is suspected.

Research studies carried out by Hallett and Stevenson (1980), Dingwall *et al*. (1983), Dale *et al*. (1986) and Corby (1987) all commented critically on standards of assessment at case conferences in the late 1970s and early 1980s. Hallett and Stevenson made much of inter-professional defen-siveness and dysfunctional group processes as impediments to good early assessment and decision-making. Dingwall *et al*. came to the conclusion that most assessments made at case conferences were, for a variety of structural reasons, including inter-professional conflict, likely to result in an under-estimation of the degree of risk to a child. Dale *et al*. (1986) considered that there were grave dangers of professionals becoming polarized over case conference decisions and exacerbating already existing difficulties. Corby (1987), while finding little inter-professional disagreement over cases of seri-ous abuse, reported a good deal of confusion in more marginal cases about why some children were registered and others were not. Decisions did not seem to be reached on the basis of a rational assessment of the degrees of risk (see also Campbell 1991).

There are few research accounts of what has been happening in case con-ferences since 1986. Higginson's (1992) research suggests that decision-making is still not based on a close assessment of potential risk. To a large extent she attributes this to the weakness of the research knowledge base that is available to provide guidance in this area. There is still much con-troversy about whether information derived from research about who abuses whom (see Chapter 5) should be used by professionals in their decision-making and how, and this will be discussed further in the next sec-tion on long-term assessment. In short-term assessments, such information does not seem to be explicitly used and yet, implicitly, factors such as the seriousness of the abuse, the cooperativeness of the parents, history of pre-vious abuse or contact with welfare agencies all play some part in the pro-cess (Medden 1985). It has been argued that at the least such factors should be made explicit so that their worth to the assessment process can be openly evaluated (Corby and Mills 1986).

Sexual abuse

The research and practice so far discussed have been concerned mainly with physical abuse and neglect. Short-term assessment in the field of child sexual abuse has followed a very different line. Children, not adults, are the subject of assessment in such cases.

How effective such assessments have been is very much open to ques-tion. There have been no systematic evaluations of this process. What we do know is that these approaches have created a great deal of controversy. The Cleveland report provides some evaluation of these methods as used there, though we have no way of rating the standards of practice because of the lack of information from other areas. It reached the conclusion that this type of disclosure work was indeed too confused in its aims and that the social workers often did not have the skills or knowledge required for such a com-plex task.[3] A further criticism levelled at the assessments employed by

Cleveland social workers was that they focused too narrowly on the abused child to the exclusion of wider family considerations:

> Social workers concentrated their efforts on the immediate need to protect the child rather than an assessment of the family. We would suggest that a child's needs and best interests cannot be fully considered in isolation from knowledge about, and full understanding of, all the circumstances relating to its parents. Their strengths and weaknesses as individuals, their functioning as a couple, their capacity as parents, and the known risks which any facet of their behaviour or attitude may have for the child concerned or any other children in the family must be taken into account. Balanced judgements cannot be made without careful appraisal. It is a sad fact that in very few social work files of the families seen by us, was there evidence of social workers taking a full social history of the family so as to inform their own views and decisions and more widely, those of the case conferences they attended. (Cleveland 1988: 75 paras 4.157, 4.158)

A third issue raised by the Cleveland inquiry report in relation to early assessment and decision-making was the danger that investigations of the kind carried out there could lead to secondary abuse, i.e. they might have a harmful effect in addition to the original abuse unless they were carefully planned and took into account the psychological needs of the child. This issue had previously been raised in the USA (Tyler and Brassard 1984).

Summary
Research into and accounts of short-term assessment and decision-making in child protection work point to a different approach being adopted depending on whether the subject of inquiry is a case of physical or sexual abuse. In the former, assessment tends not to be based on research findings and tends to result in decisions that favour non-removal of the child. The opposite seems to be true in the case of child sexual abuse. However, there is a need for considerable caution in assuming that practice carried out in Cleveland in 1987 is typical of what is happening nationally now. There are no studies evaluating the effectiveness of the approaches outlined above.

It should be noted that the 1989 Children Act has brought in changes that will affect short-term assessment work, which until now has often been hampered by conflict, denial and hostility. These changes include a new order called the Child Assessment Order (section 43), which will empower social workers to carry out assessments in situations where parents are denying them access to a child. Another change empowers local authorities to defray the expenses of an alleged abuser living away from home pending the outcome of an investigation (schedule 2.5). Finally, the latest *Working Together* guidelines (DoH 1991b: paras 5.14.6 and 5.14.7), which reflect closely the concerns of the Cleveland inquiry, point to the need for specialized training and greater sensitivity to the needs of children and parents, and stress that the interviewer should always be open to the possibility that events have not taken place. Again, it remains to be seen how child abuse investigations and early assessments will be conducted post-Cleveland.

Longer-term assessment and intervention

The focus in this section is on those cases where serious abuse has taken place and decisions have to be taken about the long-term future of a child. The bulk of cases that come into the child protection system involve moderate abuse and low standards of child care. In most of these cases decisions are reached to monitor families, provide support services and review progress at a later date. With regard to the much smaller number of children who are seriously abused, difficult decisions have to be reached about whether it is best for them to remain with or, since in such cases emergency removal is likely to have occurred, return to their parents and, if so, under what circumstances, with what services and safeguards.

Physical abuse

In the field of physical abuse and neglect, this has perhaps been the most pressing issue of all. In most of the cases publicly inquired into, the main concerns have not been the effectiveness of initial assessments and inter- ventions (the Darryn Clarke inquiry and the Kimberley Carlile inquiry are the most notable exceptions[4]). Most of the children in public inquiry cases have died while legally in the care of or under the supervision of the authorities, but actually living at home with their parents. The focus of concern has been whether these children should have remained in care or been returned to their parents' care and whether the supervision they received was of a reasonable standard.

Generally the practice of the statutory agencies has been heavily criticized for being too parent-centred in its thinking in this area and for not being sufficiently thorough in its assessments. Unfortunately, this view stems mainly from the cases that went wrong. We simply do not have enough general research information to help us decide how valid this judgement is over a wider spectrum of child protection work. Greenland (1987), whose work is also referred to in Chapter 5, devised a checklist (see Appendix), which he recommended for use in making long-term decisions about children who had been seriously abused. He stresses that 'it seems reasonable to assume a high-risk situation exists when an infant has suffered a serious non-accidental injury and more than half the check-list items, in any order, are checked' (p. 171).

Much of the research on rehabilitation of seriously abused children is derived from medical settings and is pessimistic about the effectiveness and advisability of this course of action. Hensey et al. (1983), for instance, argue that 'the children who best survived their experience after being taken into care were those for whom an early decision was made to sever parental contact and to place the child permanently with a substitute family.' King and Taitz (1985) come to a similar conclusion with regard to children failing to thrive. Lynch and Roberts (1982) are also doubtful about the value of rehabilitation unless it is accompanied by individual therapy for children. In their study they found that re-injury was rare, but that the development of the children remained at a low level after they had returned to their parents.

Two studies paint a slightly more optimistic picture and point to ways of making rehabilitation more effective.

The first study, that by Dale *et al.* (1986) of the Rochdale NSPCC Special Unit, has been very influential in recent policy and practice developments in child protection work. Using a strategic family therapy approach, social workers in this unit assess parents whose children have been removed from home following abuse, to decide whether rehabilitation is a safe prospect. Their work is based firmly on the need for therapeutic control, without which they see no hope of success. Such control is needed over both other involved agencies and clients. With regard to the latter, they stress that virtually all their clients are involuntary and they are unequivocal about the need for a firm, almost combative, approach:

> Working with involuntary clients is often a very emotionally draining experience. It is not suitable for workers who imagine that change occurs simply as a result of their being 'nice' to their clients. It is not for workers who measure their success in terms of the number of Christmas cards they get from their clients. (Dale *et al.* 1986: 75)

They stress that most abusing parents deny or minimize the abuse they have done to their children. Children, according to them, cannot be safely rehabilitated if this is the case. Such parents are 'dangerous'. The assessment that the unit carries out focuses on making parents accept full responsibility for their actions. Emphasis is also placed on helping parents to develop an understanding of their own histories and of the strengths and weaknesses of current relationships with their own extended families and with spouses and partners. Openness is seen to be mandatory and resistance is to be broken down. Failure to achieve these goals usually results in a decision not to return the child to the parents. Similarly, over-compliance is viewed with scepticism and may end with the same outcome. The carrot for all the parents is the return of their children. The unit found that 65 per cent of children from 26 families were initially rehabilitated to their parents. Ten per cent of these children were subsequently returned to care. There were no re-injuries (over an unspecified time period) among those children who remained at home. Monitoring and follow-up was considered necessary only at a minimal level.

How applicable this approach is to mainstream agencies is an open question. It would be hard for a statutory social services department to control local networks in the way that the Rochdale Special Unit did and the therapeutic approach that they adopted might not be tolerated. The NSPCC's reputation and voluntary status probably accounts for the fact that the Rochdale workers practised in the way that they did. There are also some question marks over the ethics of this type of intervention in which therapeutic control is so heavily stressed.

The second study with implications for improved rehabilitative work is reported on by Farmer (1992). Case records of a sample of 150 abused and neglected children placed home on trial were studied to see what factors were associated with success or failure. Forty-five per cent of placements were considered to be beneficial to the children and 19 per cent detrimental. Abuse or neglect reoccurred in just over a quarter of all cases. Successful rehabilitation was seen to be linked to purposeful social work involvement, planning and regular visiting. It was also linked to the number of placements that the child had experienced while in care. Those who had been placed with only one foster-parent did better than those with more than one placement. It could be that these were the least problematical cases in the first place. What this study demonstrates is that social workers in mainstream services can achieve successful rehabilitations without attempting to bring about major changes in parental attitude. They need to select the cases with the best prospects, have regular direct contact with families and work purposefully and in a planned way to achieve rehabilitative goals.

Recent developments
There have been two significant recent developments with regard to long-term assessments in cases of physical abuse and neglect. The first is the publication by the Department of Health in 1988 of *Protecting Children – a Guide for Social Workers Undertaking a Comprehensive Assessment*. This guide is recommended for use in the 1991 *Working Together* guidelines to aid decision-making, particularly where children have been abused and re-moved from home, and rehabilitation is being considered. It consists of 167 questions based largely on research knowledge. It focuses on the child, its parents and their immediate networks. Its concerns are the history and current functioning of the family, the quality of parent–child and parent–parent (where applicable) interactions, the integration of the family into the locality and with the extended family, and issues of race, culture, finance and material deprivation.

There seem to be two major problems with this guide. First, it seems to lack awareness of the difficult conditions in which social workers operate. Social workers, whatever their legal powers in a situation, have to negotiate a *modus vivendi* with their clientele. It is extremely difficult for a worker who has removed a child from home to carry out the type of assessment this document proposes. The second problem is that many of the questions, though posing as neutral, in fact have obvious implications and are likely to create a defensive response. The following questions taken from the guide illustrate both these problems:

Question 93: What arrangements have you made for the care of the children while you are under the influence of drink or drugs?
Question 112: How would you describe your sex life?
Question 115: Do you think this relationship will last for a long time (many

years), a moderate length of time (1–5 years), a short time
(3–12 months) or temporary (up to 3 months)?

While there is little doubt that social work assessments need to be more
explicit and parents and children need to know the reasons for decisions, this
guide does not seem to be a useful tool in its present form (see McBeath and
Webb 1990/91).

The second development is that there are new legal regulations covering
situations where children are returned home-on-trial to their parents while
still subject to care orders (The Accommodation of Children (Charge and
Control) Regulations 1988). These regulations require social workers to
consult a wide range of other health and welfare agencies before such
placements can be made.

Sexual abuse assessments in statutory agencies

There is little research information about the way in which statutory agencies
carry out longer-term assessments in the field of child sexual abuse. The
impression is that there is much less optimism about the chances of
preventing intra-familial sexual abuse re-occurring than seems to be the case
with regard to physical abuse and neglect. Much emphasis is placed on the
response of the non-abuser to the abused child, the age of the child and her or
his degree of assertiveness and ability to protect herself or himself in future
(see Waterhouse and Carnie 1992). Statutory social workers so far seem to
have focused much more on the child and the reactions of the non-abusing
parent than they have on the abuser. Assessment and treatment of abusers,
where it occurs, is more likely to be in the domain of psychologists and,
therefore, to occur separately from assessment work done with the rest of the
family. Denial of abuse is a major impediment to work with abusers.

The Great Ormond Street approach
Ben-Tovim et al. (1988) have devised a form of assessment, based on family
therapy principles, that involves all members of the family. They argue that
intra-familial abuse is a product of faulty family functioning and is sustained
by secrecy, and therefore that it is a prerequisite to successful treatment that
family members communicate openly with each other about what has
happened in the past and what they wish for the future. This entails the
abuser admitting to all family members what he has done and the opening up
of emotional blockages. Openness and explicitness are seen as essential
counters to the secrecy that has helped to maintain the abusive situation, and
they must be achieved regardless of the pain and anxiety created in the
process (Furniss 1991). Often by the stage at which this assessment is carried
out the family has broken up, usually as a result of a prison sentence being
imposed on the abuser.

This form of assessment entails monthly family meetings over a period
of one year to 15 months and is supplemented by children and parents

attending separate groups or in some cases receiving individual therapy. Ben-Tovim *et al.* conducted a follow-up (no time period specified) of families who were assessed between 1981 and 1984 (55 per cent of the families completed the full course of assessment). They found that 83 of 120 children (69 per cent) had not been re-abused, whereas 19 (16 per cent) had, and it was not clear whether re-abuse had taken place in the remaining cases. Most of the family make-ups had changed by the time of follow-up. Fifteen per cent of abusing parents had returned home after their prison sentence.

Clearly Ben-Tovim's work has similarities with that of Dale *et al.* (1986) in the case of physical abuse. Both focus on the need for full acknowledgement of the abuse. Both see faulty family dynamics as at the root of abuse and both merge assessment to a large extent with therapy. Both also require considerable time, resources and expertise. Both control the inflow of work, in terms of type and quantity of cases worked with. Clearly statutory agencies cannot under current circumstances replicate this sort of assessment practice, particularly given the growth in child sexual abuse discovery over the past few years (see Chapter 4). The issue for policy-makers is, if approaches of this kind are seen as desirable, who should implement them and how they should be resourced.

Summary

In overview, the picture of longer-term assessment and decision-making in the child protection field is as follows. With regard to physical abuse and neglect, statutory agencies do not follow a particular theory. They operate under a philosophy that oscillates between a preference for rehabilitation where possible in the belief that ultimately a child is better off in its own family and a preference for non-rehabilitaton as the safest course of action in terms of the protection of the child. Assessment and decisions are frequently based on the actions of parents after the abuse and, particularly, on their cooperativeness and desire to retain the care of their child. The general view emanating from public inquiry reports is that social workers are not rigorous enough in their assessment of future risk. However, research shows some degree of success with rehabilitation provided certain factors hold true (Farmer 1992). Other researchers, particularly from the more medically oriented professions, see clean-break approaches as more beneficial for children. Dale *et al.* (1986) favour intensive assessment as a precursor to decision-making. This, for them, provides clear evidence of the likelihood of successful rehabilitation or not.

With regard to sexual abuse, the picture is less clear. Social workers seem to be less likely to favour rehabilitation with the continuing presence of an abuser in the household than is the case in physical abuse and neglect. Ironically, given what has happened with physical abuse, they have been seen to be over-zealous in this regard. There is little clear evidence of how mainstream assessments are being carried out. It seems that the focus is more on the abused child than on the family as a whole. Ben-Tovim's approach is in contrast to this and provides the only British effectiveness figures in this field.

The effectiveness of intervention and treatment

Some reference has already been made to the effectiveness of professional intervention into child abuse in the previous section. Prediction studies were seen to be of limited effect. The work of Ben-Tovim et al. (1988) and Dale et al. (1986) provided some details of intervention outcomes that were mainly positive. Both these studies reported on interventions carried out outside the statutory sector. There have been very few attempts to evaluate the effectiveness of statutory work intervention in Britain (see Corby 1987: 113–27).

There are some important issues to consider in measuring effectiveness. The first relates to the indicators used to measure success or failure. Several researchers (Lynch and Roberts 1982; Calam and Franchi 1987) have argued that non-recurrence of abuse is not an adequate measure because, as they have found, the emotional quality of care for a child may continue to be low even though he or she is no longer subjected to physical violence. Second, there is the issue of the length of time allowed between intervention and the measurement of outcome. Most studies follow up cases within two years at the most, which may be too short a time to measure lasting effects. Third, there is the problem of establishing causal links between intervention and outcome in that both successful and unsuccessful results could be the consequence of variables that have nothing at all to do with the intervention programme.

Physical abuse and neglect

The American experience
Most of the information about the effectiveness of child protection intervention is to be found in American research studies.

Kempe and Kempe (1978), reporting on their therapeutic approach, found that of the cases they treated, there was a 20 per cent outright failure rate. Of the remainder, 40 per cent of parents were considered to have grown and developed into more mature and positive individuals and carers, and 40 per cent, while not achieving this form of change, at least did not re-abuse their children.

Green et al. (1981) reached similar findings to Kempe and Kempe. In a study of 79 parents who had seriously abused their children, they found that intensive psychotherapeutic help led to some improvement in 40.5 per cent of the sample, by which they meant that they had learned to control their aggression and not re-abuse. Significant improvement, including the development of greater insight into themselves and the development of empathy and understanding of others, took place in 27.8 per cent of the sample. The remaining 32 per cent showed no change in their behaviour and attitudes: 16 per cent had re-abused their children at follow-up and it was not clear whether re-abuse had happened or not in the remaining 16 per cent. They found higher rates of success among parents who stayed longer in treatment. Other factors related to treatment failure were the seriousness of the effects of the abuse and parents having gross misperceptions of their children's level of maturity and undertanding.

Cohn and Daro (1987) reported on the evaluation of federally funded projects set up between 1970 and 1980 to develop treatment-based responses to the problem of physical abuse and neglect. Most of these projects were based on the approach pioneered by Kempe and Kempe (1978). However, they did not achieve the same rates of success. While in treatment, rates of re-abuse reported ranged between 30 and 47 per cent. Overall, 42 per cent of parents treated were thought to have reduced potential for neglect, but high drop-out rates were common. The more successful programmes were those that did not rely exclusively on individual therapy but had a range of other inputs, including community support schemes of the kind reported on by Gough in Britain (1988), group work inputs including the work of Parents Anonymous[5] and parent education classes. Cohn and Daro also found that programmes which used temporary substitute care or ensured the removal of the perpetrator were among the most successful. Some of the later programmes included sexual abuse treatment. Generally these programmes achieved higher success rates than those dealing with physical abuse and neglect. Cohn and Daro are of the view that overall the results are disappointing and point to the need to focus more on prevention than treatment.

Untreatable families?
Jones (1987) reviews a range of British and American studies, including that of Green *et al.*, and finds some support for the view that intensive casework treatment with a psychotherapeutic element is associated with less re-abuse than purely child protective programmes, whereas Cohn and Daro proposed that such approaches were most successful in combination with other forms of help and support. However, Jones's main purpose is to identify those families that do not respond to treatment and that he terms 'untreatable'. These include those who have carried out serious forms of abuse, such as non-accidental poisoning, burns, neglect resulting in psycho-social short stature syndrome and cases attributed to Munchausen's syndrome by proxy. Other factors associated with untreatability are parents who were severely mal-treated themselves as children, parents with personality disorders or suffering from psychotic illness, parents who deny abuse, lack empathy and drop out of treatment programmes. The problem with this type of list is that it is too baldly stated and, therefore, as it stands, of little use in the world of practice, where there is an expectation that parents will be at least considered for a second chance. While there may have been a tendency for social workers to have been over-committed to rehabilitation in the past, there are also dangers

in unequivocally labelling people as untreatable. For instance, is it justifiable to view parents who drop out of programmes as being untreatable as a result? Clearly there is a need to examine the nature of the programmes to see if they have played a part in the outcome, independent of the parents' personality.

Treatment drop-out

Gabinet (1983a) examined the issue of treatment drop-out in relation to a child protection focused family centre in Cleveland, Ohio, which provided support for mothers, group activities and some parental education. She found that of 100 families referred to the centre in 1979, 53 failed to attend despite being given three appointments. Another five were seen fewer than five times. This lack of take-up was also reflected in the programmes reviewed by Cohn and Daro. Gabinet (1983b) argues that the failure of the family centre she studied was due to the fact that its focus on child protection was seen as threatening and unhelpful by those assigned to it.[6] She advocates a more general child-care oriented service with more power being shared with parents using such centres.

Compulsory treatment

An alternative approach is to compel treatment. Such methods, as applied to child sexual abuse offenders, have been reported as having some success in Holland (Christopherson 1981) and the USA (Giaretto 1981), where treatment can be required as an alternative to custodial sentencing. In the field of physical abuse and neglect such an approach has been adopted in the USA with mixed results. Rivara (1985) reports higher completion rates where court orders apply, as do Wolfe et al. (1980). However, Green et al. (1981) found that court-ordered treatment was negatively correlated with successful outcome. Gabinet's study (1983a) did not include court-ordered cases, but she found that over half of those families who had been sent to the centre with the threat of their children being removed if they refused did not attend.

These issues are of particular importance to British child protection work given changes in legislation that empower courts under certain conditions to make attendance at day centres a requirement of a supervision order.[7]

The effectiveness of day nursery provision

Day nurseries can also provide therapeutic treatment for children and for parents, depending on the way in which they are organized. Culp et al. (1987) in the USA report significant improvements in a range of social, physical and psychological skills among a group of 35 three-year-old children attending a therapeutic day centre compared with a control group receiving normal services. The input was intensive and a range of services was provided, including individual and group therapy for parents and children, which was supplemented by a crisis line and other community supports.

On the other hand, Crittenden (1983) suggests that more traditional approaches, which use nurseries as forms of stress-relieving respite care and also as a way of monitoring the safety and welfare of the child, may achieve the opposite of what they intend. In a small study of 22 children who had been abused and assessed as in need of protective day care, she found that nine were unable to be placed because of practical difficulties, such as shortage of places, transport or funds. At one year follow-up, more of these children were still living at home than of those who had been allocated places. At four years there were no differences between the two groups in terms of where the children were living. Crittenden concludes:

> Rather than staving off family break-up by reducing the pressure of caring full-time for the children and giving the family an opportunity to learn adequate caretaking skills, protective day care may be exacerbating the process of family rejection and anger, thus making the home a less safe place for the children. (Crittenden 1983: 300)

It should be pointed out that she reaches this conclusion from the viewpoint of an attachment theorist. Another factor may account for the apparent failure of the day nursery to improve the long-term welfare of these children. Crittenden in passing points out that all the mothers objected to the plans that were made for them and their children and complied only to avoid a court hearing.

Summary

Studies into the effectiveness of a wide range of intervention methods in the USA suggest that individual counselling or psychotherapy for parents seems to have some influence on outcomes in terms of improved general care of children and in terms of re-injury rates. Overall, however, the results are not as good as the initial work of Kempe and his associates suggested. Providing supplementary forms of help and support, such as community help, group and crisis line support, improves the effectiveness of individual therapy. Imposing treatment on unwilling clients seems to result in mixed outcomes. There is some support for the view that programmes that involve and empower parents are more effective. Where and in what circumstances compulsion is effective or necessary remains to be seen.

Sexual abuse

With regard to sexual abuse there are very few British studies that evaluate their effectiveness, with the already mentioned exception of Ben-Tovim *et al.* (1988).

In the USA Giaretto (1981) and his colleagues (Giaretto *et al.* 1978) have evaluated the effectiveness of their work. Using a humanistic-based thera-peutic approach with all members of the family (including the perpetrator), which has the formal backing of the legal system (thus enforcing offender therapy), they report that treatment carried out on 600 families in the 1970s resulted in 90 per cent of abused children being returned home in less than one month. No recidivism was reported at all. They rather vaguely state that the re-establishment of normal father–daughter relationships is achieved in most families. They do not clarify whether this means that fathers in these cases have returned to the family home. These outcomes are much more successful than those reported by Ben-Tovim *et al.* (1988) (see previous section), who took up Giaretto's approach and adapted it to the British scene. There could be several reasons for this disparity in results. First, the type of family or problem being worked with could be very different. Giaretto and his colleagues report that their clients are largely white and middle-class, whereas the majority of those treated by Ben-Tovim *et al.* come from the lower social classes. Giaretto and his colleagues initiate work with offenders at a much earlier stage, i.e. as soon as possible after disclosure. Finally, there is the effect of cultural and institutional differences. In comparison with the climate in which Giaretto operates, the British response to intra-familial sexual abuse seems punitive and over-controlled by the police and criminal law.

Gomes-Schwartz *et al.* (1990) report on the effectiveness of their crisis intervention approach with children who have been sexually abused. They found that their approach was beneficial for over three-quarters of their clients and, above all, served the important function of laying good foundations for later involvement. However, it was not sufficient in itself and in almost all cases long-term follow-up was required. In particular, families often had many other problems, which were seen to need a wider range of long-term supports and help. Short-term intervention alone was seen to be more applicable to families where sexual abuse was the sole reason for outside intervention. They argue that treatment programmes must recognize parents' needs for support and that collaboration between treatment and child protective services is essential for successful outcomes.

Therapeutic work with intra- and extra-familial sex offenders is on the increase in Britain. Sandham (1992) writes that roughly half of all probation services in England and Wales operate such schemes and there are a growing number of non-statutory approaches. Studies of effectiveness are few in number. Furby *et al.* (1989) provide an overview of the effectiveness of such treatment programmes in Britain and the USA and come to the rather pessimistic conclusion that there is no evidence that they reduce the re-occurrence of sex offending.

Summary
The range and quality of effectiveness studies of sexual abuse intervention work are very variable. There is little firm evidence to determine the effectiveness of the different approaches. The American studies considered point to the need for a non-punitive climate in which to carry out more positive work.

9 | Current issues in child protection work

In this chapter attention will be focused on issues currently being debated by researchers and practitioners in the field of child protection. Most will have been touched upon so far in the course of this book, but it is intended to develop them further here. Inevitably the issues considered are a selection from the wide range that exist. Choice has been determined as much as possible by relevance to mainstream statutory practice in the child protection field. The topics to be discussed are as follows:

1 The strengths and weaknesses of current child abuse theory and research.
2 Child abuse as a unitary concept.
3 The challenge and potential contribution of the feminist perspective to child protection policy and practice.
4 Balancing the rights of parents and the needs of children in child protection practice.
5 The need to develop an anti-racist approach to child protection work.
6 The strengths and weaknesses of inter-professional cooperation as a strategy for dealing with child abuse.
7 The future of the child protection system.

The strengths and weaknesses of current child abuse theory and research

A considerable amount of theory and research has been discussed so far in this book. There are several problems associated with these contributions that should be considered by those who make use of them.

First, as has been seen, child abuse is a topic that is dealt with by a wide range of professional and academic specialities. Child abuse research reflects the theory bases and ways of thinking of these different specialities. All have insights to offer, but there is need for careful weighing and assessment of the way in which these different interests and ideological standpoints influence the outcomes. A good example of this need is in the field of prediction studies considered in the previous chapter. Here, psychologists and medical doctors have adopted a view, with some empirical backing, that there is a measurable correlation between certain social and psychological factors and the propensity for abuse. Their background and training, based largely on positivist research, problem-solving and notions of medical prevention and cure, lead them to use these criteria to select out potential abusers and focus treatment on them. From a sociological perspective, which sees child abuse as a socially constructed problem in which professionals are not disinterested observers, this type of approach is more open to question. The factors used by psychologists and others to identify potential abuse are by no means water-tight predictors and it is seen as more logical and moral to address those factors (for example, social stress) which are associated with abuse potential directly, rather than to use them to identify the potential abuser.

Reference has been made throughout to the cultural context in which knowledge is derived and, therefore, to the relevance of that knowledge to different cultures. The work of Korbin (1981) is particularly instructive on this issue. However, she considers sharply contrasting societies where the lesson seems more obvious. What about the transferability of such knowledge between more similar types of society? How useful, for instance, is knowledge about intervening into child sexual abuse allegations among middle-class families in Santa Clara County, California, to working with deprived and disadvantaged families in industrial inner-city areas in Britain (and vice versa)? The answer is not as negative as it might seem at first sight, because such communities share some common features, not least the view that sexual abuse of children by adults is unacceptable, harmful and unlawful. However, there may be stark differences in the acceptability and viability of methods of intervention derived from these different settings. Reports from other industrialized European countries point to a much less open approach to the issue of child sexual abuse within the family than in either the USA or Britain, reflecting the different cultures, mores and beliefs that prevail there.[1]

There has been a good deal of scepticism about the worth of much child abuse research as a result of issues such as those just considered. O'Hagan (1989), arguing from a relevance-to-practice point of view, and in the wake of the Cleveland crisis, where, as we have seen, social workers' adherence to new ideas on child sexual abuse was considered to be misguided, writes:

> All literature on child sexual abuse has contributed in varying degrees to our understanding. In this practitioner's view, however, very little of the literature is either relevant or helpful in equipping front-line professional staff to cope with the multiple problems created by the abuse. (O'Hagan 1989: 21)

O'Hagan proceeds to argue that this state of affairs is not the fault of the researchers, but of the subject matter. His view is that child sexual abuse is so multivarious in the forms that it takes that it is not easily categorized or harnessed by research-based knowledge. This seems to be somewhat pessimistic and at the same time suggests that the only way forward is to rely on practical wisdom and experience. My view is that although available research on child sexual abuse has considerable limitations, it is more useful than O'Hagan suggests. However, it has to be taken from a range of sources and carefully weighed and assessed for relevance to different contexts and different situations. There are dangers associated with unthinkingly following a single model derived from another context. The problem with such an approach seems to be whether social workers and other front-line professionals have the time, commitment and organizational support to develop the type of expertise that the more careful analytical approach being suggested here requires.

The child abuse knowledge base has been attacked from another quarter, that of researchers. Dingwall is very critical of the existing knowledge base:

> The amount of scientifically-validated research on child abuse and neglect is vanishingly small. The value of any self-styled predictive check-list is negligible. Indeed such tools probably do more harm than good because of the way they further undervalue and undermine professional judgement. Child abuse research will not progress until the scientific and the social problems are clearly distinguished. The former are the topic for the mainstream of investigations into child development, family interaction and aggression within a variety of social sciences from sociology and anthropology through psychology and ethology. The latter are perhaps more distinctively the concern of the sociologist, the political scientist and the social historian. (Dingwall 1989: 51)

While this view has much to recommend it, the implication is that there is no place for research based more specifically on child abuse, because it is a socially defined phenomenon and, therefore, does not lend itself to scientific methods of investigation. This seems a rather harsh judgement. An alternative approach is to improve definitions and to be somewhat more modest about the validity and applicability of findings.

Parton argues for child abuse as a topic to be more firmly situated in the general child care field:

> We could gain considerably by recognising in research, policy and practice that child abuse is centrally concerned with debates about the way we bring up children and is hence centrally concerned about child care. In the process the message seems to be that child abuse and child protection practice should be located in child care practice. (Parton 1989: 74)

Again, this view has much merit. In the past, separating child abuse from other child care concerns has had the negative effect of it being seen as a distinct and pathological phenomenon far removed from what happens between parents and children in so-called normal families. The linkages between child abuse and general child care far outweigh the differences and certainly there are vast overlaps between what is defined as moderate abuse and what is seen as a family experiencing child care problems and difficulties. Nevertheless, the focus on child abuse has had some positive outcomes. It has greatly increased our understanding of and sensitivity towards violence in the family and its potentially debilitating effect on future mental health. It is also argued (Belsky and Vondra 1989) that a focus on child abuse can provide insights into normative family behaviour. Finally, it is an area of work that has attracted greater political and financial attention than has generally been afforded children and family issues, albeit at a price. Thus, while it is important to locate child abuse research in the wider field of child care, nevertheless there are, in my opinion, benefits to be gained from maintaining a separate focus.

The knowledge base for child protection work has many deficiencies. Great care needs to be taken in applying such knowledge to practice, particularly with regard to approaches that make grandiose claims about predictability and effectiveness. Nevertheless, the insights and aids to thinking about child abuse provided by research are of considerable importance for practitioners trying to get to grips with the massive complexities of child protection work.

Child abuse as a unitary concept

Both research and practice until recently have treated different forms of abuse as separate phenomena. This is particularly true in the case of physical and sexual abuse. Physical abuse has traditionally been seen both by practitioners and researchers as a parent, more usually mother, focused issue. The abused child has been seen as the object of abuse and has not been considered to be in need of particular attention, except in more extreme cases. In cases of sexual abuse, on the other hand, the child has been seen as the key person whose needs are paramount.

More recently, partly as a result of increased concerns about emotional abuse, there has been a growing realization that all forms of abuse have similar psychological consequences for the child and more attention is now being paid to these and other factors that are common across the board. This is a welcome trend, in that insights gained and lessons learned from the understanding of and intervention into one form of abuse can be transferred to and tested with others. The following two issues demonstrate the potential value of thinking laterally about physical and sexual abuse.

First, it is generally accepted that every effort should be made to ensure that a child who has been sexually abused should not be doubly abused by being taken into care (unless necessary for her or his protection) and thus deprived of her or his normal support systems. The same consideration should also be given to children who have been physically abused. The situation is more complex in such cases, as there may be greater uncertainty as to who the abuser is and it is statistically more probable than in the case of sexual abuse to be the mother (an additional problem is that she is also more likely to be the main carer). Nevertheless, where possible, consideration should be given under Schedule 2 (5) of the 1989 Children Act to encouraging alleged physical abusers to live elsewhere pending the outcome of an investigation.

Second, children who are physically abused should be listened to and their accounts given the same sort of credibility as those of children who have been sexually abused. This point is vividly brought home in the Stephanie Fox inquiry report:

> In June, Stephanie is reported to have told both a Social Services receptionist and day nursery staff that a bruise on her forehead was done by her daddy. She was quite clear about what happened. Perhaps more thought might have been given to talking with the child. If this had been a suspected sexual abuse case, a 'disclosure interview' would have been a priority. Should we not also listen to physically abused children? (Fox 1990: para. 5.10, 30–1)

Focusing on similarities between forms of abuse in this way should influence practitioners to question their assumptions and working practices and to make the best use of their knowledge and experience. It is to be hoped that the more sensitive approach to child sexual abuse will have an influence on the style of intervention into physical abuse cases and also that the sharper child protection focus that now characterizes physical abuse work can, where appropriate, be applied in cases of sexual abuse. None of this should be construed as thinking that there are no differences between types of abuse at all. However, at this stage, it may be more constructive to develop practice around the commonalities.

There are signs that this is beginning to happen in British child protection practice. For instance, the 1991 *Working Together* guidelines (DoH 1991b) do not distinguish between physical and sexual abuse at all, though it is not made clear whether this is a deliberate attempt to view child abuse more holistically or not.[2] Whatever the case, the message seems to be getting across that it is important to respond to the emotional needs of all abused children and all members of a family in which any form of abuse occurs, in contrast to the earlier dichotomous approach to physical and sexual abuse.

The challenge and potential contribution of the feminist perspective to child protection policy and practice

There can be no doubt that over the past ten years the feminist perspective has made a major contribution to explaining why child abuse happens. It has provided an additional dimension to the long-running debate about whether psychological or sociological factors, such as emotional deprivation or class and poverty, lie at the root of child abuse and has reframed some of the important issues.

Initially, the aim of the feminist perspective was to reinforce the message that, in the case of sexual abuse, men were, almost exclusively, the perpetrators and needed to accept responsibility for their actions. Sexual abuse was seen from this perspective as an abuse of male power over largely female children, a state of affairs brought about and maintained by patriarchal power relations at an institutional level. This power imbalance was seen not only as an explanation of why sexual abuse happened, but also as a major factor in the way in which such abuse was responded to, and as responsible for the consequences that followed from it. Examples of these effects were the fact that abused children were often blamed for the abuse, as were mothers, and the strong resistance to the opening up of the problem from men who found the subject matter threatening to their own values. Generally, this line of argument has been negatively perceived and often seen as irrelevant to direct practice. However, it has so far served its purpose of raising awareness and exposing the issues.[3]

There are now other important messages emanating from the feminist perspective with more direct implications for practice as well as understanding. One of these is the view that forms of gender socialization play a significant part in the aetiology of child abuse and that there is, therefore, a pressing need to address this issue in child protection policy and practice. As far as sexual abuse of children is concerned, it is argued that the way in which males are socialized both generally, i.e. with the belief that strength lies in coping with one's own emotions, and particularly sexually (see Coveney *et al.* 1984), i.e. with the expectation that they have stronger sexual needs than women and must be assertive and take control, creates the climate in which such abuse can happen.

As was stressed in Chapter 5, the picture seems to be somewhat different with regard to physical abuse because of the fact that men and women are, according to known statistics, equally likely to abuse children. The feminist perspective does not deny that women are violent to children, but emphasizes how gender socialization and beliefs about motherhood tend to implicate them more than is their due. More importantly, these factors help to create conditions that give male abusers the opportunity to evade responsibility for their actions. There are clear implications of this line of thought for both child protection practitioners and child abuse researchers.

First and foremost, the term 'parent' should not be synonymous with 'mother'. There is a need to separate out the interests of parents. The term 'parents' suggests shared values, concerns and interests. This may simply not be the case and is an assumption that needs testing out.

Second, social workers and researchers must make greater efforts to include men in their practice and studies. In both sexual abuse and physical abuse work, men are generally not the focus of attention. Male sexual abusers are coming into the frame more than before. However, there still seems to be little focus on men who are physically violent towards children. If, as the feminist perspective argues, the roots of violence to both children and women lie in male socialization, then the logical target for change is being systematically missed. Reference has been repeatedly made throughout the previous chapters to the way in which research projects, particularly in the field of physical abuse, can also be gender-blind in their approach. In much research, as in practice, the focus has been on female parents because they are more visible and available in that they are more likely to attend family centres and clinics with their children and, in many cases, are the sole adult providing constant care.

Third, there is a need for male and female child protection practitioners to examine their own socialization experiences and the impact that they have on the way in which they construe and respond to child abuse work. In Cleveland, for instance, it has been convincingly argued that a clash in perspective between a male-dominated police force and two determined, strong women, Marietta Higgs and Sue Richardson, was a major factor in the prolongation of the crisis there (Campbell 1988). According to this account, these two women felt justified in taking a lead role in a problematic area in which they considered themselves to have particular expertise. The police, threatened by the issue of child sexual abuse anyway, found it hard to accept a role that was subordinate to women and, therefore, pathologized their approach.

There is a need for much greater recognition of the fact that female health and welfare practitioners are far more likely as a result of their own socialization experiences to have greater awareness than their male counterparts of the way in which women are subjected to sexual oppression. This in turn is likely to result in greater potential for empathy and, therefore, makes women more likely as a whole to be more effective practitioners in such cases. This is generally recognized in social services departments and other involved agencies. However, it is important that this does not result in sexual abuse work becoming woman's work alone. If this happens, then agencies are mirroring what happens in the wider society and reinforcing beliefs and behaviours that seem to lie at the heart of the problem.

There is a need for more official recognition of this line of thought. For instance, the Cleveland report itself makes no mention of the part played by gender socialization in the conflict between professionals there. The overview of recent inquiry reports (DoH 1991b) comments on the lack of reference to gender issues in any of the reports between 1980 and 1989.

The feminist perspective should be seen as having an important positive part to play in child protection work. It highlights major deficiencies in current practice and thinking that have persisted because the male perspective has been dominant. Close examination of all mainstream areas of work from the feminist perspective offers new and positive possibilities for intervention.

Balancing the rights of parents and the needs of children in child protection practice

Achieving what is considered to be a reasonable balance between parents' rights and the need to provide protection for children has, as was seen in

Chapter 3, been a perennial problem for the state throughout the history of child abuse prevention. The state is highly ambivalent about its role with regard to child–parent relationships (see Donzelot 1980) and this ambivalence is highlighted when things go wrong within families. Essentially, parents are considered to have overarching responsibilities for the care and upbringing of their children, and within certain parameters formally required by the state, such as the need to ensure that children attend school, they also have considerable powers. Children have few independent rights until they reach the age of 16. The prevailing view is that parents have the right to make important decisions on behalf of their children and that this right is only forfeitable if they fail to carry out their duties towards them in an acceptable way. Even then, the state is wary of intervention because of its commitment to the family as a form of socialization. Indeed, its child care policy is geared to and dependent on the maintenance of the two-parent family. This is reflected in the fact that alternatives to the family, such as foster care and residential services for children, are generally poorly resourced and stigmatized.

On the one hand, therefore, the state is keen to ensure that parents should not be discouraged from carrying out their socializing role by being too heavily penalized when things go wrong. On the other hand, it cannot tolerate serious maltreatment of children. Thus agencies such as social services departments and the NSPCC are empowered to remove the rights of parents, but only as a last resort.[4]

It is of vital importance that health and welfare practitioners have an awareness of the complex nature of the politics of intervention into family life. Whereas in theory the powers that agencies such as social services departments and the NSPCC have invested in them are unequivocal and no direct mention is made of paying due regard to the rights of parents in the process, in practice, for the reasons outlined above, the rights of parents have always been major considerations in decisions made 'in the best interests of the child'. The expectation placed on social workers and others is that they will get the balance right. Their task is to calculate the risks involved for children in each situation referred to them and balance this against what seems fair to parents. They must do this in the light of legal rules, community values and resource factors.

Judging from recent history, social workers have been seen, at least in the public eye, to have failed to maintain the right sort of balance. In physical abuse cases, such as that of Jasmine Beckford, they have been seen to lean too heavily towards consideration of parents' rights. In sexual abuse cases such as those investigated in Cleveland and the Orkneys, social workers have been seen to be acting overzealously on behalf of children.

The 1989 Children Act is the latest attempt to tackle the problems of getting the balance right. On the one hand, it has widened powers to take control of a child about whom there is serious concern and whose parents are being uncooperative. It has increased the range of cases in which a guardian *ad litem* will be appointed to act specifically on behalf of the child. It has also empowered state agencies to proceed against parents where they suspect that a child will be subjected to significant harm in the future, whereas the previous legislation required abuse to be happening in the present and strictly limited intervention into potential abuse to certain specific situations.[5] On the other hand, the rights of parents to challenge such decisions have been expanded. They have been given full party rights in care proceedings and the right to appeal against emergency protection orders. Agencies have been placed under considerable pressure to clarify the reasons for their actions. Other shifts towards giving greater weight to parents' rights are to be found in the recent *Working Together* guidelines (DoH 1991b), particularly with respect to parental participation at case conferences.

The new Children Act has been seen by some as a children's charter and by others as a bill of rights for parents. In fact it is a bit of both and this is indicative of a continuation of the perennial ambivalence of the state about intervention into parent–child relationships. The 1989 Act provides no radical rethink of the problem of child protection. If anything, it makes the balancing act between preserving the rights of parents and protecting children rather more complex and difficult to achieve than before.

Health and welfare practitioners must, therefore, continue to operate in a Janus-like way with one eye on the parents and one on the child. This is a reality that must be lived with pending wider social changes, such as the allocation of more rights of independence to children. Society should also acknowledge this task and the difficulty of getting it right.

The need to develop an anti-racist approach to child protection work

A major issue that has not to date received much attention but is likely to loom large in the future is that of how the child protection system can respond adequately to the needs of children at risk in black families. There is very little information about how child protection workers are currently responding in these situations. Some early accounts of child care intervention into black families were paternalistic and judgemental in tone and suggested that black children were more likely to be deemed at risk than white children and therefore more likely to be taken into care (Fitzherbert 1967). More recent accounts have pointed to greater tentativeness about intervening in black families where there are concerns about child care (Stubbs 1989). This is borne out to some extent in recent inquiry reports (Beckford, Henry) which have intimated that social workers have overcompensated for the structural disadvantages experienced by black families in our society to the detriment of the needs of children within them. The vital issues seem to be the need to respond sensitively and in an anti-racist way to black parents without overlooking the fact that their children might be at risk and in need of protection.

As far as possible, the approach required seems to be very similar to that needed for good work with white families, with the additional awareness of the racism that many black people experience both as a result of general structural disadvantage (see Brown 1984) and in their contact with agencies such as social services departments, most of which are largely controlled by white managers and geared to the needs of a white clientele (Rooney 1987). White workers can make mistakes (a) as a result of their ignorance of cultural differences, i.e. having no awareness of the impact of culture on child-rearing practices, and (b) as a result of making assumptions based on cultural stereotypes. White professionals working with black families where abuse is suspected should be able to consult with advisers from the same cultural background as the client and should have access to interpreters where necessary. Attempts should be made to have at least one black professional at a case conference involving a black family. Chairpersons of conferences need particular awareness of an anti-racist perspective and must be able to check racist assumptions in this setting.

Following the adoption of measures such as these to guard against racial bias, it is important to be clear in one's mind that steps may well have to be taken to remove black children from their parents for their protection. Anti-racism is about providing services that are positively sensitive to the needs of black people, including their children, and as with white families these needs may well be in conflict.

This type of thinking must be applied to all aspects of child protection work, not just initial investigations. Thus, therapeutic intervention and the provision of facilities such as day nurseries and family centres need to share an anti-racist perspective and take as much action as possible to offset alienation of black families. Child protection work provides a particular challenge in this aspect because it is an activity that is perceived as questioning the quality of care being provided for children. It therefore generates a good deal of hostility and conflict that needs to be carefully worked through. Race and culture issues complicate matters even further. The adoption of comprehensive and constructive anti-racist policies by agencies can provide a background from which this difficult area of work can be conducted positively and with greater confidence.

The strengths and weaknesses of inter-professional cooperation as a strategy for dealing with child abuse

All the public inquiry reports published since 1974 have pointed to inter-professional communication and cooperation as vital ingredients in successful child protection work, and in all the cases inquired into major deficiences have been found in this respect. The Maria Colwell report pinpointed this issue. The child protection system that was established following this inquiry was based on procedures aimed at maximizing cooperation between agencies, and this inter-disciplinary philosophy has persisted up until now. Despite the formalization of such procedures, however, problems have continued to exist:

A lesson to be learned from the 1980s is that inter-agency working is not easy, and not self evidently useful. This is not to say that an individual agency can go it alone, but separate viewpoints and confusion of roles, as well as the availability of multiple pathways for communication, are a recipe for muddle. (DoH 1991b: 41)

Stevenson (1989) analyses some of the reasons for this state of affairs and points to three possible reasons.

First, there are problems with the structural organization of child protection work. Area Child Protection Committees (ACPCs), which are appointed to coordinate the input of agencies, are poorly resourced, have limited powers with regard to influencing the parent bodies of their constituent members and have an unrealistically wide range of functions. A major problem lies in the fact that individual agencies can still carry out their statutory functions regardless of recommendations from ACPCs. Thus, in Cleveland, the various agencies interpreted their roles and duties for themselves and went their own ways regardless of ACPC guidelines. The Kimberley Carlile report defined the child protection system as 'a puppet with no-one to pull the strings' (p. 142).

Second, different professional groupings find it very difficult to work cooperatively towards a common goal. There are a variety of reasons for this, such as the lack of inter-professional contact during training, the fact that different professions have different functions, goals and philosophies, different statuses and pay, and different levels of responsibility for and commitment to the child protection system.

The third impediment to better inter-professional cooperation is the fact that there can be major differences in the views that individuals have about what should or should not be done about different children at risk regardless of their professional roles and responsibilities. Individuals bring their own experiences of family life to case conferences, their own views of what constitutes adequate care of children and their own experience of other cases where intervention of a certain kind has either proved successful or not. Factors such as these can exacerbate the difficulties of cooperation already considered.

None of these problems is insurmountable and there are signs of improved working together in many areas. Much depends on individuals developing trust and respecting each other's role requirements by working together on a series of cases and by taking part in shared training. Unfortunately this is not always possible. Continuity can be hampered by high staff turnover. If staff do not specialize, they may come into contact with each other only rarely and on-the-job training is both expensive and time-consuming.

The important question to be asked is whether the type of inter-professional coordination that we currently rely on is the best way to respond to child abuse, given the difficulties outlined above. Alternative approaches have received some consideration. The Kimberley Carlile report considered that there was a pressing need for change and outlined a range of proposals, including the setting up of permanent inter-disciplinary teams. It concluded that a thorough review of organizational structures was required:

Whatever the way forward . . . the issues should not be avoided on the grounds of their scale and complexity if the safety of children demands that they should be addressed. . . . We should not demand that individuals from the relevant professions continue striving to improve their performance, and continue bearing the responsibility for their work unless we are satisfied they are working within an overall framework that maximises their skills. (Carlile 1987: 143)

This recommendation has not been acted upon.

A second more modest proposal came from the Cleveland report, namely that *ad hoc* inter-disciplinary Special Assessment Teams should be set up to assess problematic child sexual abuse allegations. These should consist of panels of medical, police and social services personnel with sufficient authority to institute preliminary investigations and to decide whether there is enough reason to proceed with a full investigation. Very few authorities have formally adopted this approach. However, as pointed out in Chapter 8, the notion of holding preliminary meetings or strategy discussions seems to be a widespread practice and is recommended in the recent *Working Together* guidelines (DoH 1991b).

Much time and effort is spent on getting professionals to cooperate over child protection investigations. Despite some of the advances and improvements referred to above, problems and difficulties continue to exist. There is a clear need for more research into the feasibility of different types of inter-professional cooperation in the field of child protection.

The future of the child protection system

Child protection work has developed over the past 15 years from being a relatively minor offshoot of general child care work to being a major aspect of the work of social services departments and of several large voluntary child care agencies. It takes up increasingly more time and resources of the health, education, police and probation services.

As was seen in Chapter 4, officially recognized abuse as measured by child abuse registration quadrupled in the second half of the 1980s. Much of this expansion was in areas of abuse that had either been newly discovered, such as sexual and emotional abuse, or redefined as abusive, such as neglect. In addition, there was a massive increase in the numbers of children on registers because of serious, but undefined, concerns on the part of involved professionals. By 1991, over 40,000 children were on registers, with approximately 20,000 being registered each year and 20,000 de-registered. There are few signs of a slowdown in the number of cases being referred. New concerns are constantly being brought to the fore, such as abuse of children in boarding schools and residential homes, abuse of disabled children etc. This broadening of focus represents a major shift from the original concern for babies and young children being physically injured by their parents.

All agencies have invested considerable resources in child protection work. Social services departments have a variety of organizational responses. Some employ specialist teams. Some retain general child care teams in name, but in practice child protection work takes up the bulk of time. Many intake teams in social services departments spend much of their time dealing with child protection investigations. Nearly all social services departments employ child protection coordinators to chair conferences, manage the administration of the system, including registers, and service Area Child Protection Committees. Considerable secretarial support is required for administering the system and maintaining communication links within and between agencies. Police departments are devoting more time and resources to child protection work, including specialist teams in some areas, interviewing suites and joint training initiatives. Some education departments employ child protection advisers. Every school is expected to have a teacher with designated responsibility for dealing with child protection issues. Many health departments employ nursing managers with a remit to oversee all child protection work. Many major hospitals provide specialist child protection services. This represents a major shift from the period in the early 1970s when the only agency with a specific remit and structure for dealing with what was then termed child neglect was the NSPCC.

How effective this response has been is a question that has not been subjected to any systematic research. Any attempt to assess the current situation has, therefore, to be an impressionistic one. Most cases referred into the child protection system are now subjected to much closer initial scrutiny than those referred in the previous era, when there was greater reliance on the judgement of individual workers and their own initiative in working with other agencies. Most assessments of situations and decisions about intervention, planning and the allocation of resources are now subject to inter-disciplinary airing and backed by the authority of middle-level managers. The focus is much more on systematic sifting of cases to decide on risk and to ensure that the risk is managed by an accountable person, usually a social worker. In addition there is much more attention being paid to a more open approach to parents and to involving them more in the decision-making process.

The benefits of this approach are that plans are shared and agreed on by all agency workers, and in some cases parents, responsibility is clearly allocated and at a later date cases are reviewed. Cooperation between agencies is built in right at the start of the intervention so that in theory the sorts of difficulties highlighted by inquiries in the past regarding poor inter-agency communication should not exist. The effect produced is more one of a team approach that can enhance confidence.

One weakness lies in the fact that decisions are often made by those who are not responsible for resource allocation. Thus plans may be agreed, but the resources required to implement them, such as personnel time, a day centre place or suitable accommodation for a family, may not be available.

Second, there is little room for discretion or flexibility in such a system, either with regard to what cases should be put into it or with regard to changing plans without case conference approval (see Corby 1987: 135;

Finkelhor and Zellman 1991). This can lead to rigid implementation of plans, with the emphasis on authority rather than on responsiveness to the client and the changing situation.

An overriding problem is whether the system that now exists can cope with the demands placed upon it. As was seen in Chapter 4, the American system is seen by some to be so overloaded that while cases are all formally processed and plans are formulated, in many cases they are not put into action (Krugman 1991). Thus the system gives the impression of dealing with cases, but the actual input is limited. These and other problems seem to exist in the British system as well.[6] Pressure of cases can result in delayed conferences, low levels of attendance and long gaps between conferences and the sending out of minutes. There is a danger of reduced direct input into cases because of the demands placed on professionals' time by the requirements of the system. There is also the danger of routinized managerial responses taking over from professional on-the-spot assessment of situations. To what extent these problems and dangers exist is not fully known and remains an issue for research.

There is a pressing need for more systematic evaluation of child protection work in Britain. Steps should be taken to analyse the process of cases into and through the system and there needs to be proper evaluation of case outcomes. As was mentioned in Chapter 8, there is also very little research into consumer views, those of mothers, fathers and children. We need to know more about what professionals working within the child protection system think of it. Currently available evidence is impressionistic. Social workers who have a key function in the system seem to have mixed feelings about the way in which it operates. On the one hand, they would like to work with a greater degree of discretion. On the other, they welcome the support and back-up the system provides, particularly in the light of criticism of individual workers for their mistakes in the past (see Corby 1987). There is little evidence about other professionals' views. Medical doctors in Britain have been critical of case conferences for being over-bureaucratic, long-winded and time-consuming. There is very little information on a police perspective or that of health, school and probation personnel. Other important questions requiring answers are: what demands are likely to be made of the system in the future, what resources will be needed to meet these demands and how can they best be deployed?

The immediate future of the child protection system is laid out in *Working Together under the Children Act 1989* (DoH 1991b). Little change is envisaged in terms of the way the system will operate. The main function of this document is to tie up the procedures to fit in with the requirements of the new act and to incorporate lessons learned from mistakes in investigations into organized abuse. This will probably prove inadequate to the problems of child protection in the 1990s. A broad research-based review of the whole child protection system, with questions such as those raised above as its focus, is needed to assess the overall impact of child protection work. Such a review would provide a more solid foundation for future developments in this field.

Concluding comments

In the introduction to this book, my stated aim was to provide for those involved in working in the child protection field a critical review of as broad a child abuse knowledge base as possible. I had in mind the notion of providing such a knowledge base for the relatively autonomous practitioner working within the child protection system. It seemed to me that current practice in this field was more concerned with systems of managing child abuse and, to a lesser extent, intervention methods than with applying knowledge derived from research, and that the knowledge base being used in practice was extremely limited.

Some of the knowledge areas covered do not seem to have immediate application. Knowledge of the response to child mistreatment through the ages, the politics of the development of the current child protection system, the problems associated with defining abuse and the extent of the problem do not provide immediate answers to pressing problems of practice. However, I hold to the value belief that practitioners who are aware of the moral and political parameters of child protection work are likely to prove more effective (provided they have practice skills as well) than those who do not have this perspective. Similarly, a broad theoretical understanding of why abuse happens is likely to enhance child protection practice. This of course remains to be empirically tested and flies in the face of in vogue views that demonstration of competence in practice is the sole issue.

Other knowledge areas reviewed (those seeking to find out who abuses whom, and with what consequences) seem to be more closely related to the concerns of practice. While much of this research appears to have direct relevance, I have tried to point out some of the weaknesses and the problems associated with applying it to practice as well as its strengths.

In this and the previous chapter, attention has focused on practice research and policy issues. The result may well be that what on the face of it seems a simple issue, the mistreatment of children, comes across as a complex and at times confusing problem without the possibility of easy resolution. If that is the case, then I offer no apologies. My belief is that an attempt to understand these complexities is a necessary requirement for effective child protection work.

Appendix: Child protection checklists

Greenland's (1987: 185) high-risk checklist includes the following items:

For parents
1 Previously abused/neglected as a child.
2 Age 20 years or less at the birth of first child.
3 Single-parent/separated; partner not biological parent.
4 History of abuse/neglect or deprivation.
5 Socially isolated – frequent moves – poor housing.
6 Poverty – unemployed/unskilled worker; inadequate education.
7 Abuses alcohol and/or drugs.
8 History of criminally assaultive behaviour and/or suicide attempts.
9 Pregnant – post partum – or chronic illness.

For children
1 Was previously abused or neglected.
2 Under 5 years of age at the time of abuse or neglect.
3 Premature or low birth-weight.
4 Now underweight.
5 Birth defect – chronic illness – developmental lag.
6 Prolonged separation from mother.
7 Cries frequently – difficult to comfort.
8 Difficulties in feeding and elimination.
9 Adopted, foster- or step-child.

Browne and Saqi's (1988: 68) checklist includes the following items:

1 Parent indifferent, intolerant or overanxious towards child.
2 History of family violence.
3 Socio-economic problems such as unemployment.
4 Infant premature, low birth weight.

5 Parent abused or neglected as a child.
6 Stepparent or cohabitee present.
7 Single or separated parent.
8 Mother less than 21 years old at the time of birth.
9 History of mental illness, drug or alcohol addiction.
10 Infant separated from mother for greater than 24 hours post-delivery.
11 Infant mentally or physically handicapped.
12 Less than 18 months between birth of children.

It is interesting to consider these items in the light of the research findings set out in Chapter 5.

Notes

2 Childhood, child abuse and history

1 O'Hagan (1989: 21) vehemently defends a position that ignores history: 'such erudite learning, is, quite frankly, irrelevant'.

2 There are some British histories of social work. Younghusband (1978) deals with the period from 1950 to 1975. Yelloly (1980) looks at the influence of psycho-analysis on social work practice from the 1930s onwards. The most comprehensive studies are those by Woodroofe (1962) and Seed (1973).

3 See Ferguson (1990 121–2) for a discussion of this issue.

4 The best example of this kind of approach in the child protection field is the work of Linda Gordon (1989), which will be considered in more detail in Chapter 3.

5 Mackie and Taylor (1990: 198–9, 402–3) provide some useful tables outlining the legal rights and responsibilites of young people at the ages of 16 and 18.

6 Frost and Stein (1989: 10–16) provide a good thoughtful critique of Aries's work.

7 See Hunt (1970), Hoyles (1979), Thane (1981), Pollock (1983), Macfarlane (1979), Boswell (1988), Wilson (1984) and Hanawalt (1977).

8 See Shorter (1976), Stone (1977), Plumb (1975), De Mause (1976) and Badinter (1981).

9 See Macfarlane (1970: 203): 'This day a quarter past two in the afternoone my Mary fell asleepe in the Lord, her soule past into that rest where the body of Jesus, and the soules of the saints are, shee was: 8 yeares and 45 dayes old when shee dyed, my soule had aboundant cause to blesse god for her, who was our first fruites, and those god would have offered to him, and this I freely re-signed up to him (,) it was a pretious child, a bundle of myrrhe, a bundle of sweetnes, shee was a child of ten thousand, full of wisedome, woman-like grav-ity, knowledge, sweet expr[essions of god, apt in her learning,] tender hearted and loving, an [obed]ient child [to us.] it was free from [the rudenesse of] litle children, it was to us as a boxe of sweet ointment, which now its broken smells more deliciously than it did before, Lord I rejoyce I had such a present for thee, it was patient in the sicknesse, thankefull to admiracion; it lived desired and dyed lamented, thy memory is and wille bee sweete unto mee' (26 May 1650).

10 Davin's account (1990) of the way in which this combination of factors led to coercive, class-blind philanthropy is particularly interesting.
11 It should be noted that Boswell has been criticized by some historians for being over-optimistic about the fate of abandoned children (see Tilly *et al.* 1992).
12 This statement, while demonstrating public concern about child sexual abuse, also shows that there was probably a hierarchy of concerns. No mention is made of female children and those of non-citizen status.
13 Lafontaine (1990: 210) drawing from anthropological work, lends some support to such a view with regard to sexual abuse.

3 A recent political history of child abuse and neglect

1 The campaigns created by Kempe in the USA (see later) and the fund-raising practices of the NSPCC are examples of this process.
2 See Dingwall *et al.* (1984: 214).
3 See Rose (1986: Chapter 11).
4 It would be wrong, however, to suggest that there was no relevant legislation at all. The 1868 Poor Law Act made wilful neglect by a parent of a child under 14 that threatened or resulted in serious injury an offence. The weakness of this law was that only Poor Law officials were empowered to bring cases of this kind to court and they very rarely did so. The 1861 Offences Against the Person Act could also be used to prosecute parents for assaults on their children, but no particular agency was mandated to report or seek out such abuse.
5 Behlmer (1982: 172) shows that 58 per cent of the 23,124 cases reported to the NSPCC in 1896–7 emanated from the general public.
6 Between 1908 and 1920, the number of recorded cases of incest rose from a yearly average of 24 to 57. This average gradually increased to 101 by the beginning of the Second World War. By 1950, the average had increased to 237. Between then and 1985 the annual number of cases fluctuated between a low of 230 to a high of 334. The annual figures for 1985, 1986 and 1987 show a marked increase: 444, 511 and 516 (Home Office Criminal Statistics).
7 The major legislative change of this period was the 1933 Children and Young Persons Act, which followed in the tradition of previous legislation by extending the range of prosecutable offences against children. It also blurred distinctions between neglected children and young offenders by such measures as the creation of approved schools for all who came into these two categories (before this they had attended separate institutions). By 1946, when the Curtis Committee reported, this type of thinking was well established: 'According to the evidence of the Home Office, it is often an accident whether a child is before the court for an offence or as a neglected child, and it is accordingly appropriate that the same methods of treatment be equally available.'
8 See pp. 209–10, which provide an extract of an NSPCC inspector's discovery of and response to a child sexual abuse case. The case is undated, but as the children involved were committed to industrial schools, it must have been before the implementation of the 1933 Children and Young Persons Act. The case involved a 12-year-old girl, her sister, 11, and her brother, 9. Their mother was dead and they were living with their father and a 46-year-old male lodger. It was revealed that the two girls slept in the same bed as the lodger. The inspector's records described the children as being dirty and neglected. A medical examination was arranged by the inspector. 'This proved that the girl aged 12 had been interfered with.' The father

and the lodger were prosecuted. The father, a first-time offender, received a light sentence, the lodger 18 months' hard labour. The children, as mentioned above, were committed to industrial schools. The tenor of the report is very factual. The response to this case comes across as insensitive by our standards but unequivocally child protective.

9 This does not mean that the approach at the ground level was not authoritative and intrusive (see Allen and Morton 1961: Chapter 6).

10 See Greenland (1958) and Allen and Morton (1961: 89–93).

11 Nelson (1984) charts the development of child abuse as a social problem in the USA and shows how, from a topic that hardly raised a flicker of concern in the 1950s, it came to figure as a prominent part of Walter Mondale's presidential campaign in 1974.

12 Parton (1985: 61) points out that the unit produced 17 articles in professional journals between 1969 and 1973.

13 The number of place of safety orders doubled in the period after the publication of the Maria Colwell report. In March 1974 there were 353 children in care on place of safety orders. In March 1975 there were 596 and in March 1976 there were 759. Between 1977 and 1985, the annual number of place of safety orders remained at roughly the same level, ranging between a low of 5207 per year to a high of 6613. However, Dingwall and Eekelaar (1984) argue that the numbers of children committed to care as a result of abuse and neglect did not increase between 1970 and 1985. Also there was no major increase in the prosecution of parents for offences against children during this time (see Martin 1978: 209).

14 Cyril Greenland's testimony was influential in this respect. His views are elaborated in his book *Preventing CAN Deaths* (1987) and are further considered in Chapters 5 and 8. See Appendix.

15 See note 13 for the annual number of place of safety orders between 1977 and 1985. In 1986, they rose to 7191 and in 1987 to 8055.

16 See Armstrong (1978), Brady (1979), Angelou (1983). Bagley and King (1990: 1–24) give a good overview of the public impact of personal accounts of sexual abuse.

17 See Cleveland (1988: para. 4.80, 64). A ten-year-old girl and her two siblings were examined with their mother's consent by Dr Higgs in the hospital. Their father removed them. They were subsequently brought into police custody under place of safety orders and examined by a police surgeon, Dr Beeby. His diagnosis conflicted with that of Dr Higgs, who re-examined the children. The following day they were re-examined by Dr Irvine, another police surgeon. The report adds that the children 'were later examined by three more doctors'.

18 Children Act 1989, section 44(7).

19 Children Act 1989, schedule 2 para. 5.

20 Lowe (1989) demonstrates this rate of increase. In 1971 there were 622 originating summons. By 1981 there were 1903 and in 1987 there were 3605. The bulk of these increases is accounted for by local authority applications.

21 For the Nottingham case see *The Times*, 30 November 1990. For Rochdale see *The Times*, 9 August 1990, and leader article, 15 September 1990. For the Orkneys see *The Times*, 5 January 1991.

4 Defining and measuring the extent of child abuse

1 Stephanie Fox (Fox 1990) was known by the health and welfare authorities to have suffered minor bruising on 30 occasions before she died as a result of a violent

outburst by her father. They had previously declined to remove Stephanie, probably because their expectations of the family were very low and it was felt that such bruising (largely perceived to be the result of careless supervision of the child rather than of physical mistreatment) was not remarkable given the background of the Fox family. The Lester Chapman case (Chapman 1979) shows a similar rather resigned acceptance of low standards of care.

In Tyra Henry's case (Henry 1987), the social worker made assumptions about Caribbean culture that placed heavy expectations on this child's grandmother to provide care and protection for her. West Indian grandmothers were stereotypically considered to be the linch-pins of the family as far as child care was concerned. In Beatrice Henry's case, nothing could have been further from the truth. She had experienced the death of her husband and the severe mistreatment of her grandson. She was a lone parent dealing with the problems of her own three children, was inadequately housed and had multiple debts. As events proved, she was completely unable to protect Tyra.

2 There is something of a contradiction here in that, despite the general phrasing used to define child abuse in legal proceedings, lawyers are concerned that there should be clear and definite proof of abuse in court.

3 The following two vignettes, with consequences in parentheses, are taken from Giovannoni and Becerra's study and give a flavour of the general approach used: 'The parents regularly left their child alone outside the house during the day until almost dark (neighbours have spotted the child wandering five blocks from home).' 'The parents banged the child against the wall while shaking him by the shoulders (the child suffered a concussion).'

4 Section 31(2) of the 1989 Children Act states: 'A court may only make a care order or supervision order if it is satisfied –

(a) that the child concerned is suffering, or is likely to suffer, significant harm; and
(b) that the harm, or likelihood of harm, is attributable to –
   (i) the care given to the child, or likely to be given to him if the order were not made, not being what it would be reasonable to expect a parent to give to him; or
   (ii) the child's being beyond parental control.'

Section 31(9) states: ' "harm" means ill-treatment or the impairment of health or development; "development" means physical, intellectual, emotional, social or behavioural development; "ill-treatment" includes sexual abuse and forms of ill-treatment which are not physical.'

5 This failure to give an explanation of the demise of the 'grave concern' category is most surprising considering that it accounts for half the children on child protection registers. The provisional feedback to local authorities on register returns for the year ending 31 March 1991 merely states that the category will not be used for registrations after 14 October 1991 (the date of the implementation of the Children Act). While this move is to be welcomed, as it will force professionals to be more specific about their concerns, some explanation of the reasons for taking this course of action would also have been welcome.

6 See Baldwin and Oliver (1975), Smith (1975) and Greenland (1987). However, these are all retrospective studies. Although the vast majority of the severely ill-treated children they studied had had minor bruising at an earlier date, this does not mean that all children with minor bruising will be severely abused in the future.

7 See section 4.6 pp. 12–13.

8 Issues of this kind were highlighted in the Doreen Aston report (Aston 1989). Before Doreen's birth, her mother Christine Mason had had a child, Karl, who died aged 10 weeks. A post-mortem revealed that he had three fractured ribs and a subdural haemorrhage, but these injuries were not thought to have contributed to his death, which was finally recorded as a cot death (see p. 8, paras 11 and 12). The authors of the report felt that the cot death decision led social workers and others to overlook the fact that the child had been abused and, therefore, that subsequent children might be particularly at risk.

9 Polansky and colleagues argue in later works that there are common agreed standards of care. They developed what they termed a 'childhood level of living scale' (Polansky *et al.* 1978) and found that there was considerable agreement among lay people about what was neglectful (Polansky and Williams 1978). Polansky *et al.* (1983: 345) conclude from these previous studies that 'it appears there is such a thing as an American standard of minimal child care that is commonly held and that may be invoked in the definition of child neglect for legal and social work purposes.' Such ideas do not, however, seem to have influenced practice greatly.

10 Political factors may also play a part in this relative lack of urgency. Wolock and Horowitz (1984) argue that neglect of children is far more common than physical abuse in the USA, but receives far less attention. This 'neglect of neglect', as they term it, results from the fact that closer inspection of many children's lives would reveal the extent to which poverty contributes to neglect and this would create political embarrassments for governments.

11 Pages 69–74 of the Beckford inquiry report provide useful detailed material on the failure-to-thrive syndrome. At birth, Jasmine weighed 5 lb 11 oz. By four months, she had reached an average weight for a child of her age and, therefore, would have been expected to maintain this average growth throughout her early childhood. After ten months, Jasmine had slipped back and her weight was well below the average. It was below the third centile (i.e. Jasmine was among the 3 per cent most poorly developed of all children). At age 15 months Jasmine weighed 18 lb 6 oz, even further down in the third centile. At 20 months, when she experienced her first serious injury, she was still well down in the third centile. At the age of 27 months, after she had been in foster care for seven months, Jasmine had grown considerably and weighed 25 lb 5 oz (on the 25th centile). At this point she was returned to her mother and stepfather. She was not weighed again until her death 27 months later. She weighed 23 lb.

12 There is much current concern about the perceived extent of sexual abuse of children by adolescents. (see Chapter 5). There is some uncertainty as to whether such offenders should be seen as abusers or whether they should be responded to as in need of help themselves. Are such offenders sexually mature?

13 See Finkelhor *et al.* (1986: 66).

14 It is important to distinguish between the terms 'prevalence' and 'incidence'. Prevalence studies measure how many people in a given sample have experienced a particular phenomenon at least once over a particular period of time. Incidence studies measure the number of occurrences of a particular phenomenon in a given sample of people over a particular period of time. Thus, if a sample of 100 people were asked if they had been sexually abused at least once before the age of 15, and 20 said that they had, the prevalence rate of abuse of such children would be 20 per cent. If these 100 people were asked how often they had been sexually abused before the age of 15, the answer would probably be higher. They might report

abuse on 60 occasions. The incidence rate of abuse would then be 60 per 100 people over the first 15 years of their lives. Lafontaine (1990: Ch. 2) gives a fuller, very useful account of these and other issues relating to prevalence and incidence studies.

15 Those families with just one- and two-year-old children were omitted because one of the study's objectives was to measure sibling violence. How this affects the interpretation of the findings (i.e. are they an under- or over-estimate of the total) is unclear. In 1990–1, the registration rate for children physically abused in the first year of their lives was higher than for all the other age groupings.

16 It must be remembered that this rate covers 15 years of childhood but does not take into account the number of abuse incidents that a child may have experienced. The MORI Poll survey found that 63 per cent of those abused had been abused once, 23 per cent were subject to multiple abuse by the same person and 14 per cent subject to multiple abuse by a number of people. Estimating accurately the gap between officially responded to cases and the true number is, therefore, a highly problematic endeavour.

5 Who abuses whom

1 In the case of Wayne Brewer, who was killed by his stepfather, Nigel Briffett, his mother was heavily implicated. In a report written for court when Wayne was made the subject of a care order, the social worker commented on her as follows: 'Her inability to restrain her husband, together with the rather negative handling of the child, characterised by her unwillingness to readily handle him, and to generally care for and stimulate him, indicate that she has not really been able to accept responsibility for him' (Brewer 1977).

2 The views put forward on this subject in the Cleveland report are of interest. The term 'collusive mother' is not explicitly used. However, the implications are clear. 'Again quoting Professor Sir Martin Roth, "In many cases mothers play a role in the genesis of the sexual abuse of their daughters. They may be too physically ill or inadequate in personality to provide proper care and protection for their children. In other cases mothers elect the eldest or one of the oldest daughters to the role of 'child mother'. The girl in her early teens or even earlier is expected to take the responsibility for the caring of the younger children whose mothering role is allowed to slide into a sexual relationship with the father. This is tolerated with little or no protest. I refer to lack of protest of [sic] the part of the mother for a variety of reasons and the mother may in such cases deny what is happening. She conceals the truth from herself as well as others; the relationship continues and when the situation is brought to light it may be insisted by the mother that it had been unknown to her"' (Cleveland 1988: para. 29, 8).

3 Mattinson and Sinclair (1979) point to the lack of involvement of males by social workers in marital work! Corby (1987: 91) found that little work was done with fathers or male parent substitutes in child protection work. The Stephanie Fox inquiry commented on the fact that very little was known about her natural father, Stephen Fox. 'So far as Stephen Fox is concerned, he was, and is, as we shall see, a shadowy figure. We believe that it would have been very useful to know more of his wider family relationships, to bring him out of the shadows. This is not to suggest that pointers would necessarily have emerged towards the final appalling violence. We do, however, believe that if, as surely must be the case, the social workers wanted to facilitate change in the behaviour of these parents, they had to

understand more about it' (Fox 1990: para 4.9, 24). Cultural factors account for part of this pattern of intervention in that males (particularly in the lower classes) are not normally expected to be closely involved in child care matters. In female-headed lone-parent families, men's involvement with children and family matters is probably even more peripheral. However, there does seem to be a tendency for social workers and other professionals (e.g. health visitors) to fall too readily into working exclusively with females in families because of assumptions about their mothering role and also because of their availability.

4 That women do physically abuse children is not being denied. For a useful case study of women who have fatally abused their children see Korbin (1989).

5 Nevertheless, Greenland (1987: 185) incorporates the category 'age 20 or less at birth of first child' in his high-risk checklist (see Appendix).

6 This trend may be being reversed somewhat by anti-racist training and policy implementation. However, these innovations are somewhat patchy and vary considerably from region to region.

7 This is a problematic issue because of the degree of secrecy that shrouds intra-familial child sexual abuse and the fact that we cannot know for certain whether or not someone who appears to have focused his abuse on one child has offended against other children or whether he might do so in the future.

8 In 1989, 26 per cent of all live births were outside marriage. In 1987 lone-parent families constituted 14 per cent of all families with dependent children (over 900,000 in all). However, although the numbers of such families rose dramatically throughout the 1970s, they have remained stable throughout the 1980s. In 1989, there were 153,000 divorces (decrees absolute) involving 148,000 children under the age of 16. Again these figures have remained stable throughout the 1980s after a steep increase in the previous decade. However, the number of under-four year olds involved in divorces has risen by 20 per cent in the 1980s (figures from the OPCS General Household Survey 1987, and from OPCS marriage statistics for 1989).

9 Christine Mason, the mother of Doreen Aston, was known to have been depressed in October 1985, seven months before Doreen was born. In January 1985, her ten-week-old son, Karl, had died in suspicious circumstances (see Chapter 4, note 8). Nine months later Christine was said to be continuing 'to give cause for concern as she was carrying the ashes of her dead child around with her' (Aston 1989: Chapter 2, para. 15, 9). There is no further reference to depression or grief reaction in the report.

Beatrice Henry, Tyra Henry's grandmother, on whom great reliance was placed by Lambeth Social Services Department for her protection, had experienced the death of her husband and the maiming and loss of her grandson in 1982 (she had also previously suffered the death of her own son). The inquiry report points out that there was 'not a line in the contemporary records and not a line in the evidence given to us which recognises that by the time of Tyra's birth, Beatrice Henry was struggling with private grief along with the difficulties of her daily life' (Henry 1987: 112). The inquiry panel recommended that social workers receive training in this area and be directed to devote attention to such matters in future.

The Koseda inquiry (Koseda 1986) noted that the cohabitation of Heidi Koseda's mother, Rosemary, with Nicholas Price 'seems to have been the start of a marked deterioration in her mental state and way of life, which culminated in serious mental illness after the discovery of Heidi's body early in 1985' (para. 1.1).

10 These other factors (except for marital or partner problems) are all included in Greenland's high-risk checklist for parents (see Appendix).

11 In the cases of Tyra Henry (Henry 1987) and Darryn Clarke (Clarke 1979) there do not seem to have been obvious signs of conflict. However, very little information seems to come to light about the relationships of parents or parent substitutes in public inquiry reports. Both Andrew Neil and Charles Courtney, who were convicted for the killing of these children, had histories of violence. The lack of conflict in their relationships with these children's mothers may have been the result of their being totally dominating and controlling figures.

12 See page 122 of the Beckford report for comments about lack of attention paid by welfare workers to the stresses of pregnancy.

13 See Dingwall (1989). These issues will be further discussed in Chapter 8.

14 Doreen Aston, Stephanie Fox and Tyra Henry and their families were all under financial and material stress at the times of their births and in their early childhoods. This was particularly apparent in the case of Stephanie Fox. The Fox family, consisting of mother, father, Stephanie aged two, and twins, aged eight months, were eventually provided with accommodation on the nineteenth floor of a tower block. They suffered chronic financial problems, despite help being given by social workers under section 1 of the 1980 Child Care Act. The report, while acknowledging this help, comments: 'Despite the desperate circumstances of families in crisis of this kind, we believe that section 1 financial help should be used whenever possible as part of a consistent plan to promote the well-being of children in families, rather than as a routine response to crisis calls for help' (Fox 1990: 72). It remains to be seen whether section 17 and Schedule 2 of the 1989 Children Act, which deal with material aid, will be implemented in this constructive way.

15 Stephen Menheniott was 19½ years old when he died as a result of multiple injuries inflicted   him over a long period of time by his father. Because of his age, this case could be seen to be the murder of a young adult, but this judgement would belie the true nature of Stephen's abuse. The events of his life and death all carry the hallmarks of a case of child abuse. His father, Thomas Menheniott, was brought up in public care institutions. Nearly all his eight children had had long spells in care. He had convictions for neglect and ill-treatment of his children and had been acquitted after being charged with incest. Stephen was a rather pathetic, immature young man. He had spent the bulk of his life in residential care attending schools for the maladjusted and had developed few lasting relationships. He was returned to his father's 'care' at the age of 15½. He was clearly exposed to prolonged physical abuse and intimidation.

6 The causation of child abuse

1 There has been increasing emphasis throughout the 1980s on the 'management' of child abuse by developing systems to ensure that cases are properly identified, registered and monitored. There has been a concomitant shift away from trying to assess the reasons for abuse happening and using this assessment as the basis for the treatment of the problem (see Corby 1987; Horne 1990). This has been a direct result of the heavy criticism that professionals in the child protection field (especially social workers) have been subjected to from public inquiries into child deaths by abuse. It also reflects the influence of systems-based managerial approaches, which have gained more and more acceptance generally in the welfare field (Davies 1981).

2 Sociobiology emerged as an identifiable discipline in the 1970s (Wilson 1975). It is essentially a new form of social Darwinism, but is more subtly argued than its

predecessor. Sociobiologists' main proposition is that social sciences have been too narrow in their interpretations of human behaviour, associating it almost exclusively with cultural and social influences. In this process, the fact that humans are, like any other form of living species, biologically driven, has been forgotten. From a sociobiological perspective, biological forces, particularly gene preservation, are paramount influences on behaviour (Dawkins 1976). Social scientists have responded by arguing that sociobiology has theoretical flaws and adverse political effects, such as the potential for encouraging racism, sexism and far right views such as eugenics (Sahlins 1977; Montagu 1980). In many ways, this conflict is part of the continuing nature–nurture debate which has existed formally since the emergence of the social sciences in the eighteenth century.

3 For a mainstream analysis see Stafford-Clark (1965), Fancher (1973) and Jahoda (1977). Kline (1981) provides details of empirical studies into Freudian theory. Feminist critiques of Freudian theory are to be found in Mitchell (1974: 61–108) and Sydie (1987: 125–67).

4 Steele and Pollock (1974: 128–30), in discussing the non-abusing parent, point out that 'The other parent almost invariably contributes, however, to the abusive behaviour either by openly accepting it or by more subtly abetting it, consciously or unconsciously.' They list various forms in which this happens, one of which seems to have been apparent in several of the inquiry report cases in Britain (e.g. Darryn Clarke, Jasmine Beckford, Kimberley Carlile): 'One parent feeling overwhelmed and frustrated may turn the infant over to the other with admonitions to do something more drastic to stop the baby's annoying behaviour.' How voluntary such behaviour is, is open to question. The non-abusing parent may be forced to hand over the child for such inappropriate discipline. With regard to the contribution of children to their own abuse they stress that 'characteristics presented by the infant, such as sex, time of birth, health status, and behavior are factors in instigating child abuse.'

5 Steele and Pollock's views on the influence of socio-economic factors on the incidence of child abuse are that they are marginal: 'Basically they are irrelevant to the actual act of child beating. Unquestionably, social and economic difficulties and disasters put added stress on people's lives and contribute to behavior which might otherwise remain dormant. But such factors must be considered as incidental enhancers rather than necessary and sufficient causes' (p. 108).

6 One exception is a study of intervention into failure to thrive cases (Iwaniec *et al.* 1985).

7 Corporal punishment has been outlawed in schools in Sweden since 1952 and legislation was passed in 1979 prohibiting the use of physical force on children within the family (see Gelles and Edfeldt 1986).

8 Smith (1991) outlines the parts of the Children Act that specifically enhance a children's rights perspective. Two examples are: (a) section 22, which emphasizes the need to consult children of sufficient age and understanding with regard to all decisions that affect them (this section is very similar to section 18 of the 1980 Child Care Act); (b) section 44(7), which gives a child of sufficient age and understanding the right to refuse a medical examination under an emergency protection order (a direct result of events in Cleveland, where it was felt that children were exposed to many assessments and examinations without having any recourse if they objected).

   In general, the 1989 Children Act is a move towards greater consideration of children as subjects rather than objects. However, the legislation still leaves a lot of room for adultist views to prevail.

9 Lynch (1976) provides a useful integrative model called 'critical path analysis'. This

incorporates the first three of Belsky's systems, but not the macrosystem, which takes into account broader societal issues.

7 The consequences of child abuse

1 See also Zimrin (1986) and Rutter (1985).

2 Death is also a consequence of child abuse cases. The extent of death by child abuse as reported in official statistics is discussed in Chapter 4.

3 Transmission of abuse from one generation to another is also an important (though highly contentious) long-term effect. This has already been dealt with in Chapter 5.

4 Green (1978) found significantly higher rates of self-abusive behaviour among a sample of physically abused children compared with neglected and non-abused children.

5 Jasmine Beckford's stepfather, Morris, spent the first nine years of his life with his grandmother in Jamaica before being reunited with his parents in Britain. At age 13, he and his sister were severely beaten by both parents and forced to sleep in an outhouse with no bed and one blanket between them before being taken into care (Beckford 1985: 42). It is not known how Tyra Henry's father, Andrew Neil, was treated as a child. His mother left home when he was aged seven. He was noted to have hysterical fits at age ten and physically assaulted a two-year-old baby when he was aged 13 (Henry 1987: 8–10). Unfortunately, not enough is known about the background of fathers in many other public inquiry cases for a variety of reasons (see Chapter 5). Closer attention to their biographical details (and those of the mothers) would undoubtedly add to our understanding of the causes of such gross violence to children.

6 Carmen et al. (1984: 382) show considerable awareness of the potential impact of physical and sexual abuse on women: 'In our sample, the abused females directed their hatred and aggression against themselves in both overt and covert ways. These behaviours formed a continuum from quiet resignation and depression to repeated episodes of self-mutilation and suicide attempts. . . . Markedly impaired self-esteem was prominent among these patients, as they conveyed a sense that they were undeserving of any empathic understanding or help by clinicians.' These reactions were in contrast to the outwardly directed aggression that was most common among the mentally ill males in this study with a history of abuse. From this perspective, the form of the reaction to abuse is heavily influenced by social and socialization factors. Similarly, being black and abused in predominantly white-dominated societies also influences the consequences and the response to the abuse (see Angelou 1984).

7 There is still a major problem in deciding what is or is not appropriate or excessive sexual behaviour, particularly with regard to older children.

8 Browne and Finkelhor (1986) also note that children who experience abuse by more than one person are more likely to experience harmful effects.

9 Gordon (1989) points out that some of what have been termed 'negative' effects of child sexual abuse, such as running away and inappropriate sexual behaviour, could be seen as positive reactions to the situations many of the girls in the records she studied were faced with. ' "Sex delinquency" was an escape route not only of victims, but often of highly responsible victims, trying to avoid telling their secrets and exploding their families' (p. 240).

8 Research into child protection practice

1 The Doreen Aston report is particularly useful for developing an understanding of the role of the health visitor in child protection work and the pressures created in working in difficult environments with limited resources.

2 Porter (1984) provides a checklist of factors linked with child sexual abuse, as do Finkelhor and Baron (1986). These do not seem so far to have been applied to child protection practice in the way that has been the case with regard to physical abuse and neglect. This could be explained by the now widely accepted view that action should only be taken in cases of intra-familial abuse when there is clear evidence.

3 The contrast with the situation in the field of physical abuse is ironic. In the Beckford report social workers were criticized because of their lack of knowledge about relevant research and the findings of previous inquiry reports. In Cleveland, they were rebuked for applying knowledge derived from research in an uncritical fashion.

4 Darryn Clarke was never seen by social workers before his death. The focus of the inquiry was on the response to the initial allegation and the reasons for the delay in tracing a child who was said to be at risk. Similarly, Kimberley Carlile was not known to the social services department to whom allegations of ill-treatment were made. However, in this case there had been prior social work involvement by other social services departments. The inquiry concentrated on the delays and difficulties associated with assessing whether Kimberley was at risk or not.

5 Parents Anonymous groups were first set up in California in 1969 (see Holmes 1978). Small voluntary groups of parents who have abused their children meet a professional group helper to share and discuss feelings and issues. The aim is to help such parents improve their self-image and provide support for each other. Parents are encouraged to contact each other regularly outside the group and to follow up parents who drop out. There is no direct equivalent in Britain. Organizations such as Parents Against Injustice and the Family Rights Group are pressure groups organized to challenge the child protection system.

6 See Ong (1985) for missed opportunities in an NSPCC day/nursery centre.

7 See Schedule 3, sections 2 and 3 of the 1989 Children Act. These sections deal with the powers of supervision orders. The court has the power to require the subject of a supervision order to attend a specified place (e.g. a day nursery) under the directions of the supervisor. Provided he, she or they consent, the responsible person(s) can also be required to attend a specified place under the directions of the supervisor (e.g. a family day or residential centre). Failure to comply with these requirements can result in the supervisor returning to court to seek a variation in the order (section 39).

9 Current issues in child protection work

1 The British system of intervention into child abuse, particularly sexual abuse, is considered to be more authoritative and intrusive than in other European countries where, as a rule, there seems to be greater emphasis on containing problems within the family and less involvement of the criminal justice system (see Bunting 1991). In countries such as Belgium, Holland and Germany, for instance, the police have a much lower profile in such work than is true in Britain. Supporters of the British system argue that to tackle child abuse properly it must be seen as a crime and they consider the continental system to be behind the times. On the other hand,

advocates for the continental approach see it as more flexible and advanced, and likely to achieve better results than the more punitive British method.

2 It is difficult to understand the intentions of the *Working Together* guidelines in this respect. Virtually all the examples used in these guidelines seem to have the case of sexual abuse in mind. For instance: 'Awareness of the needs of the child should focus the enquiry on the child. Every effort should be made to help him or her to relax and feel at ease. Consideration should be given to a child having a parent, relative, friend or supporter present during the investigative interviews, as the circumstances of the case determine. . . . The interviewer must listen carefully to what the child has to say and communication with him or her must be in a responsive and receptive manner. He or she must work at the child's pace and use language that the child can understand and thus enable the child to talk about and give as clear an account as possible of events that have taken place' (DoH 1991b: 5.14.7). An interview of this kind has not been typical practice in the case of physical abuse. This is not to argue that it is not a good idea. However, if it is the intention of the guidelines to encourage similar approaches for physical and sexual abuse investigations, then it should state its objective unequivocally.

3 Gordon's (1989) study of the recent history of intervention into child abuse in Boston in the USA charts the link between the existence of strong feminist movements and greater attention being paid to abuse of children and women in families: 'For most of the 110 years of this history, it was the women's-rights movement that was most influential in confronting, publicizing, and demanding action against family violence. Concern with family violence usually grew when feminism was strong and ebbed when feminism was weak' (Gordon 1988: 4).

4 The last resort principle is not legally defined as such, but section 1(5) of the 1989 Children Act states that the court 'shall not make any order or any of the orders unless it considers that doing so would be better for the child than making no order at all.' Under the previous legislation (the 1969 Children and Young Persons Act) the court had a similar duty, namely to consider whether the making of an order was necessary to ensure sufficient care or control of a child.

5 Before the 1989 Children Act, there were three ways of taking action on the grounds of likely risk in the future: under sections 1(2)(b) and 1(2)(bb) of the 1969 Children and Young Persons Act and under wardship proceedings (section 7, Family Law Reform Act 1967).

6 In London, there were reports of 600 registered child abuse cases being unallocated in 1990. See the 1990 Social Services Inspectorate report, *Child Protection in London. Aspects of Management Arrangements in Social Services Departments*. London: HMSO.

Bibliography

Adams-Tucker, C. (1981) 'A socioclinical overview of 28 sex-abused children', *Child Abuse and Neglect*, 5, 361–7.

Allen, A. and Morton, A. (1961) *This is Your Child: the Story of the NSPCC*. London: Routledge & Kegan Paul.

Allen, R. and Oliver, J. (1982) 'The effects of child maltreatment on language development', *Child Abuse and Neglect*, 6, 299–305.

Ammerman, R., von Hasselt, V., Hersen, M. McGonigle, J., Lubetsky, M. (1989) 'Abuse and neglect in psychiatrically hospitalised multi-handicapped children', *Child Abuse and Neglect*, 13, 335–43.

Anderson, S., Bach, C. and Griffin, S. (1981) 'Psychosocial sequelae in intra-familial victims of sexual assault and abuse'. Paper presented at the 3rd International Congress on Child Abuse and Neglect, Amsterdam.

Angelou, M. (1983) *I Know Why the Caged Bird Sings*. London: Virago.

Armstrong, L. (1978) *Kiss Daddy Goodnight*. New York: Dell.

Argles, P. (1980) Attachment and child abuse. *British Journal of Social Work*, 10, 33–42.

Aries, P. (1962) *Centuries of Childhood*. Harmondsworth: Penguin.

Asen, K., George, E., Piper, R. and Stevens, A. (1989) 'A systems approach to child abuse: management and treatment issues', *Child Abuse and Neglect*, 13, 45–57.

Association of the Directors of Social Services (1987) Press release, July.

Aston, Doreen (1989) *The Doreen Aston Report*. Area Review Committee of the London Boroughs of Lambeth, Lewisham and Southwark.

Auckland, Susan (1975) *Report of the Committee of Inquiry into the Provision of Services to the Family of John George Auckland*. London: HMSO.

Augoustinos, M. (1987) 'Developmental effects of child abuse', *Child Abuse and Neglect*, 11, 15–27.

Badinter, E. (1981) *The Myth of Motherhood: an Historical View of the Maternal Instinct*. New York: Macmillan.

Bagley, C. and King, K. (1990) *Child Sexual Abuse: the Search for Healing*. London: Tavistock/Routledge.

Bagley, C. and Ramsay, R. (1986) 'Sexual abuse in childhood: psychosocial outcomes and implications for social work practice', *Journal of Social Work and Human Sexuality*, 4, 33–47.

Baher, E., Hyman, C., Jones, C., Kerr, A. and Mitchell, R. (1976) *At Risk: an Account of the Battered Child Research Department*. London: Routledge & Kegan Paul.

Baker, A. and Duncan, S. (1985) 'Child sexual abuse: a study of prevalence in Great Britain', *Child Abuse and Neglect*, 9, 457–67.

Baldwin, J. and Oliver, J. (1975) 'Epidemiology and family characteristics of severely-abused children', *British Journal of Social and Preventive Medicine*, 29, 205–21.

Bandura, A. (1965) *Principles of Behaviour Modification*. New York: Holt, Rinehart and Winston.

Banning, A. (1989) 'Mother–son incest: confronting a prejudice', *Child Abuse and Neglect*, 13, 563–70.

Barash, D. (1981) *Sociobiology: the Whisperings Within*. London: Fontana.

Barratt, A., Trepper, T. and Fish, L. (1990) 'Feminist informed family therapy for the treatment of intra-familial child sexual abuse', *Journal of Family Psychology*, 4, 151–66.

Becker, S. and Macpherson, S. (eds) (1988) *Public Issues, Private Pain: Poverty, Social Work and Social Policy*. London: Social Services Insight Books.

Beckford, Jasmine (1985) *A Child in Trust*. The report of the panel of inquiry into the circumstances surrounding the death of Jasmine Beckford. London Borough of Brent.

Behlmer, G. (1982) *Child Abuse and Moral Reform in England 1870–1908*. Stanford, CA: Stanford University Press.

Beitchman, J., Zucker, K., Hood, J., Da Costa, G. and Akman, D. (1991) 'A review of the short-term effects of child sexual abuse', *Child Abuse and Neglect*, 15, 537–56.

Beitchman, J., Zucker, K., Hood, J., Da Costa, G., Akman, D. and Cassavia, E. (1992) 'A review of the long-term effects of child sexual abuse', *Child Abuse and Neglect*, 16, 101–18.

Belsky, J. (1980) 'Child maltreatment: an ecological integration', *American Psychologist*, 35, 320–5.

Belsky, J. and Vondra, J. (1989) 'Lessons from child abuse: the determinants of parenting', in D. Cicchetti and V. Carlson (eds) *Child Maltreatment: Theory and Research on the Causes and Consequences of Child Abuse and Neglect*. Cambridge: Cambridge University Press.

Benedict, M. and White, R. (1985) 'Selected perinatal factors and child abuse', *American Journal of Public Health*, 75, 780–1.

Ben-Tovim, A., Elton, A., Hildebrand, J., Tranter, M. and Vizard, E. (eds) (1988) *Child Sexual Abuse within the Family: Assessment and Treatment: the Work of the Great Ormond Street Team*. London: Wright.

Besharov, D. (1981) 'Towards better research on child abuse and neglect: making definitional issues an explicit methodological concern', *Child Abuse and Neglect*, 5, 383–90.

Birchall, E. (1989) 'The frequency of child abuse – what do we really know?', in O. Stevenson (ed.) *Child Abuse: Public Policy and Professional Practice*. Hemel Hempstead: Harvester Wheatsheaf.

Boswell, J. (1988) *The Kindness of Strangers: the Abandonment of Children in Western Europe from Late Antiquity to the Renaissance*. Harmondsworth: Penguin.

Bowlby, J. (1951) *Maternal Care and Mental Health*. A report prepared on behalf of the World Health Organization as a contribution to the United Nations programme for the welfare of homeless children. Geneva: World Health Organization.

Bowlby, J. (1971) *Attachment and Loss: Volume 1. Attachment*. Harmondsworth: Penguin.

Bowlby, J., Fry, S. and Ainsworth, M. (1965) *Child Care and the Growth of Love*. Harmondsworth: Penguin.

Bradshaw, J. (1990) *Child Poverty and Deprivation in the United Kingdom*. London: National Children's Bureau.

Brady, K. (1979) *Father's Days: a True Story of Incest*. New York: Dell.

Brekke, J. (1987) 'Detecting wife and child abuse in clinical settings' *Social Casework*, 68, 332–8.

Brewer, Wayne (1977) *Report of the Review Panel Appointed by Somerset Area Review Committee to Consider the Case of Wayne Brewer*. Somerset Area Review Committee.

Briere, J. (1984) 'The long-term effects of childhood sexual abuse: defining a post-sexual-abuse syndrome', Paper presented at the 3rd National Conference on the Sexual Victimization of Children, Washington, DC.

Bristow, E. (1977) *Vice and Vigilance*. Dublin: Gill & Macmillan.

Brown, C. (1984) *Black and White Britain: the Third PSI Survey*. London: Heinemann.

Brown, C. (1986) *Child Abuse Parents Speaking: Parents' Impressions of Social Workers and the Social Work Process*. Bristol School of Applied and Urban Studies Working Paper 63.

Brown, G. and Harris, T. (1978) *Social Origins of Depression: a Study of Psychiatric Disorder in Women*. London: Tavistock.

Brown, T. and Waters, J. (1985) *Parental Participation at Case Conferences*. Rochdale: B.A.S.P.C.A.N.

Browne, A. and Finkelhor, D. (1986) 'Initial and long-term effects: a review of the research', in D. Finkelhor and associates (ed.) *A Sourcebook on Child Sexual Abuse*. Beverly Hills, CA: Sage.

Browne, K. and Saqi, S. (1988) 'Approaches to screening for child abuse and neglect', in K. Browne, C. Davies and P. Stratton (eds) *Early Prediction and Prevention of Child Abuse*. Chichester: Wiley.

Bunting, M. (1991) 'Our kids on the block', *Guardian*, 12 July, 23.

Burgdorff, K. (1981) *Recognition of and Reporting of Child Maltreatment from the National Study of Incidence and Severity of Child Abuse and Neglect*. Washington, DC: National Center on Child Abuse and Neglect.

Calam, R. and Franchi, C. (1987) *Child Abuse and Its Consequences*. Cambridge: Cambridge University Press.

Campbell, B. (1988) *Unofficial Secrets*. London: Virago.

Campbell, M. (1991) 'Children at risk: how different are children on Child Abuse Registers?', *British Journal of Social Work*, 21, 259–75.

Carlile, Kimberley (1987) *A Child in Mind: Protection of Children in a Responsible Society*. The report of the commission of inquiry into the circumstances surrounding the death of Kimberley Carlile. London Borough of Greenwich.

Carmen, E., Rieker, P. and Mills, T. (1984) 'Victims of violence and psychiatric illness', *American Journal of Psychiatry*, 141, 378–83.

Carty, H. (1988) 'Brittle or battered?', *Archives of Disease in Childhood*, 63, 350–2.

Chapman, Lester (1979) *Lester Chapman Inquiry Report*. Berkshire County Council.

Christopherson, J. (1981) 'Two approaches to the handling of child abuse: a comparison of the English and Dutch systems', *Child Abuse and Neglect*, 5, 369–74.

Christopherson, J. (1983) 'Public perception of child abuse and the need for prevention: are professionals seen as abusers?', *Child Abuse and Neglect*, 7, 435–42.

Cicchetti, D. and Aber, L. (1980) 'Abused children–abusive parents: an overstated case', *Harvard Educational Review*, 50, 244–55.

Clark, B., Parkin, W. and Richards, M. (1990) 'Dangerousness: a complex practice issue', in The Violence against Children Study Group, *Taking Child Abuse Seriously*. London: Unwin Hyman.

Clarke, Darryn (1979) *The Report of the Committee of Inquiry into the Actions of the Authorities and Agencies Relating to Darryn James Clarke*. DHSS Cmnd 7739. London: HMSO.

Cleveland County Council (1988) *Report of the Inquiry into Child Abuse in Cleveland 1987*. DHSS Cmnd 412. London: HMSO.

Cobley, C. (1991) 'Child victims of sexual abuse and the criminal justice system in England & Wales', *Journal of Social Welfare Law*, 5, 362–74.

Cohen, C. and Adler, A. (1986) 'Assessing the role of social network interventions with an inner-city population', *American Journal of Orthopsychiatry*, 56, 278–88.

Cohen, F. and Densen-Gerber, J. (1982) 'A study of the relationship between child abuse and drug addiction in 178 parents: preliminary results', *Child Abuse and Neglect*, 6, 383–7.

Cohn, A. and Daro, D. (1987) 'Is treatment too late? What ten years of evaluative research tell us', *Child Abuse and Neglect*, 11, 433–42.

Colwell, Maria (1974) *Report of the Committee of Inquiry into the Care and Supervision Provided in Relation to Maria Colwell*. London: HMSO.

Conte, J. and Schuerman, J. (1987) 'Factors associated with an increased impact of child sexual abuse', *Child Abuse and Neglect*, 11, 201–11.

Corby, B. (1987) *Working with Child Abuse*. Milton Keynes: Open University Press.

Corby, B. (1990) 'Making use of child protection statistics', *Children and Society*, 4, 304–14.

Corby, B. (1991) 'Sociology, social work and child protection', in M. Davies (ed.) *The Sociology of Social Work*. London: Routledge.

Corby, B. and Mills, C. (1986) 'Child abuse: risks and resources', *British Journal of Social Work*, 16, 531–42.

Coveney, L., Jackson, M., Jeffries, S., Kaye, L. and Mahoney, P. (1984) *The Sexuality Papers: Male Sexuality and the Social Control of Women*. London: Hutchinson.

Creighton, S. (1984) *Trends in Child Abuse*. London: NSPCC.

Creighton, S. (1985, 1986, 1987) *Initial Findings from NSPCC Register Research 1984, 1985, 1986*. London: NSPCC.

Creighton, S. and Noyes, P. (1989) *Child Abuse Trends in England & Wales 1983–1987*. London: NSPCC.

Crittenden, P. (1983) 'The effect of mandatory protective day care on mutual attachment in maltreating mother–infant dyads', *Child Abuse and Neglect*, 7, 297–300.

Crittenden, P. and Ainsworth, M. (1989) 'Child maltreatment and attachment theory', in D. Cicchetti and V. Carlson (eds) *Child Maltreatment: Theory and Research into the Causes and Consequences of Child Abuse and Neglect*. Cambridge: Cambridge University Press.

Crozier, J. and Katz, R. (1979) 'Social learning treatment of child abuse', *Journal of Behavioral Therapy and Experimental Psychiatry*, 10, 213–20.

Culp, R., Heide, J. and Taylor-Richardson, M. (1987) 'Maltreated children and developmental scores: treatment versus non-treatment', *Child Abuse and Neglect*, 11, 29–34.

Curtis Committee (1946) *Report of the Care of Children Committee*. Cmnd 6922. London: HMSO.

Dale, P., Davies, M., Morrison, T. and Waters, J. (1986) *Dangerous Families: Assessment and Treatment of Child Abuse*. London: Tavistock.

Dale, P., Morrison, T., Davies, M., Noyes, P. and Roberts, W. (1983) 'A family therapy approach to child abuse: countering resistance', *Journal of Family Therapy*, 5, 117–43.

Davies, M. (1981) *The Essential Social Worker: a Guide to Positive Practice*. London: Heinemann.

Davin, A. (1990) 'The precocity of poverty', in *The Proceedings of the Conference on Historical Perspectives on Childhood*, University of Trondheim.

Davis, G. and Leitenberg, H. (1987) 'Adolescent sex offenders', *Psychological Bulletin*, 101, 417–27.

Dawkins, R. (1976) *The Selfish Gene*. Oxford: Oxford University Press.

Deblinger, E., McLeer, S., Atkins, M., Ralphe, M. and Foa, E. (1989) Post-traumatic stress in sexually abused, physically abused and non-abused children. *Child Abuse and Neglect*, 13, 403–8.

De Francis, V. (1969) *Protecting the Child Victim of Sex Crimes Committed by Adults*. Denver: American Humane Association.

De Mause, L. (ed.) (1976) *The History of Childhood*. London: Souvenir Press.

Demos, J. (1986) *Past, Present and Personal*. Oxford: Oxford University Press.

Denicola, J. and Sandler, J. (1980) 'Training abusive parents in child management and self-control skills', *Behavior Therapy*, 11, 263–70.

Department of Health and Social Security (1980) *Child Abuse: Central register systems LASSL (80)4*. London: HMSO.

Department of Health and Social Security (1982) *Child Abuse: A Study of Inquiry Reports 1973–1981*. London: HMSO.

Department of Health and Social Security (1985a) *Social Work Decisions in Child Care: Recent Research Findings and Their Implications*. London: HMSO.

Department of Health and Social Security (1985b) *Review of Child Care Law: Report to Ministers of an Interdepartmental Working Party*. London: HMSO.

Department of Health and Social Security (1986) *Child Abuse – Working Together*. A draft guide to arrangements for inter-agency cooperation for the protection of children. London: HMSO.

Department of Health and Social Security (1988) *Working Together: a Guide to Interagency Cooperation for the Protection of Children from Abuse*. London: HMSO.

Department of Health (1988) *Protecting Children: a Guide for Social Workers Undertaking a Comprehensive Assessment*. London: HMSO.

Department of Health (1989, 1990, 1991c) *Survey of Children and Young Persons on Child Protection Registers, Year Ending 31 March 1988, 1989, 1990, England*. London: HMSO.

Department of Health (1991a) *Child Abuse: a Study of Inquiry Reports 1980–1989*. London: HMSO.

Department of Health (1991b) *Working Together under the Children Act 1989: a Guide to Arrangements for Inter-agency Cooperation for the Protection of Children from Abuse*. London: HMSO.

Department of Health (1991d) *Children in Care in England & Wales, March 1989*. London: HMSO.

Department of Health (1992) *Survey of Children and Young Persons on Child Protection Registers, Year Ending 31 March 1991, England, Provisional Feedback*. London: HMSO.

Dibble, J. and Straus, M. (1980) 'Some structural determinants of inconsistency between attitudes and behavior: the case of family violence', *Journal of Marriage and the Family*, 42, 71–82.

Dingwall, R. (1989) 'Some problems about predicting child abuse and neglect', in O. Stevenson (ed.) *Child Abuse: Public Policy and Professional Practice*. Hemel Hempstead: Harvester Wheatsheaf.

Dingwall, R. and Eekelaar, J. (1984) 'Rethinking child protection', in M. Freeman (ed.) *The State, the Law and the Family*. London: Tavistock.

Dingwall, R., Eekelaar, J. and Murray, T. (1983) *The Protection of Children: State Intervention and Family Life*. Oxford: Blackwell.

Dingwall, R., Eekelaar, J. and Murray, T. (1984) 'Childhood as a social problem: a survey of the history of legal regulation', *Journal of Law and Society*, 11, 207–32.

Dominelli, L. (1986) 'Father–daughter incest: patriarchy's shameful secret', *Critical Social Policy*, 16, 8–22.

Donnison, D. (1954) *The Neglected Child and the Social Services*. Manchester: Manchester University Press.

Donzelot, J. (1980) *The Policing of Families: Welfare versus the State*. London: Hutchinson.

Driver, E. and Droisen, A. (eds) (1989) *Child Sexual Abuse: Feminist Perspectives*. Basingstoke: Macmillan.

Dubanoski, R., Evans, I. and Higuchi, A. (1978) 'Analysis and treatment of child abuse: a set of behavioral propositions', *Child Abuse and Neglect*, 2, 153–72.

Egeland, B. (1988) 'Breaking the cycle of abuse: implications for prediction and intervention', in K. Browne, C. Davies and P. Stratton (eds) *Early Prediction and Prevention of Child Abuse*. Chichester: Wiley.

Egeland, B., Sroufe, L. and Erickson, M. (1983) 'Developmental consequences of different patterns of maltreatment', *Child Abuse and Neglect*, 7, 459–69.

Egeland, B. and Vaughan, B. (1981) 'Failure of bond formation as a cause of abuse, neglect and maltreatment', *American Journal of Orthopsychiatry*, 51, 78–84.

Elmer, E. (1977) *Fragile Families, Troubled Children*. Pittsburgh: University of Pittsburgh Press.

Elwell, M. and Ephloss, P. (1987) 'Initial reactions of sexually abused children', *Social Casework*, 68, 109–16.

Emery, R. (1982) 'Marital turmoil: interparental conflict and the children of discord and divorce', *Psychological Bulletin*, 92, 310–30.

Ennew, J. (1986) *The Sexual Exploitation of Children*. Cambridge: Polity Press.

Erickson, M., Egeland, B. and Pianta, R. (1989) 'Effects of maltreatment on the development of young children', in D. Cicchetti and V. Carlson (eds) *Child Maltreatment: Theory and Research on the Causes and Consequences of Child Abuse and Neglect*. Cambridge: Cambridge University Press.

Faller, K. (1989) 'Why sexual abuse? An exploration of the intergenerational hypothesis', *Child Abuse and Neglect*, 13, 543–8.

Fancher, R. (1973) *Psychoanalytic Psychology: the Development of Freud's Thought*. London: Norton & Co.

Farmer, E. (1992) 'Restoring children on court orders to their families: lessons for practice', *Adoption and Fostering*, 16, 7–15.

Fehrenbach, P., Smith, W., Monastersky, C. and Deister, R. (1986) 'Adolescent sex offenders: offender and offense characteristics', *American Journal of Orthopsychiatry*, 56, 225–33.

Fehrenbach, P. and Monastersky, C. (1988) 'Characteristics of female adolescent sexual offenders', *American Journal of Orthopsychiatry*, 58, 148–51.

Ferguson, H. (1990) 'Rethinking child protection practices: a case for history' in the Violence against Children Study Group, *Taking Child Abuse Seriously*. London: Unwin Hyman.

Finkelhor, D. (1979) *Sexually Victimized Children*. New York: Free Press.

Finkelhor, D. (1984) *Child Sexual Abuse: New Theory and Research*. New York: Free Press.

Finkelhor, D. and associates (eds) (1986) *A Sourcebook on Child Sexual Abuse*. Newbury Park, CA: Sage.

Finkelhor, D. and Baron, L. (1986) 'High risk children' in D. Finkelhor and associates (eds) *A Sourcebook on Child Sexual Abuse*. Newbury Park, CA: Sage.

Finkelhor, D., Hotaling, G., Lewis, I. and Smith, C. (1990) 'Sexual abuse in a national survey of adult men and women: prevalence characteristics and risk factors', *Child Abuse and Neglect*, 14, 19–28.

Finkelhor, D. and Korbin, J. (1988) 'Child abuse as an international issue', *Child Abuse and Neglect*, 12, 3–23.

Finkelhor, D., Williams, L. and Burns, N. (1988) *Nursery Crimes: Sexual Abuse in Daycare*. London: Sage.

Finkelhor, D. and Zellman, G. (1991) 'Flexible reporting options for skilled child abuse professionals', *Child Abuse and Neglect*, 15, 335–41.

Fitzherbert, K. (1967) *West Indian Children in London*. London: Bell.

Flin, R. (1990) 'Child witnesses in criminal courts', *Children and Society*, 4, 264–83.

Fox, Stephanie (1990) *The Report of the Inquiry into the Death of Stephanie Fox*. London Borough of Wandsworth.

Freeman, M. (1983) *The Rights and Wrongs of Children*. London: Francis Pinter.

Freeman, M. (1988) 'Time to stop hitting our children', *Childright*, 51, 5–8.

Friedrich, J. and Boriskin, J. (1976) 'The role of the child in abuse: a review of the literature', *American Journal of Orthopsychiatry*, 46, 580–9.

Friedrich, W. (1979) 'Predictors of coping behaviour of mothers of handicapped children', *Journal of Consulting and Clinical Psychology*, 47, 1140–1.

Friedrich, W., Urquiza, A. and Beilke, R. (1986) 'Behaviour problems in sexually abused young children', *Journal of Pediatric Psychology*, 11, 47–57.

Frodi, A. and Lamb, M. (1980) 'Child abusers' response to infant smiles and cries', *Child Development*, 51, 238–41.

Frodi, A. and Smetana, J. (1984) 'Abused, neglected and non-maltreated preschoolers' ability to discriminate emotion in others: the effects of IQ', *Child Abuse and Neglect*, 8, 459–65.

Fromuth, M. (1986) 'The relationship of childhood sexual abuse with later psychological and sexual adjustment in a sample of college women', *Child Abuse and Neglect*, 10, 5–15.

Frost, N. and Stein, M. (1989) *The Politics of Child Welfare: Inequality, Power and Change*. New York: Harvester Wheatsheaf.

Furby, L., Weinrott, W. and Blackshaw, L. (1989) 'Sex offender recidivism: a review', *Psychological Bulletin*, 105, 3–30.

Furniss, T. (1991) *The Multi-professional Handbook of Child Sexual Abuse: Integrated Management, Therapy and Legal Intervention*. London: Routledge.

Gabinet, L. (1983a) 'Child abuse treatment failures reveal need for redefinition of the problem', *Child Abuse and Neglect*, 7, 395–402.

Gabinet, L. (1983b) 'Shared parenting: a new paradigm for the treatment of child abuse', *Child Abuse and Neglect*, 7, 403–11.

Garbarino, J. (1977) 'The human ecology of child maltreatment: a conceptual model for research', *Journal of Marriage and the Family*, 39, 721–35.

Garbarino, J. (1982) *Children and Families in Their Social Environment*. New York: Aldine.

Garbarino, J. and Crouter, A. (1978) 'Defining the community context for parent-child relations: the correlates of child mistreatment', *Child Development*, 49, 604–16.

Garbarino, J. and Gilliam, G. (1980) *Understanding Abusive Families*. Lexington, MA: Lexington Books.

Garbarino, J. and Sherman, D. (1980) 'High risk neighbourhoods and high risk families: the human ecology of child mistreatment', *Child Development*, 51, 188–98.

Garbarino, J. and Vondra, J. (1987) 'Psychological maltreatment: issues and perspectives', in M. Brassard, R. Germain and S. Hart (eds) *Psychological Maltreatment of Children and Youth*. Oxford: Pergamon Press.

Gardner, L. (1972) 'Deprivation dwarfism', *Scientific American*, 227, 76–82.

Gelles, R. (1982) 'Towards better research on child abuse and neglect: a response to Besharov', *Child Abuse and Neglect*, 6, 495–6.

Gelles, R. (1989) 'Child abuse and violence in single parent families: parent absence and economic deprivation', *American Journal of Orthopsychiatry*, 59, 492–501.

Gelles, R. and Cornell, C. (1985) *Intimate Violence in Families*. Beverly Hills, CA: Sage.

Gelles, R. and Edfeldt, A. (1986) 'Violence towards children in the United States and Sweden', *Child Abuse and Neglect*, 10, 501–10.

George, C. and Main, M. (1979) 'Social interaction of young abused children: approach, avoidance and aggression', *Child Development*, 50, 306–18.

Germain, G. and Gitterman, A. (1980) *The Life Model of Social Work Practice*. Cambridge, MA: Harvard University Press.

Giaretto, H. (1981) 'A comprehensive child sexual abuse treatment program', in P. Mrazek and C. Kempe (eds) *Sexually Abused Children and Their Families*. New York: Pergamon Press.

Giaretto, H., Giaretto, A. and Sgroi, S. (1978) 'Co-ordinated community treatment of incest', in A. Burgess, A. Groth, L. Holmstrom and S. Sgroi (eds) *Sexual Assault of Children and Adolescents*. Lexington, MA: Lexington Books.

Gil, D. (1970) *Violence against Children*. Cambridge, MA: Harvard University Press.

Gil, D. (1975) 'Unravelling child abuse', *American Journal of Orthopsychiatry*, 45, 346–56.

Gil, D. (1978) 'Societal violence and violence in families', in J. Eekelaar and S. Katz (eds) *Family Violence*. Toronto: Butterworth.

Gillham, B. (1991) *The Facts about Sexual Abuse*. London: Cassell.

Giovannoni, J. and Becerra, R. (1979) *Defining Child Abuse*. New York: Free Press.

Giovannoni, J. and Billingsley, A. (1970) 'Child neglect among the poor: a study of parental adequacy in families of three ethnic groups', *Child Welfare*, 49, 196–204.

Glaser, D. and Frosh, S. (1988) *Child Sexual Abuse*. Basingstoke: Macmillan.

Goldstein, J., Freud, A. and Solnit, A. (1979) *Beyond the Best Interests of the Child*. New York: Free Press.

Goldston, D., Turnquist, D. and Knutson, J. (1989) 'Presenting problems of sexually abused girls receiving psychiatric services', *Journal of Abnormal Psychology*, 98, 547–60.

Gomes-Schwartz, B., Horowitz, J. and Cardarelli, A. (1990) *Child Sexual Abuse: the Initial Effects*. Beverley Hills, CA: Sage.

Goode, W. (1971) 'Force and violence in the family', *Journal of Marriage and the Family*, 33, 624–36.

Goodwin, J., McCarthy, T. and DiVasto, P. (1981) Prior incest in mothers of abused children. *Child Abuse and Neglect*, 7, 163–70.

Gordon, L. (1989) *Heroes of Their Own Lives: the Politics and History of Family Violence, Boston 1880–1960*. London: Virago.

Gordon, M. and Creighton, S. (1988) 'Natal and non-natal fathers as sexual abusers in the UK: a comparative analysis', *Journal of Marriage and the Family*, 50, 99–105.

Gorham, D. (1978) 'The maiden tribute of Babylon reexamined: child prostitution and the idea of childhood in late-Victorian England', *Victorian Studies*, 21, 354–79.

Gough, D. (1988) 'Approaches to child abuse prevention', in K. Browne, J. Davies and P. Stratton (eds) *Early Prediction and Prevention of Child Abuse*. Chichester: Wiley.

Gray, J., Cutler, C., Dean, J. and Kempe, C. (1977) 'Prediction and prevention of child abuse and neglect', *Child Abuse and Neglect*, 1, 45–58.

Green, A. (1978) 'Self-destructive behaviour in battered children', *American Journal of Psychiatry*, 135, 579–82.

Green, A., Gaines, R. and Sandgrund, A. (1974) 'Child abuse: pathological syndrome of family interaction', *American Journal of Psychiatry*, 131, 882–6.

Green, A., Power, E., Steinbok, B. and Gaines, R. (1981) 'Factors associated with successful and unsuccessful intervention with child abusive families', *Child Abuse and Neglect*, 5, 45–52.

Greenland, C. (1958) 'Incest', *British Journal of Delinquency*, 9, 62–5.

Greenland, C. (1987) *Preventing CAN Deaths: an International Study of Deaths Due to Child Abuse and Neglect*. London: Tavistock.

Griffiths, D. and Moynihan, F. (1963) 'Multiple epiphyseal injuries in babies ("battered baby syndrome")', *British Medical Journal*, 5372, 1558–61.

Groth, A. and Burgess, A. (1979) 'Sexual traumas in the life histories of rapists and child molesters', *Victimology*, 4, 10–16.

Hallett, C. and Stevenson, O. (1980) *Child Abuse: Aspects of Interprofessional Cooperation*. London: Allen & Unwin.

Halston, A. and Richards, D. (1982) 'Behind closed doors', *Social Work Today*, 14, 7–11.

Hampton, R., Gelles, R. and Harrop, J. (1989) 'Is violence in black families increasing? A comparison of 1975 and 1985 national survey rates', *Journal of Marriage and the Family*, 89, 969–80.

Hanawalt, B. (1977) 'Childrearing among the lower classes of late medieval England', *Journal of Interdisciplinary History*, 8, 1–22.

Hearn, J. (1990) 'Child abuse and men's violence' in the Violence against Children Study Group, *Taking Child Abuse Seriously*. London: Unwin Hyman.

Henry, Tyra (1987) *Whose Child? The report of the public inquiry into the death of Tyra Henry*. London Borough of Lambeth.

Hensey, O., Williams, J. and Rosenbloom, L. (1983) 'Intervention in child abuse: experience in Liverpool', *Developmental Medicine and Child Neurology*, 25, 606–11.

Herman, J. (1981) *Father–Daughter Incest*. Cambridge, MA: Harvard University Press.

Higginson, S. (1992) 'Decision-making in the assessment of risk in child abuse cases', M Phil thesis, Cranfield Institute of Technology.

Hobbs, C. and Wynne, J. (1986) 'Buggery in childhood – a common syndrome of child abuse', *The Lancet*, ii, 792–6.

Hoffman-Plotkin, D. and Twentyman, C. (1984) 'A multimodal assessment of behavioral and cognitive deficits in abused and neglected pre-schoolers', *Child Development*, 55, 794–802.

Holman, B. (1988) *Putting Families First: Prevention and Child Care*. Basingstoke: Macmillan.

Holmes, S. (1978) 'Parents anonymous: a treatment method for child abuse', *Social Work*, 23, 245–7.

Holt, J. (1974) *Escape from Childhood*. Harmondsworth: Penguin.

Home Office (1923) *Report of the Work of the Children's Branch*. London: HMSO.

Home Office (1950) *Children Neglected or Ill-treated in Their Own Homes*. Joint circular with the Ministry of Health and Ministry of Education. London: HMSO.

Horne, M. (1990) 'Is it social work?', in the Violence against Children Study Group, *Taking Child Abuse Seriously*. London: Unwin Hyman.

Houlbrooke, R. (1984) *The English Family 1450–1700*. London: Longman.

Housden, L. (1955) *The Prevention of Cruelty to Children*. London: Cape.

House of Commons (1984) *Children in Care Volume 1*. Second report from the Social Services Committee. Session 1983–4. London: HMSO.

Howe, D. (1980) 'Inflated states and empty theories in social work', *British Journal of Social Work*, 10, 317–40.

Howe, D. (1991) 'Knowledge, power and the shape of social work practice', in M. Davies (ed.) *The Sociology of Social Work*. London: Routledge.

Howes, C. and Espinosa, M. (1985) 'The consequences of child abuse for the formation of relationships with peers', *Child Abuse and Neglect*, 9, 397–404.

Hoyles, M. (1979) 'Childhood in historical perspective' in M. Hoyles (ed.) *Changing Childhood*. London: Writers & Readers Publishing Cooperative.

Hrdy, S. (1977) *The Langurs of Abu*. Cambridge, MA: Harvard University Press.

Hunt, D. (1970) *Parents and Children in History*. New York: Basic Books.

Hunter, R. and Kilstrom, N. (1979) 'Breaking the cycle in abusive families', *American Journal of Psychiatry*, 136, 1320–2.

Hyman, C. (1978) 'Some characteristics of abusing families referred to the NSPCC', *British Journal of Social Work*, 8, 629–35.

Ingleby Report (1960) *Report of the Committee on Children and Young Persons*. Cmnd 1191. London: HMSO.

Isaacs, C. (1982) 'Treatment of child abuse: a review of behavioral interventions', *Journal of Applied Behavioral Analysis*, 15, 273–94.

Iwaniec, D., Herbert, M. and McNeish, A. (1985) 'Social work with failure to thrive children and their families: part II. Behavioural social work intervention', *British Journal of Social Work*, 15, 375–89.

Jacobson, R. and Straker, G. (1982) 'Peer group interaction of physically abused children', *Child Abuse and Neglect*, 6, 321–7.

Jahoda, M. (1977) *Freud and the Dilemmas of Psychology*. London: Hogarth Press.

Jampole, L. and Weber, M. (1987) 'An assessment of the behaviour of sexually abused and nonsexually abused children with anatomically correct dolls', *Child Abuse and Neglect*, 11, 187–92.

Jaudes, P. and Diamond, L. (1985) 'The handicapped child and child abuse', *Child Abuse and Neglect*, 9, 341–7.

Jaudes, P. and Morris, M. (1990) 'Child sexual abuse: who goes home?', *Child Abuse and Neglect*, 14, 61–8.

Jayaratne, S. (1977) 'Child abusers as parents and children: a review', *Social Work*, 22, 5–9.

Jenkins, H. and Asen, K. (1992) 'Family therapy without the family: a framework for systemic practice', *Journal of Family Therapy*, 14, 1–14.

Johnson, T. (1988) 'Child perpetrators: children who molest other children: preliminary findings', *Child Abuse and Neglect*, 12, 219–29.

Johnson, T. (1989) 'Female child perpetrators: children who molest other children', *Child Abuse and Neglect*, 13, 571–86.

Johnston, M. (1979) 'The sexually mistreated child: diagnostic evaluation', *Child Abuse and Neglect*, 3, 943–51.

Jones, D., Pickett, J., Oates, M. and Barbor, P. (1987) *Understanding Child Abuse*, 2nd edn. Basingstoke: Macmillan.

Jones, D. P. H. (1987) 'The untreatable family', *Child Abuse and Neglect*, 11, 409–20.

Jones, D. P. H. (1991) 'Ritualism and child sexual abuse', *Child Abuse and Neglect*, 15, 163–70.

Jonker, F. and Jonker-Bakker, P. (1991) 'Experiences with ritualist child sexual abuse: a case study from the Netherlands', *Child Abuse and Neglect*, 15, 191–6.

Joseph, Sir Keith (1972) 'The next ten years', *New Society*, 5 October, 8–9.

Kadushin, A. and Martin, J. (1981) *Child Abuse - an Interactional Event*. New York: Columbia University Press.

Kaufman, J. and Zigler, E. (1987) 'Do abused children become abusive parents?', *American Journal of Orthopsychiatry*, 57, 186–92.

Kaufman, J. and Zigler, E. (1989) 'The intergenerational transmission of child abuse', in D. Cicchetti and V. Carlson (eds) *Child Maltreatment: Theory and Research on the Causes and Consequences of Child Abuse and Neglect*. Cambridge: Cambridge University Press.

Kelly, L. (1988) *Surviving Sexual Violence*. Cambridge: Polity Press.

Kelly, L., Regan, L. and Burton, S. (1991) 'An exploratory study of the prevalence of sexual abuse in a sample of 16–21 year olds', Child Abuse Studies Unit, The Polytechnic of North London.

Kempe, C. and Helfer, R. (eds) (1980) *The Battered Child*, 3rd edn. Chicago: Chicago University Press.

Kempe, C., Silverman, F., Steele, B., Droegemueller, W. and Silver, H. (1962) 'The battered child syndrome', *Journal of the American Medical Association*, 181, 17–24.

Kempe, R. and Kempe, C. (1978) *Child Abuse*. London: Fontana.

Kinard, E. (1980) 'Mental health needs of abused children', *Child Welfare*, 49, 45–62.

King, J. and Taitz, L. (1985) 'Catch-up growth following abuse', *Archives of Disease in Childhood*, 60, 1152–4.

Kline, P. (1981) *Fact and Fantasy in Freudian Theory*. London: Methuen.

Kolko, J., Moser, J. and Weldy, S. (1988) 'Behavioral/emotional indicators of sexual abuse in child psychiatric in-patients: a controlled comparison with physical abuse', *Child Abuse and Neglect*, 12, 529–41.

Korbin, J. (ed.) (1981) *Child Abuse and Neglect: Cross Cultural Perspectives*. Berkeley: University of California Press.

Korbin, J. (1989) 'Fatal maltreatment by mothers: a proposed framework', *Child Abuse and Neglect*, 13, 481–9.

Koseda, Heidi (1986) *Report of the Review Panel into the Death of Heidi Koseda*. London Borough of Hillingdon.

Krug, R. (1989) 'Adult male report of childhood sexual abuse by mothers: case descriptions, motivations and long-term consequences', *Child Abuse and Neglect*, 13, 111–19.

Krugman, R. (1991) 'Child abuse and neglect: critical first steps in response to a national emergency', *American Journal of Diseases in Childhood*, 145, 513–15.

Lafontaine, J. (1988) *Child Sexual Abuse: an ESRC Research Briefing*. London: Economic and Social Research Council.

Lafontaine, J. (1990) *Child Sexual Abuse*. Cambridge: Polity Press.

Lamphear, V. (1985) 'The impact of maltreatment on children's psychosocial adjustment: a review of the research', *Child Abuse and Neglect*, 9, 251–63.

Larrance, D. and Twentyman, C. (1983) 'Maternal attribution and child abuse', *Journal of Abnormal Psychology*, 92, 449–57.

Lauderdale, M., Valrunas, A. and Anderson, M. (1980) 'Race, ethnicity and child maltreatment: an empirical analysis', *Child Abuse and Neglect*, 4, 163–9.

Lealman, G., Haigh, D., Phillips, J., Stone, J. and Ord-Smith, C. (1983) 'Prediction and prevention of child abuse – an empty hope?', *The Lancet*, i, 1423–4.

Letourneau, C. (1981) 'Empathy and stress: how they affect parental aggression', *Social Work*, 26, 383–90.

Leventhal, J., Egester, E. and Murphy, J. (1984) 'Reassessment of the relationship of perinatal risk factors and child abuse', *American Journal of Diseases in Childhood*, 138, 1034–9.

Lewis, D., Mallouh, C. and Webb, V. (1989) 'Child abuse, delinquency and violent criminality', in D. Cicchetti and V. Carlson (eds) *Child Maltreatment: Theory and Research on the Causes and Consequences of Child Abuse and Neglect*. Cambridge: Cambridge University Press.

Lewis, M. and Schaeffer, S. (1981) 'Peer behaviour and mother-infant interaction', in M. Lewis and S. Schaeffer (eds) *The Uncommon Child*. New York: Plenum Press.

Lindberg, F. and Distad, L. (1985) 'Survival reponses to incest: adolescents in crisis', *Child Abuse and Neglect*, 9, 413–15.

Lowe, N. (1989) 'The role of wardship in child care cases', *Family Law*, 19, 38–45.

Lukianowicz, N. (1971) 'Battered children', *Psychiatrica Clinica*, 4, 257–80.

Lusk, R. and Waterman, J. (1986) 'Effects of sexual abuse on children', in K. Macfarlane and J. Waterman (eds) *The Sexual Abuse of Young Children*. New York: Holt, Rinehart & Winston.

Lynch, M. (1975) 'Ill health and child abuse', *The Lancet*, ii, 317–19.

Lynch, M. (1976) 'Child abuse – the critical path', *Journal of Maternal and Child Health*, July, 25–9.

Lynch, M. (1988) 'The consequences of child abuse', in K. Browne, C. Davies and P. Stratton (eds) *Early Prediction and Prevention of Child Abuse*. Chichester: Wiley.

Lynch, M. and Roberts, J. (1977) 'Predicting child abuse: signs of bonding failure in the maternity hospital', *British Medical Journal*, i, 624–6.

Lynch, M. and Roberts, J. (1978) 'Early alerting signs', in A. Franklin (ed.) *Child Abuse: Prediction, Prevention and Follow-up*. Edinburgh: Churchill Livingstone.

Lynch, M. and Roberts, J. (1982) *The Consequences of Child Abuse*. London: Academic Press.

Lyon, T. (1989) 'Legal developments following the Cleveland report in England – a consideration of some aspects of the Children Bill', *Journal of Social Welfare Law*, 1989, 200–6.

McAuley, R. and McAuley, P. (1977) *Child Behaviour Problems: an Empirical Guide to Management*. London: Macmillan.

McBeath, G. and Webb, S. (1990/91) 'Child protection language as professional ideology in social work', *Social Work and Social Sciences Review*, 2, 122–45.

McCord, J. (1983) 'A 40 year perspective on the effects of child abuse and neglect', *Child Abuse and Neglect*, 7, 265–70.

Macfarlane, A. (1970) *The Family Life of Ralph Josselin*. Cambridge: Cambridge University Press.

Macfarlane, A. (1979) '"The family, sex and marriage in England 1500–1800" by Laurence Stone', *History and Theory*, 18, 103–26.

Macfarlane, K. and Waterman, J. (1986) *The Sexual Abuse of Young Children*. New York: Holt, Rinehart & Winston.

Mackie, J. and Taylor, L. (1990) *A Parents' Guide to the Law*. Harmondsworth: Penguin.

Mackenzie, T., Collins, N. and Popkin, M. (1982) 'A case of fetal abuse?', *American Journal of Orthopsychiatry*, 52, 699–703.

Macleod, M. and Saraga, E. (1988) 'Challenging the orthodoxy: towards a feminist theory and practice', *Feminist Review*, 28, 15–55.

Main, N. and Goldwyn, R. (1984) 'Predicting rejection of her infant from mother's representation of her own experience: implications for the abused–abusing inter-generational cycle', *Child Abuse and Neglect*, 8, 203–17.

Maisch, H. (1973) *Incest*. London: Andre Deutsch.

Mantell, D. (1988) 'Clarifying erroneous child sexual abuse allegations', *American Journal of Orthopsychiatry*, 58, 618–21.

Martin, H. (1972) 'The child and his development', in C. Kempe and R. Helfer (eds) *Helping the Battered Child and His Family*. Philadelphia: Lippincott.

Martin, J. (1978) 'Family violence and social policy', in J. Martin (ed.) *Violence and the Family*. Chichester: Wiley.

Martin, J. and Elmer, E. (1992) 'Battered children grown up: a follow-up study of individuals severely maltreated as children', *Child Abuse and Neglect*, 16, 75–87.

Masson, H. and O'Byrne, P. (1990) 'The family system approach: a help or hindrance?', in the Violence against Children Study Group, *Taking Child Abuse Seriously*. London: Unwin Hyman.

Masson, J. (1984) *Freud: the Assault on Truth*. London: Faber & Faber.

Mattinson, J. and Sinclair, I. (1979) *Working with Marital Problems in a Social Services Department*. Oxford: Blackwell.

Meadow, R. (1977) 'Munchausen syndrome by proxy: the hinterland of child abuse', *The Lancet*, 57, 92–8.

Meadow, R. (1985) 'Management of Munchausen syndrome by proxy', *Archives of Disease in Childhood*, 60, 385–93.

Meadow, R. (1989) 'Suffocation', *British Medical Journal*, 298, 1572–3.

Medden, B. (1985) 'The assessment of risk: child abuse and neglect case investigations', *Child Abuse and Neglect*, 9, 57–62.

Mehl, A., Coble, L. and Johnson, S. (1990) 'Munchausen syndrome by proxy: a family affair', *Child Abuse and Neglect*, 14, 577–86.

Meiselman, K. (1978) *Incest*. San Francisco: Jossey Bass.

Menheniott, Stephen (1978) *Report of the Social Work Service of the DHSS into Certain Aspects of the Management of the Case of Stephen Menheniott*. London: HMSO.

Michenbaum, D. (1977) *Cognitive Behavior Modification: an Integrative Approach*. New York: Plenum Press.

Miller, A. (1985) *Thou Shalt Not Be Aware*. London: Pluto Press.

Minuchin, S. (1974) *Families and Family Therapy*. Cambridge, MA: Harvard University Press.

Mitchell, J. (1974) *Psychoanalysis and Feminism*. London: Allen Lane.

Montagu, A. (1980) *Sociobiology Reexamined*. Oxford: Oxford University Press.

Montgomery, J. (1989) 'The emotional abuse of children', *Family Law*, 19, 25–9.

Montgomery, S. (1982) 'Problems in the perinatal prediction of child abuse', *British Journal of Social Work*, 12, 189–96.

Moore, J. (1985) *The ABC of Child Abuse Work*. Aldershot: Gower.

Mrazek, P., Lynch, M. and Ben-Tovim, A. (1983) 'Sexual abuse of children in the UK', *Child Abuse and Neglect*, 7, 147–53.

Mrazek, P. and Mrazek, D. (1987) 'Resilience in child maltreatment victims: a conceptual exploration', *Child Abuse and Neglect*, 11, 357–66.

Mueller, E. and Silverman, N. (1989) 'Peer relations in maltreated children', in D. Cicchetti and V. Carlson (eds) *Child Maltreatment: Theory and Research on the Causes and Consequences of Child Abuse and Neglect*. Cambridge: Cambridge University Press.

Murphy, J., Jenkins, J., Newcombe, R. and Sibert, J. (1981) 'Objective birth data and the prediction of child abuse', *Archives of Disease in Childhood*, 56, 295–7.

Murphy, J., Jellinek, M., Quinn, D., Smith, G., Poitrast, F. and Goshko, M. (1991) 'Substance abuse and serious child mistreatment: prevalence, risk and outcome in a court sample', *Child Abuse and Neglect*, 15, 197–211.

Nash, C. and West, D. (1985) 'Sexual molestation of young girls', in D. West (ed.) *Sexual Victimisation*. Aldershot: Gower.

National Center on Child Abuse and Neglect (1981 and 1986) *National Study of the Incidence and Severity of Child Abuse and Neglect*. Washington, DC: NCCAN.

Nelson, B. (1984) *Making an Issue of Child Abuse: Political Agenda Setting for Social Problems*. Chicago: Chicago University Press.

Nelson, S. (1987) *Incest: Fact and Myth*. Edinburgh: Strathmullion.

Neursten, L., Goldering, J. and Carpenter, S. (1984) 'Non-sexual transmission of sexually transmitted diseases – an infrequent occurrence', *Pediatrics*, 74, 67–76.

Newberger, C. and White, K. (1989) 'Cognitive foundations for parental care', in D. Cicchetti and V. Carlson (eds) *Child Maltreatment: Theory and Research on the Causes and Consequences of Child Abuse and Neglect*. Cambridge: Cambridge University Press.

Newlands, M. and Emery, J. (1991) 'Child abuse and cot deaths', *Child Abuse and Neglect*, 15, 275–8.

Newson, J. (1978) *Seven Years Old in the Home Environment*. Harmondsworth: Penguin.

Oates, R., Forrest, D. and Peacock, A. (1985) 'Self-esteem of abused children', *Child Abuse and Neglect*, 9, 159–63.

Oates, R., Peacock, A. and Forrest, D. (1984) 'The development of abused children', *Developmental Medicine and Child Neurology*, 26, 649–56.

Office of Population and Census Statistics (1974–1989) *Mortality Statistics 1974–1989*. London: HMSO.

O'Hagan, K. (1989) *Working with Child Sexual Abuse*. Milton Keynes: Open University Press.

Oliver, J. (1985) 'Successive generations of child maltreatment', *British Journal of Psychiatry*, 147, 484–90.

O'Neill, Dennis (1945) *Report by Sir Walter Monckton on the Circumstances which Led to the Boarding-out of Dennis and Terence O'Neill at Bank Farm, Minsterley and the Steps Taken to Supervise Their Welfare*. Cmnd 6636. London: HMSO.

Ong, B. (1985) 'The paradox of "wonderful children": the case of child abuse', *Early Child Development and Care*, 21, 91–106.

Oppenheimer, R., Palmer, R. and Brandon, S. (1984) 'A clinical evaluation of early abusive experiences in adult anorexic and bulimic females: implications for preventive work in childhood', Paper presented to the Fifth International Congress on Child Abuse and Neglect. Montreal.

Orme, T. and Rimmer, J. (1981) 'Alcoholism and child abuse: a review', *Journal of Studies on Alcohol*, 42, 273–87.

Ostbloom, N. and Crase, S. (1980) 'A model for conceptualising child abuse causation and intervention', *Social Casework*, 61, 164–72.

Ounsted, C., Roberts, J., Gordon, M. and Milligan, B. (1982) 'The fourth goal of perinatal medicine', *British Medical Journal*, 284, 879–82.

Packman, J. (1975) *The Child's Generation: Child Care Policy from Curtis to Houghton*. Oxford: Blackwell.

Packman, J. (1986) *Who Needs Care?* Oxford: Blackwell.

Parker, H. J., Bakx, K. and Newcombe, R. (1988) *Living with Heroin: the Impact of a Drugs Epidemic on an English Community*. Milton Keynes: Open University Press.

Parker, H. and Parker, S. (1986) 'Father-daughter sexual abuse: an emerging perspective', *American Journal of Orthopsychiatry*, 56, 531–49.

Parton, C. and Parton, N. (1989) 'Child protection, the law and dangerousness', in O. Stevenson (ed.) *Child Abuse: Public Policy and Professional Practice*. Hemel Hempstead: Harvester Wheatsheaf.

Parton, N. (1979) 'The natural history of child abuse: a study in social problem definition', *British Journal of Social Work*, 9, 431–51.

Parton, N. (1981) 'Child abuse, social anxiety and welfare', *British Journal of Social Work*, 11, 391–414.

Parton, N. (1985) *The Politics of Child Abuse*. Basingstoke: Macmillan.

Parton, N. (1989) 'Child abuse', in B. Kahan (ed.) *Child Care Research, Policy and Practice*. London: Hodder & Stoughton.

Parton, N. (1990) 'Taking child abuse seriously' in the Violence against Children Study Group, *Taking Child Abuse Seriously*. London: Unwin Hyman.

Parton, N. (1991) *Governing the Family: Child Care, Child Protection and the State*. Basingstoke: Macmillan.

Paterson, C. and McAllion, S. (1989) 'Osteogenesis imperfecta and the differential diagnosis of child abuse', *British Medical Journal*, 299, 1451–4.

Pavlov, I. (1927) *Conditioned Reflexes: an Investigation of the Physiological Activity of the Cerebral Cortex*. Oxford: Oxford University Press.

Pelton, L. (1978) 'Child abuse and neglect: the myth of classlessness', *American Journal of Orthopsychiatry*, 48, 608–17.

Peters, J. (1976) 'Children who are victims of sexual assault and the psychology of offenders', *American Journal of Psychotherapy*, 30, 395–421.

Pfohl, S. (1977) 'The "discovery" of child abuse', *Social Problems*, 24, 310–23.

Pierce, R. and Pierce, L. (1985) 'The sexually abused child: a comparison of male and female victims', *Child Abuse and Neglect*, 9, 191–9.

Pincus, A. and Minahan, A. (1973) *Social Work Practice: Models and Methods*. Itasca, Illinois: Peacock.

Plumb, J. (1975) 'The new world of children in eighteenth century England', *Past and Present*, 67, 64–95.

Polansky, N., DeSaix, C. and Sharlin, S. (1972) *Child Neglect: Understanding and Reaching the Parents*. New York: Child Welfare League of America.

Polansky, N., Chalmers, M., Buttenweiser, E. and Williams, D. (1978) 'Assessing adequacy of child caring: an urban scale', *Child Welfare*, 57, 439–49.

Polansky, N. and Williams, D. (1978) 'Class orientations to child neglect', *Social Work*, 27, 397–401.

Polansky, N., Chalmers, M., Buttenweiser, E. and Williams, D. (1979) 'The isolation of the neglectful family', *American Journal of Orthopsychiatry*, 49, 149–52.

Polansky, N., Ammons, P. and Weathersby, B. (1983) 'Is there an American standard of child care?', *Social Work*, 28, 341–6.

Pollock, L. (1983) *Forgotten Children: Parent–Child Relations from 1500 to 1900*. Cambridge: Cambridge University Press.

Porter, R. (ed.) (1984) *Child Sexual Abuse within the Family*. London: Tavistock.

Pritchard, C. (1992) 'Didn't we do well?', *Social Work Today*, 23 January, 16–17.

Reavley, W. and Gilbert, M. (1979) 'The analysis and treatment of child abuse by behavioral psychotherapy', *Child Abuse and Neglect*, 3, 509–14.

Reidy, T. (1977) 'The aggressive characteristics of abused and neglected children', *Journal of Clinical Psychology*, 33, 1140–5.

Reite, M. (1987) 'Infant abuse and neglect: lessons from the laboratory', *Child Abuse and Neglect*, 11, 347–55.

Rivara, F. (1985) 'Physical abuse in children under 2: a study of therapeutic outcomes', *Child Abuse and Neglect*, 9, 81–7.

Roberts, J., Lynch, M. and Golding, J. (1980) 'Postneonatal mortality in children from abusing families', *British Medical Journal*, 281, 102–4.

Roberts, J. (1988) 'Why are some families more vulnerable to child abuse?' in K. Browne, C. Davies and P. Stratton (eds) *Early Prediction and Prevention of Child Abuse*. Chichester: Wiley.

Rooney, B. (1987) 'Racism and resistance to change: a study of the Black Social Workers Project, Liverpool Social Services Department', University of Liverpool.

Rose, L. (1986) *The Massacre of the Innocents*. London: Routledge & Kegan Paul.

Rose, L. (1991) *The Erosion of Childhood: Child Oppression in Britain 1860–1918*. London: Routledge.

Rowe, J. and Lambert, L. (1973) *Children Who Wait*. London: ABAFA.

Rush, F. (1980) *The Best Kept Secret*. Englewood Cliffs, NJ: Prentice-Hall.

Russell, D. (1984) *Sexual Exploitation: Rape, Child Sexual Abuse and Workplace Harrassment*. Beverly Hills, CA: Sage.

Russell, D. (1986) *The Secret Trauma: Incest in the Lives of Girls and Women*. New York: Basic Books.

Rutter, M. (1978) *Maternal Deprivation Reassessed*. Harmondsworth: Penguin.

Rutter, M. (1985) 'Resilience in the face of adversity: protective factors and resistance to psychiatric disorder', *British Journal of Psychiatry*, 147, 598–611.

Sack, W., Mason, R. and Higgins, J. (1985) 'The single-parent family and abusive child punishment', *American Journal of Orthopsychiatry*, 55, 253–9.

Sahlins, M. (1977) *The Use and Abuse of Biology*. London: Tavistock.

Sandham, J. (1992) 'Book Review "Gender, Sex-Offenders and Probation Practice" (L. Dominelli)', *British Journal of Social Work*, 22, 220–2.

Scarre, G. (1980) 'Children and paternalism', *Philosophy*, 55, 117–24.

Scott, M. (1989) *A Cognitive-behavioural Approach to Clients' Problems*. London: Tavistock.

Seagull, E. (1987) 'Social support and child maltreatment: a review of the evidence', *Child Abuse and Neglect*, 11, 41–52.

Seebohm Report (1968) *Report of the Committee on Local Authority and Allied Personal Social Services*. London: HMSO.

Seed, P. (1973) *The Expansion of Social Work in Britain*. London: Routledge & Kegan Paul.

Sharpe, J. (1984) *Crime in Early Modern England 1550–1750*. London: Longmans.

Shorter, E. (1976) *The Making of the Modern Family*. London: Collins.

Silbert, M. and Pines, A. (1981) 'Sexual child abuse as an antecedent to prostitution', *Child Abuse and Neglect*, 10, 283–91.

Sivan, A., Schor, D., Koeppl, G. and Noble, L. (1988) 'Interaction of normal children with anatomical dolls', *Child Abuse and Neglect*, 12, 295–304.

Skinner, A. and Castle, R. (1969) *78 Battered Children: a Retrospective Study*. London: NSPCC.

Skinner, B. (1953) *Science and Human Behaviour*. Basingstoke: Collier Macmillan.

Sluckin, W., Herbert, M. and Sluckin, A. (1983) *Maternal Bonding*. Oxford: Blackwell.

Smith, F. (1979) *The People's Health*. London: Croom Helm.

Smith, J. (1984) 'Non-accidental injury to children I: a review of behavioural intervention', *Behaviour Research and Therapy*, 22, 331–47.

Smith, J. and Rachman, S. (1984) 'Non-accidental injury to children II: a controlled evaluation of a behavioural management programme', *Behaviour Research and Therapy*, 22, 349–66.

Smith, P. (1991) 'The child's voice', *Children and Society*, 5, 58–66.

Smith, S. (1975) *The Battered Child Syndrome*. London: Butterworth.

Smith, S., Hanson, R. and Noble, S. (1974) 'Social aspects of the Battered Baby Syndrome', *British Journal of Psychiatry*, 125, 568–82.

Sommerville, J. (1982) *The Rise and Fall of Childhood*. Beverly Hills, CA: Sage.

Stafford-Clark, D. (1965) *What Freud Really Said*. London: McDonald.

Staffordshire County Council (1991) *The Pindown Experience and the Protection of Children*. The report of the Staffordshire child care inquiry 1990, Staffordshire County Council.

Steele, B. and Pollock, C. (1974) 'A psychiatric study of parents who abuse infants and small children', in R. Helfer and C. Kempe (eds) *The Battered Child*, 2nd edn. Chicago: University of Chicago Press.

Steele, B. (1986) 'Notes on the lasting effects of early child abuse throughout the life cycle', *Child Abuse and Neglect*, 10, 283–91.

Stevenson, O. (1989) 'Multi-disciplinary work in child protection', in O. Stevenson (ed.) *Child Abuse: Public Policy and Professional Practice*. Hemel Hempstead: Harvester Wheatsheaf.

Stocks, T. (1988) 'Has family violence decreased? A reassessment of the Straus and Gelles data', *Journal of Marriage and the Family*, 50, 281–91.

Stone, L. (1977) *The Family, Sex and Marriage in England 1500–1800*. London: Weidenfeld & Nicolson.

Straus, M. (1979) 'Family patterns and child abuse in a nationally representative sample', *Child Abuse and Neglect*, 3, 213–25.

Straus, M. and Gelles, R. (1986) 'Societal change and change in family violence from 1975 to 1985 as revealed by 2 national surveys', *Journal of Marriage and the Family*, 48, 465–79.

Straus, M., Gelles, R. and Steinmetz, K. (1980) *Behind Closed Doors: Violence in the American Family*. New York: Anchor Press.

Stubbs, P. (1989) 'Developing anti-racist practice – problems and possibilities', in C. Wattam *et al.* (eds) *Child Sexual Abuse*. Harlow: Longman.

Sweet, J. and Resick, P. (1979) 'The maltreatment of children: a review of theories and research', *Journal of Social Issues*, 35, 40–59.

Sydie, R. (1987) *Natural Women, Cultured Men*. Milton Keynes: Open University Press.

Thane, P. (1981) 'Childhood in history', in M. King (ed.) *Childhood, Welfare and Society*. London: Batsford.

Theringer, D., Burrows Horton, C. and Millea, S. (1990) 'Sexual abuse and exploitation of children and adults with mental retardation and other handicaps', *Child Abuse and Neglect*, 14, 301–12.

Tilly, L., Fuchs, R., Kertzer, D. and Ransel, D. (1992) 'Child abandonment in European history: a symposium', *Journal of Family History*, 17, 1–22.

Tong, L., Oates, K. and McDowell, M. (1987) 'Personality development following sexual abuse', *Child Abuse and Neglect*, 11, 371–83.

Toro, P. (1982) 'Developmental effects of child abuse and neglect: a review', *Child Abuse and Neglect*, 6, 423–31.

Treacher, A. and Carpenter, J. (1984) *Using Family Therapy: a Guide for Practitioners in Different Professional Settings*. Oxford: Blackwell.

Truesdell, D., McNeil, J. and Deschner, J. (1986) 'Incidence of wife abuse in incestuous families', *Social Work*, 31, 138–40.

Tyler, A. and Brassard, M. (1984) 'Abuse in the investigation and treatment of intrafamilial child sexual abuse', *Child Abuse and Neglect*, 8, 47–53.

Tymchuk, A. and Andron, L. (1990) 'Mothers with mental retardation who do or do not abuse their children', *Child Abuse and Neglect*, 14, 313–23.

Wald, M. (1982) 'State intervention on behalf of endangered children – a proposed legal response', *Child Abuse and Neglect*, 6, 3–45.

Waterhouse, L. and Carnie, J. (1992) 'Assessing child protection risk', *British Journal of Social Work*, 22, 47–60.

West, D. and Farrington, D. (1977) *The Delinquent Way of Life: 3rd Report of the Cambridge Study in Delinquent Development*. London: Heinemann.

Westcott, H. (1991) 'The abuse of disabled children: a review of the literature', *Child Care, Health and Development*, 17, 243–58.

White, K., Benedict, M., Wulff, L. and Kelley, M. (1987) 'Physical disabilities as risk factors for child maltreatment: a selected review', *American Journal of Orthopsychiatry*, 54, 530–43.

Wiedemann, T. (1989) *Adults and Children in the Roman Empire*. London: Routledge.

Wiehe, V. (1989) 'Child abuse: an ecological perspective', *Early Child Development and Care*, 42, 141–5.

Wild, N. (1986) 'Sexual abuse of children in Leeds', *British Medical Journal*, 292, 1113–16.

Wilson, E. (1975) *Sociobiology: the New Synthesis*. Cambridge, MA: Harvard University Press.

Wilson, S. (1984) 'The myth of motherhood a myth: the historical view of European child rearing', *Social History*, 9, 181–98.

Wohl, A. (1978) 'Sex and the single room: incest among the Victorian working classes', in A. Wohl (ed.) *The Victorian Family*. London: Croom Helm.

Wolfe, D. (1985) 'Child-abusive parents: an empirical review and analysis', *Psychological Bulletin*, 97, 462–82.

Wolfe, D., Aragona, J., Kaufman, K. and Sandler, J. (1980) 'The importance of adjudication in the treatment of child abusers: some preliminary findings', *Child Abuse and Neglect*, 4, 127–35.

Wolfe, D., Sandler, J. and Kaufman, K. (1981) 'A competency-based parent training program for child abusers', *Journal of Consulting and Clinical Psychology*, 49, 633–40.

Wolff, R. (1981) 'Origins of child abuse and neglect within the family', *Child Abuse and Neglect*, 5, 223–9.

Wolock, L. and Horowitz, B. (1984) 'Child maltreatment as a social problem: the neglect of neglect', *American Journal of Orthopsychiatry*, 54, 530–43.

Woodroofe, K. (1962) *From Charity to Social Work in England and the United States*. London: Routledge & Kegan Paul.

Yelloly, M. (1980) *Social Work Theory and Psychoanalysis*. New York: Van Nostrand Reinhold.

Young, L. (1964) *Wednesday's Child: a Study of Child Neglect and Abuse*. New York: McGraw-Hill.

Younghusband, E. (1978) *Social Work in Britain 1950–1975*. London: Allen & Unwin.

Zimrin, H. (1986) 'A profile of survival', *Child Abuse and Neglect*, 10, 339–49.

Index

EMOTIONAL AND PSYCHOLOGICAL ABUSE OF CHILDREN

Kieran O'Hagan

Recent public inquiries, research and new legislation have all compelled child care professionals to widen their focus beyond the narrow parameters of the physical health of the child. Emotional and psychological health are now rightly regarded as crucial. This book aims to enable practitioners to articulate precisely what is meant by the terms 'emotional' and 'psychological' abuse; to be able to identify it, and to formulate effective strategies for dealing with it. The author identifies certain categories of parent and parental circumstances which are conducive to the emotional and psychological abuse of children. He makes clear, however, that parents are not the only carers who abuse children in this way. He explores such abuse within an historical, global and cultural context, and examines recent inquiry reports which have exposed the emotional and psychological abuse of children within the child care and child protection systems. Numerous case histories are provided, and one is explored in detail within the context of new child care legislation.

Contents
Court out – Knowing or feeling – Definitions of emotional and psychological abuse – Global, cultural and historical contexts – Case histories – Parents – Observation, communication and assessment – The emotional and psychological abuse of Michelle – Implications for management and training – Bibliography – Index.

176pp   0 335 09884 3 (Paperback)   0 335 09889 4 (Hardback)

SURVIVING SECRETS
THE EXPERIENCE OF ABUSE FOR THE CHILD,
THE ADULT AND THE HELPER

Moira Walker

In recent years considerable attention has been paid to the subject of abuse in childhood. Less attention has been paid to what happens to the vast number of women and men who have reached adulthood with this experience haunting them. Moira Walker overviews the experience and its implications, dealing with physical, sexual and psychological abuse. An essential part of the content is based on interviews with survivors of child abuse, voicing their views on the effects of the experience and the effectiveness of the help offered. At the same time, *Surviving Secrets* seeks to understand the context in which abuse takes place, the society which itself contains and sustains abuse at various levels. It is a moving account of the experience and effects of childhood abuse, and a handbook for all those in the caring professions, in voluntary organizations and elsewhere who are helping survivors of abuse.

Contents
Introduction – A web of secrets: generations of abuse – Adults reflect: the child's experience – Childhood abuse: the adult's experience – Sharing secrets: the child's and the adult's experience – The development of Multiple Personality Disorder – Stages in the process of counselling and therapy – Particular issues in the process of therapy – Issues for the helper – References – Index.

224pp   0 335 09763 4 (Paperback)   0 335 09764 2 (Hardback)

CHILD ABUSE REVISTED
CHILDREN, SOCIETY AND SOCIAL WORK

David M. Cooper

Child abuse work has attracted an enormous amount of bad publicity in recent years which has increasingly brought serious disadvantages not only to the children and families involved, but also to social and other workers in the field. Social workers have been manoeuvred into a narrower form of state intervention that may be counter-productive at times, leaving them widely criticized and demoralized and thus less able to help children.

This book presents a major and possibly controversial re-assessment of child abuse work in Britain since the early 1970s. It draws on evidence from a wide range of areas: recent social and political history, changes in child care law, the theory base for much child abuse work, the professional development of social work and the national pressure group PAIN (Parents Against INjustice). These areas are explored before moving on to a proposed alternative approach to child abuse work where prevention and support are given priority over 'panic and rescue'. The legal, political and professional implications of this alternative approach are considered in detail, making the book a valuable resource for a wide range of students and professionals interested in child abuse and child care law.

Contents
Preface – Acknowledgements – Society – Law – Social work – Knowledge – Parents – Children – The future – Bibliography – Index.

128pp   0 335 15726 2 (Paperback)   0 335 15727 0 (Hardback)

WORKING WITH CHILD ABUSE
SOCIAL WORK PRACTICE AND THE CHILD ABUSE SYSTEM

Brian Corby

Child abuse, and the official response to it, is currently a highly emotive issue. Child abuse has been recognized as a major social problem in Britain since the early 1970s but recent much-publicized deaths and, in particular, the report of the inquiry into the death of Jasmine Beckford have added to the pressure to improve our methods of coping with child abuse. Most of this pressure is falling on the statutory social work departments.

Brian Corby draws on his four years research study (of the day-to-day practice of social workers with families suspected of abusing their children) to critically examine current practice and the overall system developed in the 1970s for dealing with the problem of child abuse. The questions he raises include:

- does the child abuse system work in a reactive rather than a positive fashion?
- are social workers denied autonomy, fearful of making mistakes and too concerned with covering themselves?
- are parents suspected of child abuse too easily deprived of their civil liberties or are children inadequately protected against them?
- is the case conference a venue for inter-professional rivalry rather than an effective forum for reaching decisions about child abuse cases?
- do social workers currently have the necessary specialist knowledge and training to deal with child abuse cases effectively?
- are crisis interventions successful – what are their longer term outcomes?

In the light of this research and analysis, Brian Corby goes on to suggest important policy changes in our handling of the complexities of child abuse. He provides essential reading for trainees and professionals in the field of child abuse and for students of social work and administration.

Contents
Introduction – Child abuse: the context – The research issues – The parents, their children and the social workers – Detecting and investigating child abuse – Official decision-making at case conferences – After the case conference: working with families – What happens to abuse cases: outcomes after two years – Present and future – Appendices – Index.

176pp   0 335 15395 X (Paperback)   0 335 15396 8 (Hardback)